NEGOTIATING THE MAINSTREAM

NEGOTIATING THE MAINSTREAM

A SURVEY
OF THE
AFRO-AMERICAN
EXPERIENCE

Harry A. Johnson, editor

American Library Association
Chicago 1978

Library of Congress Cataloging in Publication Data
    Main entry under title:

    Negotiating the mainstream.

      Bibliography: p.
      Includes index.
        1. Afro-Americans—Addresses, essays, lectures.
    I.   Johnson, Harry Alleyn.
    E185.N38   973'.04'96073   77-29041
    ISBN 0-8389-0254-5

Printed in the United States of America

7-5-78

Contents

Preface

This volume, over two years in preparation, is a testament by distinguished black American authors to the Afro-American's search for truth in the pursuit of life, liberty, and happiness in these United States. Recent research studies concerning the Afro-American have been conducted by anyone possessing the time or the resources. We have tried, instead, to perceive Afro-Americans as they see themselves, and to present these views from their unique vantage point.

The volume is intended to be a survey of Afro-American experiences in terms of principal contemporary problems viewed from a conceptual vantage point, and "negotiating the mainstream in America" is the common theme weaving the chapters into a common unity. The focus, obviously, is on substantive topics of concern to all Americans, but especially Afro-Americans seeking freedom from oppression, as America enters its third century as a nation.

Competent black scholars, well established in their respective fields, have deliberated on the selected topics. Their organization and writing styles differ, but each has approached the respective topic with a historical view, including those events, milestones, and movements significant in forcing change in America. Each has approached the current scene and contemporary thought with a combination of scholarship and sobriety. Although writing at times with compassion, insight, and opinions, the authors analyze and liberally document their themes for the reader.

And so, with deep gratitude to my fellow black writers who agreed that this book was long overdue, I extend my heartfelt thanks. We invite the reader to seek in these pages some personal challenges, with a view that there is room in the American mainstream for all of its citizens.

HARRY ALLEYN JOHNSON

Harry A. Johnson   **Public Education:
The Battle
and Its Aftermath**

From the Dark Continent, brought in chains, Negroes formed the laboring class for a rustic and pioneering people. The education given to these black Americans during the period of the great Tobacco Lords and the Cotton South unmasked basic conflicts in the white Christian consciousness while simultaneously revealing the great courage and perseverance of Negro people.

Early in this period emerged the difficult question: "Should slaves be Christianized, and if so, what would be their status on the American continent?" This question precipitated one of the great moral dilemmas of early colonial life. Since Christian theory advocated the equality of all men in the sight of God, the Christian way of life could neither condone nor sanction slavery. From the introduction of slavery to the period of insurrection in the early 1800s, therefore, the white power structure gave reluctant approval to the *educational* Christianization of their slaves.

The first of the colonial settlers in America to offer Negroes the same educational and religious privileges that they provided for themselves were the Quakers. Believing in the brotherhood of man and the fatherhood of God, they brought the Negroes into their church as equals. The Spanish and French Catholic missionaries were also at the forefront in introducing Christian education to Negroes, while the English colonists, because of the example of the Catholics, sought ways to justify some degree of education for blacks. Perhaps the most reluc-

Harry A. Johnson is dean of Learning Resources, Virginia State College, Petersburg.

1

tant were the Puritans, who felt that the church should be reserved for the elect, and on this basis excluded Negroes.

Eventually freedmen schools, missions, churches, and benevolent and religious organizations for blacks were established, albeit often reluctantly, in the colonies. Strong new voices like that of Patrick Henry, who demanded liberty or death, gave some credence to the concept of education and freedom of mind for blacks. In some parts of the world, impetus for the struggle for human rights was emerging. Although publications in London as early as 1673 give some evidence that the Puritans favored conversion, such individuals as John Elliot and Cotton Mather of New England favored instruction of Negroes and Samuel Sewall, a Massachusetts judge, not only favored instruction but was outspoken, for that day, against slavery itself. The fact is well established, however, that the education of Negroes in colonial America came not as an effort at education but rather as one aimed at Christianization.

In 1704 a catechizing school was founded in New York City at Trinity Church and instruction was given there by Elie Neau until 1712. (As early as 1634 Paul LeJeune, a Jesuit missionary in Canada, claimed that he was teaching a young Negro the alphabet.) The Ursuline nuns attempted to teach Negroes and Indians in 1727, and in 1734 a school for Negroes was established and conducted on Chartres Street in New Orleans. The Society for the Propagation of the Gospel in Foreign Parts was organized by the members of the established church in London in 1701 to do missionary work among Indians and Negroes. As missionaries, members went out to instruct children in the scriptures. One of the first schoolmasters of that organization was the Reverend Samuel Thomas of Goose Creek Parish in South Carolina, who took up his work there in 1695 and by 1705 could count among his communicants twenty Negroes who, with several others, "well understood the English tongue."

As mentioned, the most dedicated educational efforts were made by Quakers. Anthony Benezet, a Quaker, began an evening school in his home in Philadelphia in 1750 and conducted instruction there for twenty years.[1] Benezet, in establishing a free school in 1770 with Moses Patterson as the first teacher, left a fortune for the continuation of this school (known as the Benezet House, located on Locust Street in Philadelphia). The Quakers had many men of conscience such as Benezet, and in 1776 abolished the holding of slaves by Quakers. In the North

1. W. A. Low, "The Education of Negroes Viewed Historically," in *Negro Education in America,* eds. Virgil A. Clift, Archibald W. Anderson, and H. Gordon Hullfish (New York: Harper Brothers, 1962) , p. 21.

among free Negroes, the desire for education was manifested in schools such as the African Free School, which was opened in New York by the Manumission Society in 1781. In 1798, a school for Negro pupils was set up in Boston in the home of a prominent Negro named Primis Hall; Paul Cuffee, a prosperous Negro, set up a school in Massachusetts in the late 1700s.

> The motives of those individuals who educated Negroes can be separated into approximately three categories: first, masters who wanted educated Negroes to increase their plantation's productivity; second, the zealous missionaries who, because they believed they were bringing the divine message from God, taught slaves English and the principles of the Christian religion. The third, and possibly most human and balanced of all, was that of sympathetic human beings who wanted to help the oppressed. Many of the leaders of the abolition movement were in this category.[2]

The philanthropic efforts of many individual whites, organized groups, and black leaders combined to provide the thrust for the education of Negroes in the South in the antebellum period, which saw the emergence of such groups as the Phoenix Society, the Manumission Society, and the abolitionist societies. Benjamin Franklin, a firm supporter of Anthony Benezet, was made president of the Abolition Society of Philadelphia, which in 1774 founded a successful colored school that was maintained for one hundred years. The organized church played an important part in the education of blacks; as previously mentioned, the French and Spanish Catholics did more than the Anglicans. The *Code Noir*, for example, obligated all planters to have their Negroes instructed and baptized, and provided slaves with days of rest as observed by the Catholic church. Though members of the Anglican church had difficulty reconciling their view that no Christian could be a slave with the actual fact of slavery, the Bishop of London declared that educating a slave to be a Christian did not automatically warrant manumission.

Many white plantation owners helped the cause of education by providing an education for their mulatto offspring. This was especially true of Catholic, Spanish, and French planters. In addition, planters provided skilled training for many of their slaves so that they might better run the plantation. Some plantations were self-sustaining. The clothing worn, tools used, food consumed, and houses inhabited were produced by slave labor. This practice was reflected in the slave trade:

2. Carter G. Woodson, *The Education of the Negro Prior to 1861* (Washington, D.C.: Associated Publishers, 1919) , pp. 59–60.

slaves were sold on the auction block as artisans, carpenters, black-smiths, seamstresses, and weavers.[3]

A separate school for colored children was established as a part of the Boston Public School system in 1820. In the 1849 case of *Roberts v. the City of Boston,* brought to test the legality of maintaining a separate system for Negroes, the Supreme Court of Massachusetts stated: "For half a century, separate schools have been kept in Boston for colored children, and the primary school in Belknap Street was established in 1820." The court approved of the separate school system. Earlier, in 1846, George Putnam and other Boston Negroes petitioned the school committee to abolish separate schools for Negroes. The board answered this petition by stating that they deemed separate schools not only "legal and just" but also "best adopted to promote the education of that class [i.e., Negroes] of our population."[4]

Because Negroes of the North found it so difficult to move from labor-oriented jobs to the skilled and apprentice jobs, a way had to be found for their training. Abolitionists, Negro leaders, and friends of the colored race were successful in getting persons of African descent admitted into the "manual labor schools" containing facilities for both practical and classical education, although such schools usually emphasized industrial training. This tendency was reflected in the action of free Negro leaders through their delegates to the convention assembled in Philadelphia in 1830. They were convinced that schools should be reconstructed "on the manual labor system," the only way of progress for free Negroes of the North.[5] At about the same time, the Phoenix Society of the city of New York was established to promote the improvement of blacks in morals, literature, and the mechanical arts.

During the period preceding emancipation, South Carolina was the first state to warn against educating slaves. A law passed 10 May 1740 stated:

> That all and every Persons whatsoever, who shall hereafter teach or cause any Slave or Slaves to be taught to write, or shall use or employ a Slave as a Scribe in any manner of writing whatsoever, hereafter taught to write; every such Person and Persons shall, for every such offense forfeit the sum of One Hundred Pounds Current Money.[6]

3. James B. Sellers, "Slavery in Alabama," *Birmingham News,* 8 May 1947 (Tuscaloosa: University of Alabama Press, 1950) , p. 27.
4. Horace Mann Bond, *The Education of the Negro in the American Social Order* (New York: Prentice-Hall, 1934) , p. 374.
5. "Minutes of the Fourth Annual Convention for the Improvement of the Free People of Color" (Philadelphia, 1831) , p. 26.
6. Earle H. West, *The Black American and Education* (New York: Charles E. Merrill, 1972) , p. 10.

The following year the North Carolina General Assembly enacted a law prohibiting the teaching of slaves to read, write, use figures, or receive books or pamphlets. Negroes were also forbidden to preach in North Carolina, an effort to prohibit any enlightenment through hearing a sermon or speech by slave or freedman. The citizens of Southampton, Virginia, in support of Virginia's stand regarding the education of Negroes following Nat Turner's Rebellion in 1831, "resolved that the education of persons of color is expedient and improper as it is calculated to cause them to be dissatisfied with their conditions and furnishes the slave with the means of absconding from his master."[7]

The precedent-setting case of *Robert* v. *the City of Boston* established the beginning of "separate but equal" laws in the United States. By it, a black child was barred by law from entering a white school. Ironically Boston, the foremost city providing a haven for Negroes, established this precedent. However, only six years later the Massachusetts General Statutes, Section 10, made clear that "no person shall be excluded from a public school on account of the race, color or religious opinions, of the applicant or scholar."

Carter G. Woodson, in his account of the movement to offer higher education to Negroes, notes that after the establishment of Liberia in 1847, "the more liberal colonizationists endeavored to furnish free persons of color the facilities for higher education with the hope that their enlightenment would make them so discontented with this country that they would emigrate to Liberia."[8] As further inducement to return to Africa, funds were established for Liberia to induce American blacks to return to Africa for an education.

Meanwhile, however, many white colleges were opening their doors to Negroes to study law, medicine, and religion. By 1852, colored students had attended such institutions as Bowdoin College in Maine, Dartmouth Theological School, Harvard University, Rush Medical College in Chicago, Athens College in Ohio, Rutland College in Vermont, the Medical School at New York University, and several others. Gerrit Smith, one of the great philanthropists of the mid-nineteenth century, gave funds to colleges for the education of blacks. Smith believed that blacks should have the opportunity to obtain either a common or classical education which could be used in this country or abroad.

This period saw the development of Negroes skilled in many areas. Henry Harris of Clarksdale, Mississippi, was sent by his master to an

7. Ibid., p. 36.
8. Woodson, p. 5.

iron foundry in Tuscaloosa, Alabama, where he learned welding. The slave Gregory, reared in Charleston, South Carolina, was observed by his owner to have a love for tools and was apprenticed to a master carpenter who taught him the skillful use of the hammer and saw.[9] Such permissiveness contributed to the development of a group of skilled workers within the free Negro and slave population. The number of workers employed in skilled occupations provides clear evidence of this fact. Using the 1848 industrial census of Charleston, South Carolina, for example, Phillips showed that free Negroes were employed in all but eight of the fifty occupations composing the skilled group, and slaves were employed in all but thirteen.[10] Negroes in the South were fairly dominant as carpenters and joiners, barbers, hairdressers, and bankers. Slaves represented between 47 percent and 67 percent of all such employed workers in the area.

The indulgence of white masters unwittingly led many slaves to literacy. House servants needed to learn how to tell the time of day and distinguish between the household newspapers, and foremen had to learn to keep records. Young slave children worked their way to literacy through "play school" with their young masters and mistresses. Frederick Douglass, for example, kept crumbs of food with which to trade with hungry white boys in exchange for a lesson from Webster's spelling book.

Motivated by the desire to make slaves more obedient, large plantation owners encouraged Sunday schools and quite often required Bible reading as a part of home study programs. Supporting these efforts were southern religious leaders who insisted that literacy was the potential savior of the slave system. Most prominent among these religious leaders was the Reverend George F. Pierce, Bishop of the Methodist Episcopal Church, South.

In the mid-eighteenth century, the Presbyterians took a bold step in developing religious leadership among Negroes by making formal training directly available to them. In 1740 Hugh Bryan, a wealthy and deeply pious Presbyterian, opened a Negro school in Charleston. By 1755, other schools had been opened in Virginia, where Presbyterians were teaching the slaves to read and spell.[11]

During the pre-Civil War period courageous black men and women

9. Orlando K. Armstrong, *Old Massa's People* (Indianapolis: Bobbs-Merrill, 1951), p. 96.

10. Ulrich B. Phillips, "The Slave Labor in the Charleston District," *Political Science Quarterly* 22:434–35 (1970).

11. Henry Allen Bullock, *A History of Negro Education in the South* (Cambridge, Mass.: Harvard University Press, 1967), p. 11–12.

became teachers regardless of vocation. They never had the prerogative of teaching and educating Negroes directly, but were able to accomplish enlightenment only indirectly, as through the church. Benjamin Banneker (1731–1806), scientist, was likened to Thomas Jefferson in his versatility. Banneker was an astronomer, clockmaker, and mathematician. He helped plan and design the nation's capital in Washington, D.C. Born free near Baltimore and befriended by Quakers, he studied astronomy, mastering it in his fifties. In 1791 President Washington appointed him to assist Andrew Ellicott III, and other men in surveying Washington, D.C. This first black presidential appointee was also one of the first blacks to point the way to education for both free and enslaved Negroes in America.

John Chavis (1763–1838), a teacher and one of the first black leaders of the early slave years, was born free near Oxford, North Carolina. In physical appearance he was described as a "pure black African." He attended Princeton University and later taught white pupils from the leading families of North Carolina. In the late 1790s he enrolled at Washington Academy, now Washington and Lee University, and by 1808 he was conducting schools for whites by day and blacks by night. Chavis taught Greek, Latin, English, mathematics, and other subjects to boys and girls in Wake, Granville, and Quang counties in North Carolina. Restrictions imposed after Nat Turner's Revolt ended his teaching and ministry. James Derham, born in 1762, became the first black physician in America. A slave, Derham was owned by three successive physicians; Dr. Dove, a New Orleans physician, permitted him to buy his freedom and encouraged him to set up his own practice. One of the first educated blacks in America, he was an inspiration to both whites and blacks.

Prince Hall (1735–1807), founder of the oldest social organization among Negroes in America, left his name and imprint on the Prince Hall Masons and their great struggle for social and charitable deeds. John Brown Russwurm (1799–1851), founder of the first black newspaper in America, *Freedom* (founded at Bowdoin College, Maine, 1826), left for Africa in 1829, becoming the first superintendent of public schools in Liberia.

Thriving in small pockets in the colonies, Christian education for Negroes increased in the nineteenth century with the establishment of schools in Virginia and other colonies in the North and South. This continued until the period of insurrection led by Nat Turner, John Brown's Raid, and other forms of resistance to slavery, when the attitude toward education of any sort for Negroes changed.

After Nat Turner's uprising, a wave of repression swamped the South. Toppin compares the treatment of Negro slaves in America and those of Latin America and the resistance of American slaves to the system:

> Early in 1800 Gabriel, a slave in Henrico County, and Jack Bowler organized several thousand slaves to attack Richmond on August 30. . . . A slave preacher in Southampton County, Virginia, Nat Turner, confesses to having visions, saying, "the Spirit instantly appeared to me and said '. . . Christ has laid down the yoke.' " . . . On August 21, 1831, . . . within twenty-four hours proceeding from house to house, they killed sixty whites, secured guns and horses, and gained fifty followers. . . . A remarkable free Black named Denmark Vesey organized some ten thousand slaves for an assault on Charleston in July, 1822. A slave leader, Peter Poyas, urged his followers, "Do not open your lips! Die silent, as you shall see me do."[12]

After the insurrection, "black" codes were devised curtailing the movements of Negroes, and forbidding their education under penalty of law. Reduced to little more than animals, Negroes in the South remained in their own Dark Ages for generations. However, the southern slave codes proved to be only a temporary obstacle: Negroes stole away to clandestine places to learn; children of the masters taught their young friends; teachers and preachers, by devious means, overcame the opposition to teaching. Some schools were operating in Danville and Richmond, Virginia, as late as 1855, and the liberal Berea College in Kentucky was at the forefront in admitting Negro students. The sentiments of this reactionary period, however, reached into the North, where the subsequent anti-abolition riots curtailed the efforts of freedmen to operate schools in many places and caused teachers to be driven from their schools and the burning of such gathering places. In 1835 Daniel Payne was forced to close his little school of sixty students in Charleston, South Carolina, and John Chavis, another Charleston native, had to close his school. These and many other incidents were evidence of the effects of the slave code in both North and South.

Following the Civil War, freedmen's schools immediately began to feel the effects of the anti-Negro sentiment. The impact was first felt through the provincial governors, supported by Presidents Lincoln and Johnson. The black codes permitted all branches of government the opportunity to support public animosity and revenge, causing extensive violence and seriously hampering the education of Negroes.

Edward Stanley, upon becoming governor of North Carolina in 1862,

12. Edgar A. Toppin, *A Biographical History of Blacks in America since 1528* (New York: David McKay, 1971), p. 90.

closed the freedmen's schools in that state. The Florida legislature of 1865 passed an act that affected the schools more emphatically: Florida placed a one-dollar tax on all Negroes to support their schools. To Negroes who were barely able to earn a subsistence wage, this was a heavy burden. Texas established a similar law, whereby the state's normal wealth supported white schools, while the income from a tax on Negroes supported a system for Africans and their children.

The South totally rejected the concept of white teachers coming South to teach Negro children. The fear was not so much that of Negro children learning to read, write, and figure, but of the spreading of the doctrine of equality of the races.

POST-CIVIL WAR YEARS AND THE ESTABLISHMENT OF JIM CROW, 1865–1935

> Lift Every Voice and Sing
> Till Earth and Heaven Ring,
> Ring with the Harmony of Liberty
>
> Let us rejoice . . .

These words, by James Weldon Johnson, echoed the sentiments of black people responding to the urgent call of freedom. The Emancipation Proclamation took effect on 1 January 1863. At the time of the 1860 census, one-eighth of the Negroes in the United States were free; among the slave-holding states, however, hardly more than 5 percent of the freedmen possessed even the simplest education.

The victory of the North left ugly scars on the South which have taken generations to heal. Negroes have borne the brunt of this long, painful healing process. Many appeals went out through the country to help freed slaves to educate themselves and become independent. Benevolent societies were established in major cities of the North; non-sectarian groups were joined by religious groups, and their help in providing clothing and food was extended to include education.[13] Leading the religious organizations was the American Missionary Association, which had been incorporated in 1849 for the purpose of operating Christian missions and educational institutions at home and abroad. Its Home Mission Society, later to create many colleges for Negroes, was established in 1832 to preach the gospel in destitute regions.

The Reconstruction period opened up opportunities for the Americanization of blacks. Emergency relief measures gave way to the Bureau of Refugees, Freedmen, and Abandoned Lands, directly under the supervision of the War Department. The bureau, headed by General

13. Woodson, p. 5.

Oliver O. Howard, had as its first commission the providing of "the foundations of education."[14] Thus, special care of Negroes passed into federal hands. From the point of view of Negro opportunities, the act was of great historical significance, since it gave needed backing to the teachers of the benevolent societies who had been making efforts to establish a unified school system for freedmen.

Strong opposition, in the meantime, continued to develop in the South against Negro education. In 1877 a white Virginian, writing under the name of "Civis," denounced education for Negroes and bitterly attacked the concept of equality:

> I oppose it [public education] because its policy is cruelty in the extreme to the negro himself. It instills in his mind that he is competent to share in the higher walks of life, prompts him to despise those menial pursuits to which his race has been doomed, and invites him to enter into competition with the white man for those tempting prizes that can be won only by a quicker and profounder sagacity, by a greater energy and self-denial, and a higher order of administrative talent than the negro has ever developed.[15]

Records of the War Department handling freed Negroes as "contraband" showed that they were cared for under military occupiers such as Commander General Rufus Saxton in the Sea Islands area, Colonel John Eaton in Mississippi, and General N. P. Banks in Louisiana. The first real program of organized education for blacks was initiated. The Freedmen's Bureau encouraged efforts to centrally organize black education. In 1862 the Boston Education Commission was founded, along with the National Freedmen's Relief Commission in New York and Philadelphia. During this same period, the American Missionary Association set up schools in the Virginia cities of Yorktown, Suffolk, Portsmouth, and Newport News. Schools were also established in Washington, D.C., Columbus, Ohio, and North and South Carolina. The first day school for Negroes under the new dispensation was set up in September of 1861.[16]

Abraham Lincoln, writing to General Banks in Louisiana on the subject of Reconstruction, wrote that "some provisions must be made for the education of the young blacks."[17] General Banks must be credited with the first systematic effort to establish free public schools for

14. Bullock, p. 23.

15. Bennet Puryear, *The Public School and Its Relation to the Negro* (Richmond, Va.: Clemmitt and Jones, printers, 1877) , p. 17.

16. Francis G. Peabody, *Education for Life, the Story of Hampton Institute* (New York: Doubleday, Page and Co., 1918) , p. 38.

17. John G. Nicolay and John Hay, *Abraham Lincoln, A History* (New York: Century Co., 1904) .

Negro children, schools which were supported by taxes levied upon the property of citizens. His General Order No. 38, with its seven points for adoption, is a milestone in the history of Negro education.[18]

The value of the Freedmen's Bureau as the agency assigned to develop Negro education has been the subject of controversy. However, the bureau must justly be credited with the establishment of a widespread and fairly well-organized system of free schools for Negroes in the South. In the five years of its operation, it was instrumental in the initiation of 4,239 separate schools. The extent of its work can further be gauged by the fact that it employed 9,307 teachers and instructed 247,333 pupils.[19] This powerful government agency was to reflect, during its five years of life, the objective of its founder. As W. E. B. DuBois stated:

> The Freedmen's Bureau became a full-fledged government of men. It made laws, executed them and interpreted them; it laid and collected taxes, defined and punished crime, maintained and used military force and dictated such measures as it thought necessary and proper for the accomplishment of its varied ends.[20]

The bureau received its support from numerous sources. During its first year, it derived nearly $2,000,000 from the sale of crops and other confiscated goods from Confederate property and from school taxes and tuition. In addition, the U.S. Congress appropriated $11,084,750 for the period 1866–67. Of this amount, over $5,000,000 went to support freedmen schools. Southern school systems, established in 1861, received their organizational identity some eight years later through the assistance of the Freedmen's Bureau. Fourteen southern states had established 575 schools by 1865, and these schools were employing 1,171 teachers for the 71,779 Negro and white children in regular attendance. Virginia, North Carolina, and Louisiana were the most forward-looking states in regard to the public school systems: they possessed approximately half the school teachers and pupils in the region at that time. The public school was designed to serve a dual purpose: to stand up for the rights of the freed Negro and to provide impetus to the formation of a new order.

Opposition to education of Negroes was not universal in the South; although the system itself was transplanted from the New England

18. Ibid.
19. J. W. Alvord, *Semi-Annual Reports on Schools for Freedmen*, no. 10 (Washington, D.C.: U.S. Government Printing Office, 1866–70).
20. W. E. B. DuBois, *The Souls of Black Folk* (Chicago: A. C. McClung and Co., 1904), p. 27.

Common School, many southerners rallied to the support of education for Negroes. In every southern state, prominent white people came forward to advocate the education of Negroes. According to tradition, E. J. Harris of Ocala, Florida, one of the oldest and most respected citizens of the town, donated property for the site of a church and school for freedmen. At Meridian, Mississippi, sites for Baptist and Methodist churches and a schoolhouse for Negroes were donated by L. A. Ragsdale, a wealthy and influential white citizen. At Canton, Mississippi, the Reverend T. J. Drane, a Baptist minister of fine reputation, organized a school for freedmen. Native white citizens who restored political, if not economic, home rule in the South in the mid-1870s promised to retain the public schools. In speeches made soon after the close of the Civil War, General Clanton of Alabama, General Gordon of Georgia, and other equally prominent leaders advocated the education of Negroes and urged white southerners to enter the classroom.[21]

These courageous southern white citizens were human beings grappling with a conscience. Their motives were clear: in the name of humanity, they advanced the cause of education as a way to not only amend for the cruelty of the past, but to provide a path for Negro self-reliance and freedom to pursue, if not happiness, at least survival. Integration or segregation did not then enter the picture.

Lyman Abbott, after attending the Fourth Annual Conference for Education in the South, a conference which brought together leaders from North and South to discuss educational problems of the southern states, stated:

> The Southerner has less prejudice against the Negro and more interest in his welfare than the Northerner has; he desires the Negroes' education, but believes that whatever it may become in the future, it should now be industrial rather than literacy.[22]

Horace Mann Bond refers to this movement among individuals and groups as the "awakening of private conscience,"[23] a fitting caption.

As the post-Civil War years advanced, a cleavage developed among southerners toward the education of blacks and whites together. A constitutional convention, meeting in Richmond in 1901–2 on the eve of Virginia's educational campaign, profoundly affected the relations between white and Negro schools and revealed the social attitudes of

21. Bond, p. 34.
22. Ibid., p. 127.
23. Ibid.

state leaders. The campaign featured a growing move to disfranchise the Negro and further entrench the "machine" which controlled education in Virginia. This Virginia machine was a rural one, dependent on its power over the railroad interests and control of the state legislature. It stressed low taxation and, therefore, neglected welfare legislation and fought against appropriations for public schools.[24] Disfranchisement of Negroes was the main business of the convention. The anti-Negro movement pervaded all deliberations, and the final changes made in the education clause legalized racial discrimination in the school system.[25]

This sentiment was widespread. Discussion at the convention reflected a general trend toward stripping Negroes of many gains they had made since emancipation. Professor Richard Heath Dabney of the University of Virginia declared it "foolish for the State to tax itself for the education of the colored people it sought to disenfranchise." State Superintendent Joseph W. Southall was reported to have said that "Negro education is a failure." Paul B. Barringer, chairman of the faculty of the University of Virginia and owner of 1,600 acres of agricultural land, stated that "the public school training for this people should be primarily a Sunday School training." This was the theme of the time, although the Reconstruction period had established that Negroes were entitled to the same basic education as whites. This principle of equality was challenged at this time in the "new" South, when many influential southern leaders were determined to keep the Negro subservient. Their aim, to keep Negroes politically inarticulate and disfranchised as in antebellum days while offering a modicum of education as a compromise, became known as the "Atlanta Compromise."

The Freedmen's Bureau, supported by federal troops still in the South, gave food and medicine to the freed slaves. The bureau built or aided in the establishment of more than 4,000 schools, with 9,000 teachers and almost 250,000 Negro students. These schools evolved into the Negro public school system in the South. Other groups offered assistance, including the American Missionary Society, American Baptist Home Mission Society, the Methodists, the Quakers, and the Presbyterian Synod. In addition, thousands of white persons from the North came to the South, dedicated to the education of the Negroes. By 1870,

24. "Virginia is as much railroad-ridden as Pennsylvania, only the People don't know it." William A. Jones, congressman of Warsaw, Va., 4 September 1906. With the Henry St. George Tucker Papers, University of North Carolina.
25. Louis R. Harlan, *Separate and Unequal* (Chapel Hill: University of North Carolina Press, 1958), p. 138.

when the Freedmen's Bureau was abolished, over 20 percent of newly freed Negroes could read and write.

In a memorable speech at the Atlantic Cotton States and International Exposition in 1895, Booker T. Washington gave persuasive sanction to the course of southern sectionalism in the new South and the role assigned, by the whites, to the Negro. The exposition opened in Atlanta on 18 September 1895, and 40,000 visitors listened to Washington, the only Negro speaker and the first of his race to address such a vast audience of southern white men and women. Frederick Douglass, acknowledged Negro spokesman and leader, had died seven months before the Atlanta Compromise; Washington, replacing him, brought a new philosophy and direction to Negro leadership. In his Atlanta Compromise speech he indicated his aversion for bookish pursuits that lacked practical application to the task of making a living. In Atlanta, he said, the Negro race would

prosper in proportion as we learn to draw the line between the superficial and the substantial, the ornamental gewgaws of life and the useful. No race can prosper til it learns that there is as much dignity in tilling a field as in writing a poem.[26]

A decade later he wrote:

In a certain way every slave plantation in the south was an industrial school. On these plantations young colored men and women were constantly being trained not only as farmers but as carpenters, blacksmiths, wheelwrights, brick masons, engineers, cooks, laundresses, sewing women and housekeepers. . . . Slavery . . . was a curse to both races, but . . . industrial training on the plantation left the Negro at the close of the war in possession of nearly all the common and skilled labor in the South. . . . For nearly twenty years after the war, except in a few instances, the value of the industrial training given by the plantations was overlooked. Negro men and women were educated in literature, in mathematics and in the sciences. . . . How often have I been discouraged as I have gone through the South, and into the homes of the people of my race, and have found women who could converse intelligently upon abstruse subjects, and yet could not tell how to improve the condition of the poorly cooked and still more poorly served bread and meat which they and their families were eating three times a day.[27]

Horace Mann Bond summarizes the objectives that Washington envisioned for Tuskegee Institute as an educational institution:

(1) the development of attitudes and habits of industry and honesty in the

26. Toppin, p. 137.
27. Ibid., p. 137–38.

disciplining of raw, country youth through institutionalized activities; (2) the development of specific skills in definite crafts and occupations; and (3) the preparation of teachers for the public and private schools of the South who might, through spreading the gospel of thrift, industry, and racial conciliation, aid in constructing a firm economic foundation upon which the future aspiration of the race might stand.[28]

To Washington, entering the mainstream of American life was neither a priority nor a concern. He was concerned with the task of finding the realistic and pragmatic route to survival. Paralleling this concern was his recognition of the Negroes' need to progress from their present position, finding jobs not only on the farm, but also in trades and as domestics; they knew which work whites preferred not to do. Washington did not concern himself with dreaming of the luxury of the mainstream, but rather with the hard reality of the survival of the Negro race in the United States.

The Atlanta Compromise, or racial adjustment policy, created, among Negro educators, exponents on both sides for nearly a century. Booker T. Washington was without doubt the spokesman for black people from the time of his Atlanta speech, but his ideology was radically different from that of Frederick Douglass. Washington, until his death in 1915, labored for the economic preparation of Negroes through his "let down your bucket where you are" philosophy. Douglass, his predecessor, was a more militant leader, one who had advised John Brown at Harper's Ferry and Abe Lincoln on emancipation.

Another Negro scholar, spokesman, and writer, William Edward Burghardt DuBois (1868–1963), had been listed in *Who's Who in America* since its first publication date in 1898. DuBois was the proud, confident and militant scholar who launched the Niagara Movement, which advocated the immediate ending of racial discrimination and segregation in the United States. He disagreed violently with Booker T. Washington's emphasis on vocational education for black people. He believed that Negroes were entitled to develop all of their faculties and talents to the utmost. Washington stressed vocational education and a "place" for Negroes in America; DuBois stressed training in the liberal arts and humanities. DuBois was to see many of his views implemented through teacher training at such prestigious institutions as Howard University and Fisk University. In an article he wrote in 1903 entitled "The Talented Tenth" DuBois outlined his ideas of education in contrast to those of Booker T. Washington on the type of schooling best suited for blacks:

28. Bond, p. 119.

The Negro race, like all races is going to be saved by its exceptional men. The problem of education, then, among Negroes must first of all deal with the Talented Tenth; it is the problem of developing the Best of this race that they guide the Masses. If we make money the object of man-training, we shall develop money-makers but not necessarily men; if we make technical skill the object of education, we may possess artisans but not, in nature, men. Men we shall have only as we make manhood the object of the work of the schools—intelligence, broad sympathy, knowledge of the world that was and is, and of the relation of men to it—this is the curriculum of that Higher Education which must underlie true life.[29]

Lincoln University in Pennsylvania and Wilberforce University in Ohio were two institutions founded before emancipation. In fact, of the historically Negro public colleges still in existence today, seventeen were in existence before 1890. They were established as "normal schools," "colleges," and "universities" for Negroes in the South by northern missionary and church groups. The American Missionary Association sponsored Talladega College in 1867 in Alabama, Fisk University in Tennessee in 1866, and Tougaloo College in 1869 in Mississippi. Although little more than elementary and secondary schools in the beginning, they were denoted as "universities" in hopes of their future.

Immediately after the Civil War, between 1865 and 1890, several black colleges were founded in the South, including the prestigious Howard University (1869), Hampton Institute (1868), and Tuskegee Institute (1881). Howard University, founded by the great humanitarian Oliver Otis Howard, former general in the Union army and the school's first president, and Hampton Institute, founded by Samuel Chapman Armstrong with only two teachers and fifteen students, were only two of many that exemplified the awakening of the private conscience of white America. General Armstrong stated that his aim was to educate the whole person; he hoped to graduate good teachers, agricultural realists, and skilled mechanics.

A school in Pine Bluff, Arkansas, became Arkansas Agricultural, Mechanical and Normal College in 1872. Morehouse came into existence in Augusta, Georgia, in 1867 under another name and later moved to Atlanta. The American Baptist Home Mission Society, founder of Morehouse, also aided in founding and supporting Virginia Union University (Virginia) in 1865, Shaw University (North Carolina) in 1865, and Benedict College (South Carolina) in 1871. Alcorn College in Mississippi came into being in 1871 through an act of the Mississippi legislature. Rust College was established in Mississippi by the Methodist

29. Ibid., p. 363.

Episcopal Church in 1867. That year also saw the opening of Barber-Scotia College in North Carolina, founded by the Presbyterian Church. Many other Negro colleges developed or were founded during the 1860s and 1870s.

Most of the historically Negro public colleges were established in the 1890s, and resulted mainly from the Morrill Act of August 30, 1890. Known as the Second Morrill Act, it specified that "the establishment and maintenance of such colleges separately for white and colored students will be held to be in compliance with the provisions of this act if the funds received in such State or Territory be equitably divided as hereinafter set forth."[30]

At the same time, Negroes received baccalaureate and professional degrees from historically white colleges and universities such as Oberlin College in Ohio, throughout the Reconstruction period. Some blacks even served as teachers at these institutions. T. McCants Steward received degrees from the University of South Carolina in 1875, and Joseph E. Jones was a professor of Greek at Richmond Theological Seminary in 1876. Unfortunately, this situation ended as state governments passed into the hands of the Democratic party.

The post-Civil War years and the years of disfranchisement saw the emergence of the Niagara Movement and the National Association for the Advancement of Colored People (NAACP). Leaders of the Niagara Movement, such as W. E. B. DuBois and John Hope, along with editors Monroe Trotter and J. Max Barber, were, as previously noted, opposed to the "let down your buckets" philosophy of Booker T. Washington. The Niagara Movement had its beginning in Fort Erie at the instigation of DuBois. Attending the founding meeting were black intellectuals, newspapermen, teachers, and professionals from fourteen states. John Hope, president of Atlanta Baptist College, was the highest ranking leader in attendance; Jesse Max Barber was the Atlanta editor of the *Voice of the Negro,* and was eventually run out of town because of his militant views. Robert S. Abbott's *Chicago Defender,* founded in 1905, became the most influential militant Negro newspaper supporting the full demands of the Niagara Movement. The significance of this movement, and later of the NAACP, on Negro education was obvious in its stressing that Negroes must have full citizenship and the right to an education to the maximum of their capacity.

Other blacks making their mark during this period included John Hope Franklin, an 1894 graduate of Brown University who went on to become architect and president of the Atlanta University merger; he

30. U.S. Dept. of Interior, vol. 1 (1894), p. 620.

was one of the first black college presidents. Hiram Revels, educated by Quakers, was a Reconstruction teacher who also served as a minister in the Methodist Church, senator from Mississippi (1869), secretary of state under Governor Powers, and in 1871 became the president of Alcorn College, a new institution for Negroes in Mississippi which later became one of the land grant colleges in the South. Daniel Hale Williams (1858–1931), known as the "Father of Negro Hospitals," was a pioneer surgeon who received early training at Northwestern University (then Chicago Medical College). He, with others, founded Provident Hospital and Training School for Nurses in Chicago, which opened to the public in 1891. Williams is credited with performing the first operation on the human heart. Isaac Love, an educator and bishop (1834–1937), raised the funds to build Love College for Negro students. Notable teachers of this period included George Washington Carver of Tuskegee Institute, whose extensive research on peanuts and sweet potatoes changed the course of agriculture in the South. Carver, born a slave in Missouri, dedicated his talents to humanity as teacher and scientist, producing over 300 different products from the peanut.

Perhaps the individual who has best recorded the history of his people is Carter G. Woodson (1875–1950). Few writers of any period have shown his depth of commitment; his life was, in fact, dedicated to correcting the stereotyped misconceptions of the history of Negroes in America. An accomplished teacher specializing in history and languages, his work at Dunbar High School in Washington, D.C., and at the Library of Congress preceded his Ph.D. from Harvard University. He later became dean of Howard University School of Liberal Arts and head of the graduate faculty. His first book, *The Education of the Negro Prior to 1861,* published in 1915, is still a major, unchallenged work.

Scholar, lecturer, and college president, William Saunders Scarborough was a former slave who attended Atlanta University and Oberlin College. He taught Latin, Greek, and mathematics, and his contributions to education included the authorship of a Greek textbook, membership on the faculty of Wilberforce University, and the presidency of that institution in 1903.

Mordecai Johnson, educator and orator, became one of the most renowned university presidents in America. As president of Howard University, he brought great prestige to that institution, increased the faculty three times over, doubled faculty salaries, and was instrumental in securing $6,000,000 in congressional support. Born in Columbus, Tennessee, and encouraged by his mother, he became a student at Morehouse College and later at Harvard University, where he astounded his commencement audience with a speech entitled "The Faith of the American Negro," which brought him national acclaim. After teaching economics and history at Harvard, Johnson served as a minister in Charleston, West Virginia.

Some individuals worked for the cause of Negro education and achievement through organizations. Claude Albert Barnett, for example, spearheaded the founding of the Associated Negro Press in 1919. This organization kept Negroes abreast of news and developments affecting them. James Weldon Johnson, executive secretary of and dedicated worker for the NAACP, led the campaign for enactment of the Dyer Anti-Lynching Bill. Walter White, NAACP executive secretary, also contributed much of his time and energies to the NAACP Legal Defense and Education Foundation, a staunch supporter of Negroes seeking rights as American citizens in various fields.

The *Journal of Negro Education,* established in 1932 at Howard University under Charles H. Thompson, provided a sounding board for black educators. At the same time, black institutions were increasing in strength, quality, and enrollment, a growth identified with both the national awakening of conscience and the economic growth of early twentieth-century America.

The dual system of education emerging in the South became a special and humiliating burden for American Negroes, however. Could the South afford two educational systems? Could these two systems possibly be equal in quality? Education for Negroes in the South was influenced from the start by the assumption that Negroes were intellectually inferior; the concept of racial inferiority was, of course, necessary to maintain the master/slave society. This stereotype was developed, maintained, and reinforced to disfranchise Negroes. The tremendous impact of the philosophy of John Dewey on American education, especially Negro education, can be recognized within this framework. John Dewey's philosophy forced educators to regard all people as worthy individuals who should be allowed to develop to their full capacities. He helped educators to free themselves of the bondage of custom and mores and examine their attitudes, prejudices, and practices. This "Freedom to Be One's Best Self," as defined by Dewey, was the "release of capacity from whatever hems it in."[31] His philosophy taught men to rebel against autocracy, no matter what form it appeared in. His philosophy also addressed itself to the practical resolution of special problems of Negro education.

Women played a very special role in the education and achievement

31. William Heard Kilpatrick, *Philosophy of Education* (New York: Macmillan, 1951) , pp. 119–347.

of black people during these years. Nannie Helen Burroughs (1883–1961), working for the Association of Colored Women, founded the Women's Industrial Club in Louisville, which emphasized the development and teaching of domestic skills to Negro girls. She also played an important part in founding the National Training School for women and girls which opened its doors in 1909, with Burroughs as president. Charlotte Hawkins Brown, a founder and prime mover of the Palmer Memorial Institute, received her early training at Wellesley in Massachusetts. She then returned to North Carolina to start a "farm life" school. She brought $100,000 in contributions to Sadalia, North Carolina, from many supporters, and eventually received additional support from the Julius Rosenwald Fund.

Virginia Randolph, born in Richmond, Virginia, in 1875, was another inspiring and dedicated teacher. Teaching in Goochland and Henrico counties, she developed a philosophy of education unique in her environment, one based on common sense. Fannie M. Richards, born of free parents in Fredericksburg, Virginia, was the first Negro schoolteacher in Detroit, Michigan. Her leadership there was forthright and visible for forty-seven years. Born a slave in Macon, Georgia, Lucy Laney (1854–1933) became the founder of a private school, Haines Normal Institute in Georgia, named for a generous financial contributor from Milwaukee. The school was opened in a church basement in Georgia in 1886.

The foremost American black woman educator, however, was Mary McLeod Bethune (1875–1955). Born of former slaves, she became first president and cofounder of Bethune-Cookman College. Special advisor to President Franklin D. Roosevelt, she went on to become special U.S. Observer to the United Nations Conference, vice-president of the NAACP, director of Negro Affairs in the National Youth Administration, and the recipient of numerous awards for her achievements. Awarded the Spingarn Medal in 1935, Mrs. Bethune was named "Mother of the Century" by the Dorie Miller Foundation the year before her death in 1955.

Although a reaction to Negro aid had set in by 1871 in both the South and the North, dedicated white Americans continued to give of themselves during this most crucial period in the history of Negro education. Trusting and believing that Negroes could elevate themselves to improve their status, become more productive citizens, and educate their own people, some whites became teachers, while others donated funds. Much of this faith in the future, however, can be attributed to Booker T. Washington's ideology, rather than the liberal arts approach advocated by W. E. B. DuBois. Donations were made by countless white individuals and many foundations; it was a single donor, S. Griffiths Morgan, who appeared in the records of Booker T. Washington, in the notation, "Educated by S. Griffiths Morgan."[32]

Pierce S. DuPont all but revolutionized the education of Negroes in the state of Delaware. By 1931, DuPont had contributed over $2,000,000 for public school buildings. The grant was given to build a schoolhouse in every county where Negro children were enrolled in school. The Peabody Education Fund, whose donations to black education eventually amounted to approximately $3,500,000, was established in 1867, and although the Peabody trustees helped defeat the Civil Rights Bill pending in Congress in 1873, the fund, by 1880, had turned its attention mainly to the training of black teachers. The first general agent of the Peabody Fund was Jabaz L. M. Curry, one of the first men of prominence in the South to advocate the training of Negroes at public expense. Andrew Carnegie, one of America's first industrial barons, was to provide $10,000,000 through philanthropic gifts for library services for numerous Negro communities and colleges in the South. A close friend of Booker T. Washington, he also made generous contributions to Hampton Institute and Tuskegee Institute. It is recorded that a sum of $720,000 was given to Tuskegee and nearly $1,000,000 to Hampton Institute. The Rockefeller Foundation founded and enriched the General Education Board in the amount of $1,000,000 in 1902. The General Education Board was founded to assist states in developing the Negro education divisions. The board later expanded to lend support through endowments to Negro colleges and normal schools. The Rockefeller family had given large sums of money to Negro education through the American Baptist Home Missionary Association, with Morehouse College in Atlanta and Spelman College for Women in Atlanta, two black institutions, the favored recipients. The General Education Board, by 1929, had expended over $20,000,000 in a variety of services to Negro education. Of that sum, over $5,000,000 represented donations to and endowment of eleven Negro colleges and normal schools: Fisk University, Hampton Institute, Knoxville, Lincoln University, Morehouse College, Shaw University, Spelman College, Talladega College, Tuskegee Institute, Virginia Union University, and Wiley College.[33]

32. Samuel Chapman Armstrong, *Twenty-two Years' Work of Hampton* (Hampton, Va.: Normal School Press, 1893), p. 58.
33. Monroe N. Work, *Negro Year Book, 1931–32* (Tuskegee, Ala.: Negro Year Book Publishing Co.), p. 227.

Other philanthropic foundations aiding black education included the Phelps-Stokes Fund. Caroline Phelps-Stokes designated in her will that the income from $900,000 should be used, among other purposes, "for the education of Negroes both in Africa and the United States." This fund has supported efforts in research and educational commissions to Africa. The John F. Slater Fund was established in 1882 with a $1,000,000 contribution from John F. Slater of Norwich, Connecticut.[34] This textile manufacturer gave funds "for uplifting the lately emancipated population of Southern States."[35] In later years, the influence of Booker T. Washington was to be felt on the fund and its subsequent emphasis upon individual training in the schools assisted by the Slater Fund.

Perhaps the most significant progress in the education of rural Negroes came through the generous contributions of Anna T. Jeanes, who established, through the persuasion of Hollis Frissell of Hampton and Booker T. Washington of Tuskegee, the Anna T. Jeanes Fund. This quiet, serious, and concerned Quaker woman of Philadelphia, at the solicitation of George Foster Peabody, gave the fund $200,000 in 1905 for the specific purpose of helping Negro rural schools in the South.[36] She stipulated that Hollis Burke Frissell of Hampton and Booker T. Washington of Tuskegee be consulted in making plans for the disposition of this money. It was through these resources that the "Jeanes" teachers and supervisors came to serve as demonstration teachers throughout the South. She left in perpetuity, in 1907, over $1,000,000 for rural and county black education.

The Julius Rosenwald Fund was established in 1917 and has done more in attracting matching funds for the education of Negroes than any other funding agency. Rosenwald, head of the Sears and Roebuck merchandising empire, made his first donation of $25,000 toward a Negro YMCA and later made smaller pledges to Tuskegee Institute. By 1932, through his donations, 5,357 buildings had been erected for 663,615 pupils, and between 24 to 40 percent of Negro children in the South were in Rosenwald schools. Rosenwald and the directors of his trust directed their attention first toward building rural schools, later toward support of high schools and colleges, and, finally, toward provisions for Negroes and whites to advance their careers. At his death, Rosenwald left 200,000 shares of Sears and Roebuck stock (worth more than $30,000,000 at the time) to the Rosenwald Foundation.

34. Benjamin Brawley, *Doctor Dillard of the Jeanes Fund* (New York: Fleming H. Revell, 1930), pp. 25–33.
35. Ibid.
36. Bond, p. 136.

Other funds to assist Negro education included the Daniel Hand Fund worth several million dollars. Set up in 1888, it supported the work of the American Missionary Association.

The early years of the twentieth century saw the "separate but equal" doctrine permeating all phases of Negro life, not only in schools and colleges, but in housing, employment, religion, and social and political life. The way of life as a Negro had been established for the next half-century.

Certainly the most visible issue in the history of Negro education has been segregation. Segregation was firmly fixed before World War I, but the heightened racism following the war solidified it, and further efforts were made to construct barriers between the races. In 1919, for example, the Georgia legislature passed laws requiring segregation, while Arizona passed laws making it optional. With such actions, segregation was not only entrenched by custom but sanctioned by law.

Schooling for Negroes in the South in this period was deplorable and wholly unequal to that of whites. It was characterized by poor facilities, poorly trained teachers, and lack of funds. In the early years of the twentieth century, Negro leaders who opposed segregation did so because it was inextricably linked with inferior educational opportunities. During this period, 47,426 Negro teachers were certified in fifteen southern states, but many had not been educated beyond the fifth grade. In 1930, more than one-third of southern Negro teachers possessed less than a high school training and fewer than 58 percent of these teachers had less than two years of college training.[37] Moreover, southern superintendents kept the pay of Negro teachers much lower than that of white teachers doing the same work.

The Negro school played an important part in inculcating those values which would place blacks in a caste condition. The curriculum of county and ghetto schools for Negroes was oriented toward rural life and established "Smith-Hughes teachers" as principals.[38] The Smith-Hughes Act of Congress established the opportunity for land grant colleges and universities to extend themselves into the rural areas to fulfill the educational needs of the people in agriculture and industry; teachers from these schools were often referred to as "Smith-Hughes teachers." Black people profited greatly, since many of them did not or could not attend college but were reached by these teachers. One-room rural schools with outside toilets and a bucket at the well became

37. Fred McCluistion, *The South's Negro Teaching Force* (Chicago: Julius Rosenwald Fund, 1932), p. 96.
38. Wilson Gee, *The School Economics of Agriculture* (New York: Macmillan, 1932), pp. 469–530.

familiar sights. Benches and slates with no books, or with books dis-
carded by white pupils, were common, and the school year depended
on the sequences of the crops; school was in session only when the crops
were in.

The eleven southern states that reported teacher salaries according to
race in 1909 paid $23,856,914 to teachers in their schools that year. Not
more than $3,818,705, or 12 percent, was paid to Negro teachers for
instructing approximately 40 percent of the children. As the Negro
schools and colleges increased their curriculums, their inadequacies
grew. The South's design for separate but equal education grew in
theoretical splendor, but actual support for Negro education grew
smaller and the graduates of black institutions were denied jobs in
mainstream America. And with the Depression, black school conditions
worsened.

Between 1930 and 1934 at least two significant developments took
place. First, the powerful Southern Association, an accrediting agency
for white institutions, felt it owed some responsibility to approving
Negro schools, and renamed its initial committee for this the Committee on the Approval of Negro Schools. Second, Negroes themselves
established a forward-looking organization, the Association of Colleges
and Secondary Schools. This new organization extended its institutional
membership to include secondary schools.

THE FEDERAL AWAKENING, 1935–1954

The era following the Great Depression was a turning point in Negro
education. Challenges in the courts and the rise of new, militant, and
well-trained Negro leaders assaulted the concept of segregation. This
period, from 1935 to 1954, was one of nonviolent rebellion, characterized by litigation. From 1900 to 1953, numerous court cases had been
presented relating to the education of Negroes in the South. These were
prosecuted almost entirely by the NAACP; all were settled on the
"separate but equal" doctrine created by the *Plessy* v. *Ferguson* case,
though little attention was paid to the "equal" aspect. Thurgood Marshall stated, "This . . . doctrine was seized upon and used by state and
federal courts in school cases again and again without effort being made
to analyze the legality of the segregation statutes involved."[39]

Under the able leadership of Marshall, the NAACP from 1930 to
1945 made its attack on the "equal" aspect of the doctrine. This was

39. Thurgood Marshall, "An Evaluation of Recent Efforts to Achieve Racial Integration in Education through Resort to the Courts," *Journal of Negro Education* 21, no.
3:316–27 (Summer 1952) .

especially pressed in the areas of graduate and professional education of Negroes in the South. Chronologically, these higher education cases included the Hocutt case against the University of North Carolina in 1933 (this case was lost); the Donald Murray case in 1935, which admitted Murray to the Law School at the University of Maryland; the Gaines case in 1938, which saw the University of Missouri open its doors to the establishment of a "Jim Crow" law school even though Gaines himself disapproved; the Bluford case in Missouri, which resulted in the establishment of a School of Journalism at Lincoln University, a historically Negro college; cases against the University of Tennessee, which were lost on the grounds that administrative remedies had not been exhausted; and the case against the University of Kentucky, which resulted in the establishment of a School of Engineering at the Negro college, Kentucky State.[40] Despite some success, however, at the close of the 1930s Negroes were admitted by court order only to the University of Maryland. In 1940 the University of West Virginia voluntarily opened its doors to a Negro.

In 1936, the NAACP began a legal campaign to equalize the salaries of Negro and white teachers in public schools in the fifteen southern states which practiced separate education. An early case was that of William B. Gibbs, who sued the Montgomery County, Maryland, Board of Education in December of 1936. This black school principal's action was followed swiftly, in 1937, by that of Elizabeth Brown, a Maryland elementary school teacher; Negro teachers in Anne Arundel County and Prince Georges County were quick to follow. The celebrated case of Aileen Black, a science and chemistry teacher in Norfolk, Virginia, was successfully contested by Melvin Alston in the same city.

The school boards in the southern states fought back with every device they could conceive of to stem this tide, but by 1941 the NAACP announced that almost half of its campaign had been completed successfully. The campaign continued in years to come, taking on thirty-eight cases.[41] Of this number, twenty-seven were won by 1948, resulting in the addition of millions of dollars to the salaries of Negro teachers. By mid-century, the NAACP had completed its drive for equal salaries for Negro teachers.

The year 1945 saw a change in strategy in the NAACP's approach to litigation. Thurgood Marshall wrote that "the only solution to the problem was an all out attack against segregation in public education.[42]

40. Ibid.
41. Florence Murray, *Negro Handbook, 1949* (New York: M. Malliet and Co.), pp. 62–63.
42. Marshall, pp. 316–27.

No longer would the "separate but equal" line be pursued. Plans were laid for a direct attack against the validity of segregation statutes which related to public graduate and professional education.

The significant pronouncement in the Gaines case was followed in less than a decade by an equally meaningful decision in the case of *Sipuel* v. *Board of Education*. The court ruled on the admission of Ada Lois Sipuel to the University of Oklahoma. It stated that the state was compelled to provide for the plaintiff, and all others similarly situated, not only equal opportunity to commence the study of law at a state institution, but that she must be able to start her program at the same time as other students. She was admitted to the University of Oklahoma Law School in 1949. This was followed by *Sweatt* v. *Painter*, which virtually ended segregation of graduate and professional education as a legal issue.

In 1951, the NAACP decided to make a direct attack against segregation on the elementary and high school levels. This decision apparently was based on the assumption that, if the invalidity of segregation statutes at these levels of public education could be established, the doctrine of "separate but equal," as currently applied to all public education, would be destroyed. Four cases were initiated and all found their way to the U.S. Supreme Court. These cases directly attacked segregation in public schools. J. Waties Waring of Charleston, South Carolina, tried the first case, that of Clarendon County, South Carolina, in 1951; this case was followed by the Topeka, Kansas, case in 1951, the Prince George, Virginia, case in 1952, and the Wilmington, Delaware, case in 1952. The case of Oliver Brown for his daughter, Linda Brown, was lost in federal court on 3 August 1951; it was accepted by the Supreme Court along with the other, similar cases.

When these cases reached the Supreme Court, the basic issue was clearly the legality of segregation. This Supreme Court was known as the "Warren Court." Chief Justice Earl Warren, in delivering the opinion of the Court in the Brown, et al., cases, said, "The plaintiffs contend that segregated schools are not equal and cannot be made equal, but that hence they are deprived of the equal protection of the law."[43]

On 17 May 1954 the U.S. Supreme Court rendered its decision in the four school segregation cases which had been initiated by the NAACP in 1951 and 1952. In the four cases against Kansas, Virginia, South Carolina, and Delaware, the historic decision was:

43. Albert P. Blaustein and Clarence Clyde Ferguson, Jr., *Desegregation and the Law* (New Brunswick, N.J.: Rutgers University Press, 1957), pp. 45–49.

We conclude that in the field of public education the doctrine of "separate but equal" has no place. Separate educational facilities are inherently unequal. Therefore, we hold that the plaintiffs and others similarly situated for whom the actions have been brought are, by reason of the segregation complained of deprived of the equal protection of the laws guaranteed by the fourteenth amendment.[44]

THE CIVIL RIGHTS REVOLUTION AND ITS IMPACT ON NEGRO EDUCATION, MID-1950–1970

The aftermath of the Supreme Court's *Brown* v. *Board of Education* decision presented Negroes with a formidable challenge. Scattered efforts were made to comply with the decision, although resistance was greater and received headline publicity. Washington, D.C., set an immediate and commendable example: in 1955 the complete integration of the District of Columbia's public schools began. By 1956 Baltimore, which had a 41 percent Negro population, had integrated 11,000 of its 51,000 Negro pupils. In West Virginia, most of the public school systems complied with the ruling; the formerly Negro West Virginia State College soon had over 400 white students admitted. In Kentucky, some Negro teachers were quietly moved to previously all-white schools. Oklahoma and Missouri officially began desegregating. Schools on federal and military posts throughout the South were integrated; the University of Louisville was opened to all races; and historic Berea College in Kentucky again opened to Negroes (it had been forbidden to enroll blacks in 1904).

Other compliances were noted. Stowe Teachers College for Negroes was consolidated in 1954 with Harris Teachers College for whites. In 1955 Thomas B. Portwood, superintendent of schools, announced that the San Antonio, Texas, school district would begin integration of children that fall. San Antonio had the advantages of good race relations and a clear-cut statement of policy, with a small Negro population and a fairly large number of Spanish Americans. School desegregation in Nashville, Tennessee, was court ordered, and W. A. Bass, the superintendent, instituted the city's "grade a year" plan in the fall of 1957. Throughout the country, other spontaneous efforts were made without resort to further litigation.

But resistance remained. The latent violence which accompanied public school and higher education desegregation throughout much of the South was manifested in Little Rock, Arkansas; at the University of Alabama; and in massive resistance and the closing of schools in Virginia. This period also saw the rise of private institutions which

44. *Brown v. Board,* 347 U.S. 483 (1954).

barred Negro children. Violent racial incidents flared up in Baltimore, Maryland, and in nearby Milford, Delaware. In Sturgis, Kentucky, rebellion started on 4 September 1956; similar violence was recorded in Mansfield, Texas, and Clinton, Tennessee. The federal government, however, avoided a direct stand until President Eisenhower forced the issue into the open at Little Rock. After Little Rock, southern politicians and educators turned to resistance through pupil placement laws. Laws of this kind were passed in Alabama, Florida, Louisiana, Mississippi, North Carolina, South Carolina, Tennessee, and Virginia. In fact, various kinds of resistance strategies were designed to slow integration, and several states even prepared to abolish their public schools rather than face the prospect of integration.

In March 1956, ninety-nine congressmen, mostly Senators and Representatives from the South, signed what was to become known as the "Southern Manifesto" opposing and denouncing the Supreme Court ruling and encouraging resistance. The manifesto said, in part:

> We regard the decision of the Supreme Court in the school cases as a clear abuse of judicial power . . . undertaking . . . to encroach upon the reserved rights of the states and the people. . . .
> This unwarranted exercise of power by the court, contrary to the Constitution is creating chaos and confusion . . . destroying the amicable relations between the white and Negro races that have been created through ninety years of patient effort by the good people of both races. It has planted hatred and suspicion where there has been heretofore friendship and understanding. . . . .
> We commend . . . those states which have declared the intention to resist forced integration by any lawful means. . . .
> We pledge ourselves to use all lawful means to bring about a reversal of this decision which is contrary to the Constitution and to prevent the use of force in its implementation.
> In this trying period, as we all seek to right this wrong, we appeal to our people not to be provoked by the agitators and troublemakers invading our states and to scrupulously refrain from disorder and lawless acts.[45]

Several southern states, however, made quick progress in opening the doors of white schools to qualified Negroes. Texas, Louisiana, and Arkansas rank high among those states that made the transition early and without too much trouble. In most instances, higher education integration in state-supported institutions came through court orders. The pattern was to admit qualified Negroes in southern states to the graduate and professional schools. Private schools, well-established and prestigious, continued to admit more Negroes to their ranks.

45. Toppin, p. 207.

The Negro colleges, surviving tenaciously from the Appomattox Surrender to the middle of the twentieth century, found themselves the forgotten champions. When white universities throughout the land were denying an education to black people, these institutions were educating and providing teaching and administrative positions to thousands of educated Negro men and women. But the years from 1950 to the early 1970s witnessed the end of these institutions through mergers with large white universities, the closing down of black state-supported colleges, annexations, and other directives which left them no longer black and no longer unique. Integration of several of these formerly black institutions has saved and strengthened them, but the financial crisis has closed the doors of many others. Enrollments in black colleges in the 1970s are, for the most part, holding steady, as can be seen in table 1. Some institutions have been eliminated, while others have merged or have been integrated into traditionally white institutions. The need for black colleges will not diminish in the future, since many students can not gain admittance to white schools because of their special requirements.

Resistance to school integration took many forms. The children themselves, both black and white, reflected the prejudice and hatred of their parents. Violence erupted in the schools. Often teachers and administrators dealt unfairly with children of another race. Virginia, as previously noted, led the way with "massive resistance." The Commonwealth of Virginia assumed direct responsibility for the control of all Virginia public schools, and pupil assignment was a part of the delaying tactics.

The most heralded conflict was that of Little Rock's Central High School in Arkansas. Governor Orval E. Faubus, a militant anti-integrationist, resisted the assignment to that school of nine Negro children. The community was polarized, and federal troops were sent into Little Rock by President Eisenhower to insure the admittance of the children. In many other instances throughout the country popular sentiment erupted into violence; where the community had prepared for change, however, the transition was smoother.

On 1 February 1960, four black students at North Carolina Agricultural and Technical College at Greensboro, North Carolina, began a sit-in at the local Woolworth's lunch counter, a preview of the new militancy among black Americans. The students went to the Woolworth store, where they could make purchases but could not eat, and sat down at the "white only" lunch counter, remaining until they were arrested. Even though the sit-in technique had been previously used by

Table 1. Enrollment Figures for Predominantly Negro Colleges and Universities, Fall 1964, 1970, and 1975

Institution	Location	Affiliation	Total Enrollment Fall, 1964	Total Enrollment Fall, 1970	Total Enrollment Fall, 1975
ALABAMA					
Alabama A & M University	Normal	State	1,465	2,755	4,034
Alabama State University (Teachers College)	Montgomery	State	2,058	1,671	3,158
Daniel Payne College	Birmingham	African Methodist Episcopal (A.M.E.)	360	450	367
Miles College	Birmingham	Christian Methodist Episcopal (C.M.E.)	816	1,139	1,127
Oakwood College	Huntsville	Seventh-Day Adventist	387	640	1,035
Stillman College	Tuscaloosa	Presbyterian U.S.	568	713	711
Talladega College	Talladega	United Church of Christ	387	533	481
Tuskegee Institute	Tuskegee	Private	2,612	3,062	3,284
ARKANSAS					
Arkansas Mechanic & Normal College	Pine Bluff	State	2,579	3,445	
Philander Smith College	Little Rock	Methodist	592	639	676
Shorter College	North Little Rock	A.M.E.	204	260	197
DELAWARE					
Delaware State College	Dover	State	720	1,393	1,784
DISTRICT OF COLUMBIA					
District of Columbia Teachers College	Washington	City	1,275	4,488	1,820
Howard University	Washington	Private	7,555	9,283	9,303

FLORIDA					
Bethune-Cookman College	Daytona Beach	Private	861	1,065	1,313
Edward Waters College	Jacksonville	A.M.E.	858	969	563
Florida A & M University	Tallahassee	State	3,322	5,024	4,871
Florida N & I Memorial College	St. Augustine	Private	329	864	
Gibbs Junior College	St. Petersburg	County		727	
GEORGIA					
Albany State College	Albany	State	1,169	1,942	1,702
Atlanta University	Atlanta	Private	623	1,219	1,136
Clark College	Atlanta	Methodist	839	1,085	1,475
Fort Valley State College	Fort Valley	State	1,411	2,338	1,807
Interdenominational Theological Center	Atlanta	Interdenominational	104	141	204
Morehouse College	Atlanta	Private	819	1,020	1,275
Morris Brown College	Atlanta	A.M.E.	928	1,456	1,530
Paine College	Augusta	Methodist & A.M.E.	402	691	649
Savannah State College	Savannah	State	1,279	2,444	2,413
Spelman College	Atlanta	Baptist	688	967	1,155
KENTUCKY					
Kentucky State University	Frankfort	State	1,226	1,754	2,174
LOUISIANA					
Dillard University	New Orleans	Private	837	968	1,117
Grambling College	Grambling	State	3,634	3,900	3,571
Southern University and A & M College	Baton Rouge	State	9,556	12,000	12,269
Xavier University	New Orleans	Roman Catholic	831	1,422	1,548

Table 1 (cont.)

Institution	Location	Affiliation	Total Enrollment Fall, 1964	Total Enrollment Fall, 1970	Total Enrollment Fall, 1975
MARYLAND					
Bowie State College	Bowie	State	566	2,259	3,323
Coppin State College	Baltimore	State	529	1,811	2,574
University of Maryland (Eastern Shore)	Princess Anne	State		732	1,192
Morgan State College	Baltimore	State	3,118	5,106	5,720
MISSISSIPPI					
Alcorn A & M College	Lorman	State	1,412	2,520	2,420
Jackson State College	Jackson	State	2,012	4,665	5,960
Rust College	Holly Springs	Methodist	549	724	731
Tougaloo Southern Christian College	Tougaloo	American Missionary Assn. & United Christian Missionary Society	497	600	783
MISSOURI					
Lincoln University	Jefferson City	State	2,411	2,447	2,537
NORTH CAROLINA					
North Carolina Agricultural & Technical State University	Greensboro	State	3,227	3,670	4,937
Barber-Scotia College	Concord	Presbyterian	315	369	470
Bennett College	Greensboro	Methodist	591	660	545
Elizabeth City State University	Elizabeth City	State	984	1,104	1,266
Fayetteville State University	Fayetteville	State	1,095	1,600	3,075

Institution	City	Affiliation			
Johnson C. Smith University	Charlotte	Presbyterian	1,022	1,148	1,209
Livingstone College	Salisbury	A.M.E. Zion	679	720	744
North Carolina Central University	Durham	State	2,651	2,856	4,391
St. Augustine's College	Raleigh	Protestant Episcopal (P.E.)	736	1,175	1,515
Shaw University	Raleigh	Baptist	721	1,154	1,625
Winston-Salem State University	Winston-Salem	State	1,115	1,401	1,962
OHIO					
Central State College	Wilberforce	State	2,521	2,564	2,131
Wilberforce University	Wilberforce	A.M.E.	415	1,182	1,052
OKLAHOMA					
Langston University	Langston	State	937	1,109	1,151
PENNSYLVANIA					
Cheyney State College	Cheyney	State	1,228	2,144	2,459
Lincoln University	Lincoln University	Private	527	1,100	1,102
SOUTH CAROLINA					
Allen University	Columbia	A.M.E.	815	670	485
Benedict College	Columbia	Baptist	1,100	1,408	1,286
Claflin College	Orangeburg	Methodist	545	775	894
Morris College	Sumter	Baptist	483	601	443
South Carolina State College	Orangeburg	State	1,720	2,227	3,040
TENNESSEE					
Fisk University	Nashville	Private	970	1,274	1,517
Knoxville College	Knoxville	United Presbyterian	843	915	818
Lane College	Jackson	C.M.E.	594	976	681
Meharry Medical College	Nashville	Private	345	532	734
Morristown College	Morristown	Methodist	252	173	181

Table 1 (cont.)

Institution	Location	Affiliation	Total Enrollment Fall, 1964	Total Enrollment Fall, 1970	Total Enrollment Fall, 1975
TENNESSEE (cont.)					
Owen College	Memphis	Baptist	302	340	
Tennessee State University	Nashville	State	4,701	5,614	4,973
TEXAS					
Bishop College	Dallas	Baptist	992	1,968	1,222
Huston-Tillotson College	Austin	Private	615	747	696
Jarvis-Christian College (merged with Texas Christian College)	Hawkins	Disciples of Christ	412	707	509
Paul Quinn College	Waco	A.M.E.	358	565	504
Prairie View A & M University	Prairie View	State		4,575	4,612
Texas College	Tyler	C.M.E.	476	534	536
Texas Southern University	Houston	State	4,216	5,485	7,141
Tyler District College	Tyler	County		3,897	
Wiley College	Marshall	Methodist	553	576	535
VIRGINIA					
Hampton Institute	Hampton	Private	1,977	2,768	2,858
St. Paul's College	Lawrenceville	P.E.	441	505	517
Virginia State College	Petersburg	State	5,381	4,970	4,848
Virginia Theological Seminary	Lynchburg	Baptist	65	70	
Virginia Union University	Richmond	Baptist	1,334	1,405	1,356
WEST VIRGINIA					
Bluefield State College	Bluefield	State	1,108	1,316	1,232
West Virginia State College	Institute	State	2,810	3,663	3,533

the Congress of Racial Equality (CORE) in 1943 in Chicago and in 1949 and 1953, it had not caught on nationally by 1960. Within weeks of the Greensboro incident, however, sit-ins spread to a dozen or more southern cities with Negro colleges nearby; in the next two years the technique was refined to almost guerrilla war proportions.

The protests and demonstrations of the 1960s were initiated by young blacks, primarily students from colleges and high schools throughout the South. The protests were directed against the whole American system of segregation; segregation at public lunch counters, theaters and movie houses, public transportation, and other degrading and humiliating apartheid patterns.

In February of 1960, 1,000 students marched throughout downtown Orangeburg, South Carolina; over 350 were arrested and placed in an open-air stockade. In the rain they sang the "Star-Spangled Banner" and held a prayer meeting. Two years later, students from the large Atlanta University complex held a sit-in at all downtown chain and drug stores timed to the split second. Virginia Union University students in Richmond, Virginia, staged a sit-in at the Thalhimers Department Store lunch counter, while their Virginia State College friends did the same at stores in the Petersburg area under the able leadership of civil rights leader David Gunter.

An estimated 20,000 persons were arrested in direct action demonstations across the South between 1960 and 1963. The situation roused northerners to support action and pickets at northern branches and headquarters of merchandising chains with segregated southern outlets and to raise funds for bail. Of perhaps more importance, the demonstrations stirred northern campuses into a vigorous pursuit of social change.

The aims of the southern protest were quickly broadened to include other areas than lunch counters. Wade-ins were staged at "white only" beaches, kneel-ins at "white only" churches, and stand-ins in theaters. The courage of the students who were taunted, clubbed, tear gassed, and jailed prompted adult support in many cities. And they received financial support from the Southern Christian Leadership Conference (SCLC), founded in 1957 and presided over by Martin Luther King.

On 1 December 1955 a gentle woman named Rosa Parks had refused to relinquish her seat on a Montgomery, Alabama, public bus. Thus began the movement that was to bring to prominence the Reverend Dr. Martin Luther King, Jr. The Negro spiritual with the refrain "we shall overcome" ushered in the civil rights movement. A deep-rooted desire for equal treatment in education, employment, and housing, and a willingness to sacrifice everything for such treatment caused 50,000 Negroes in Montgomery to walk, bypassing empty buses, and ushering in the nonviolent protest movement.

Other forms of protest had been used by Negroes during and after slavery. Nat Turner's Rebellion in Virginia was one of many attempts; Gabriel Prosser and Denmark Vesey were other early protestors. The great exodus of Negroes from the South seeking liberty and civil rights in the North was another form of protest. From Louisiana, Alabama, Georgia, and all of the other southern states, blacks headed north and west to New York, Philadelphia, Chicago and further west. Discontent with oppression was reflected in this exodus, which was accelerated after World War II.

The protest movement in all of its forms shows the persistent, uncompromising determination of Negroes to secure their rights by pressing and pressuring their country to live by its own doctrines of equality. All American life has felt the shocks of this movement, perhaps most especially in the area of education. From the little girls at Little Rock to the college students at Woolworth's lunch counter in Greensboro, the story is one of courage and because of it, schools and colleges will never be the same again.

This striving for equality eventually found a patron in John F. Kennedy, the first U.S. president to ever publicly proclaim that segregation was a moral wrong: "Thomas Paine said in the Revolution of 1776 that the cause of America is the cause of all mankind. I think . . . the cause of all mankind is the cause of America. If we fail, I think the cause of freedom fails, not only in the United States, but every place."[46] President Kennedy used the power of the federal government to protect the rights of Negroes with respect to school desegregation and discrimination in public places. During his presidency, he worked for strong civil rights legislation which embraced nondiscrimination in employment and the use of public facilities. He advocated withdrawing of federal funds from programs practicing discrimination, and this affected most of the educational programs in schools and colleges throughout the land. In 1961 he ordered his Health, Education and Welfare secretary to appoint a committee of experts to review the vocational education programs and make recommendations for their modernization. In his message to Congress on 29 January 1963 Kennedy focused on education's central position in the nation's economic progress: "A free nation can rise no higher than the standard of excellence set in its schools and colleges. Ignorance and illiteracy, unskilled workers and

46. John F. Kennedy, 19 September 1960.

school dropouts—these and other failures of our educational system breed failure in our social and economic system."[47]

In 1962, his firmness in dealing with the admission of James Meredith to the University of Mississippi brought federal troops to that university. When Governor George Wallace stood in the doorway at the University of Alabama on that June eleventh to bar Negroes from the university, President Kennedy federalized the National Guard. After Kennedy's assassination, President Lyndon B. Johnson signed the Civil Rights Act of 1964. This act embraced a number of far-reaching provisions, including the prohibition of discrimination in public educational institutions. President Johnson later also signed the Economic Opportunity Act of 1964 which provided education for disadvantaged youth ages 12 to 21, as well as for preschool education, broadly conceived for disadvantaged children ages four to five and known as "Project Head Start."

Just as the NAACP focus on litigation gave way to sit-ins and Martin Luther King's nonviolence movement, so did the latter evolve into "Black Power," a movement that caused serious division among black leaders. Bayard Rustin, the articulate black civil rights spokesman, described the dilemma surrounding Black Power:

> There are two Americas—black and white—and nothing has more clearly revealed the divisions between them than the debate currently raging around the slogan of "black power." Despite—or perhaps because of—the fact that this slogan lacks any clear definition, it has succeeded in galvanizing emotions on all sides, with many whites seeing it as the expression of a new racism and many Negroes taking it as a warning to white people that Negroes will no longer tolerate brutality and violence. But even within the Negro community itself, "black power" has touched off a major debate—the most bitter the community has experienced since the days of Booker T. Washington and W. E. B. DuBois.[48]

The Black Power movement was reflected in the field of education in schools and colleges throughout the land. White universities saw the emergence of black student union organizations that pressed for black studies programs. In predominantly black schools, "blackness" was emphasized. Black speakers, militant and proud, were invited to speak. Students literally changed the curriculum by demanding "equal time" for Nat Turner, Frederick Douglass, and Malcolm X in addition to George Washington, Abe Lincoln, and Daniel Boone. Textbooks and paperbacks flooded the market for black students yearning for their

47. John F. Kennedy, 29 January 1963.
48. Bayard Rustin, "Black Power and Coalition Politics," *Commentary* 42:35–40 (September 1966).

own history, their own identity. The rise of "black is beautiful" in the schools witnessed the appearance of a new kind of beauty queen: she was indeed black in color, with "Afro" coiffure, dressed as an African princess.

The protest movement shows interesting contrasts with the Black Power movement. The former emphasized a quiet quest for admittance, integration, and equal rights to an education in the mainstream. Black Power, on the other hand, emerged as a new kind of separatism, one which stressed relevance in education and an opportunity for an individual "black identity" outside of the mainstream. The focus on merging with white America gave way to a search for a black identity, and the opportunities in schools and colleges to express it.

CONTEMPORARY BLACK EDUCATION

By the end of the 1960s, a new mood toward education for blacks was sweeping the country. The ushering in of the 1970s saw a hardening of the arteries in the flow of civil rights and freedom. With the Nixon administration firmly entrenched, whatever guilt and conscience white America held toward previous denials for blacks became invisible. Whitney Young, Jr., synthesizes this mood swing in his memorable letter to "Jim Crow":

> Dear Jim:
>   Well, I see you're back in schools again. You're really persistent, with more lives than a cat.
>   We thought we got rid of you back in 1954, when the Supreme Court said you were unconstitutional. Of course, you hung on. We knew you would. ... Part of the reason why you came back in the school is the phony smokescreen raised about integration: Code words like "busing" were much nicer to use than the "keep the schools white," your supporters once used. ...
>   When we sent you scurrying back into the woodwork during the civil rights revolution of the "sixties," we thought we'd seen the last of you. We didn't expect that there would be a massive failure of leadership in this nation, a situation where many leaders don't lead, but rather follow those elements in the society that are least representative of its ideals and commitments.
>   So we're back where we started—fighting Jim Crow. We won once; we'll win again.
>
> Yours in battle,
> Whitney M. Young, Jr.[49]

The mid-1960s saw the end of massive resistance and the passage of the Civil Rights Bill of 1964. This bill provided school boards and

49. Whitney M. Young, Jr., "An Open Letter to Jim Crow," *Chicago Daily Defender* 65, no. 50 (18–24 April 1970).

governing bodies technical assistance in the preparation, adoption, and implementation of plans for the desegregation of public schools. Grants and contracts provided special training to improve the ability of teachers, supervisors, counselors, and other elementary or secondary school personnel to deal effectively with special educational problems caused by desegregation.

In colleges and universities, the black history movement was initiated to study the role and contributions of Americans of African descent in the development of America. California required that Afro-American history, in addition to that of other ethnic groups, be included when adopting textbooks and in teachers manuals for civics and history. Major universities in the East and Midwest set up black history courses and hurriedly staffed them to placate the demands of black students. This rush for black history often defeated its purpose, however; John O. Killens, in sounding a warning to black militants demanding black studies, stated in 1960: "What I am saying, brothers and sisters, is that some of us are shucking and jiving and hiding behind the cover of 'Militance and Relevance'. . . . The Liberation Movement needs doctors, teachers, lawyers, engineers committed to the movement, and some of you are copping out because 'it ain't relevant.' "[50]

Alvin Poussant, a black psychiatrist, sounded the same warning about black history in a 1973 publication:

A black person can't develop a positive sense of identity just from learning black history. If one can not function as a man in this society, if this society continues to politically and socially castrate the black man, all the black history and black art in the world aren't going to bring him a positive sense of identity of self-esteem.[51]

Elementary and secondary schools throughout the nation added courses in black history and black studies. Herman Brown, addressing the 56th Assemblage of the Annual Meeting of the Association for the Study of Afro-American Life and History in Washington, D.C., on 22 October 1971, set forth four needs for black studies programs:

First, Black Studies programs fulfill a need for scholarly correction of historical and cultural myths. Second, Black Studies programs provide potential elementary and secondary teachers destined to serve in black communi-

50. John O. Killens, "The Artist and the Black University," *The Black Scholar* 1:63–64 (1 November 1969) .

51. Alvin Poussant, *Why Blacks Kill Blacks* (New York: Emerson Hall Publishers, 1973) , p. 126.

ties, with much more knowledge of the ethnic background of the students with whom they will be working. Third, Black Studies programs fulfill a psychological need on the part of black students. Fourth, Black Studies programs fulfill the need to begin the process of resocialization and socialization of Americans destined to play roles in the United States over the next fifty years.[52]

White colleges and universities throughout the country entered into the 1970s with integrated student bodies. Although many black students served as token "window dressing" for federal funds, they did make their way into the mainstream of college and university life; for instance, a black girl became Miss Ohio State and a black youth became president of the University of California student body. They sat on governing campus bodies and participated in most extracurricular activities.

The rush, too, was on for capable black faculty members. Although usually brought on as instructors or assistant professors, they established themselves in the community and in the eyes of the U.S. Office of Education. Blacks often held such positions as assistant to the president, dean or registrar for Minority Affairs, recruitment supervisor, supervisor of student teachers or coordinator of black studies, sociology instructors, and the like. They were still the last to be hired in the sciences and humanities or as top administrators and teachers in their own disciplines.

In the 1970s several states incorporated their black colleges into the mainstream of higher education. Some of these formerly black institutions quickly became predominantly white, such as West Virginia State and Bluefield State College. Others, like Kentucky State College and Cheyney State College, became almost evenly divided. Many black colleges have remained almost completely black, such as the 8,000-member Norfolk State College student body and those of Texas Southern University and Grambling University. Integrated higher education and the high cost of operation caused other black institutions to close, including Storrer College, Kittrell College, Palmer Memorial Institute, and Virginia Seminary.

These changes raised the controversial question of the need for black colleges. The United Negro College Fund, whose purpose is to help small, struggling black colleges, has repeatedly attempted to answer this question, pointing out the continuing need for post-secondary education for blacks throughout this nation. One of the most eloquent

52. Herman Brown, "Black Studies," unpublished paper presented at the Convention of the Association for the Study of Afro-American Life and History, Washington, D.C., 22 October 1971.

responses was provided in 1970 by Lerone Bennett of Morehouse College in his *The Time of the Whole:*

All over America students are in revolt against the dogmas of the past and the lesson plans of yesteryear. . . . For more than one hundred years now, Morehouse and other predominantly black educational institutions have worked on the frontiers of the educational dilemmas of this country, And we owe a debt of gratitude we shall never be able to repay to men like William Jefferson, John Hope, Benjamin E. Mayes. . . . It was a climate of expectancy created by these men and others that thousands of black boys learned for the first time that they were human beings and that no one could limit their horizons and their hope. It was in this crucible that many of the great pioneers of the black liberation struggle were forged. . . . Because it took maimed and tortured minds and ministered to them and made them whole, because it took students no other college would accept and created teachers and preachers and healers, because it salvaged the unsalvageable and gave hope to the doomed and the damned and the despairing. . . . An institution that performed these wondrous things cannot and should not die.[53]

In the minds of millions of blacks, Bennett's tribute to Morehouse is symbolic; it speaks their hope for Howard, Fisk, Tuskegee, Dillard, and Grambling, for Virginia State and Virginia Union, and Xavier in New Orleans, and Morgan and Alcorn, for Lincoln, Wilberforce, Hampton and a host of others.

Some of the challenges facing Afro-American education in the seventies include:

1. The role of standardized tests
2. Visibility in predominantly white institutions
3. Black English in a standard English environment
4. Equal access to quality education
5. Economic resources to match ability and potential
6. Styles of learning
7. Self-image and confidence
8. Racist teachers and administrations
9. Busing
10. Job placement after graduation
11. Remediation and "catch up" programs
12. Relevant curriculums.

These are only some of the problems which face black students. Inte-

53. Lerone Bennett, "The Time of the Whole," *The Challenge of Blackness* (Chicago: Johnson Publishing Co., 1972) , pp. 231–47.

gration in schools and colleges has been of tremendous value to blacks, but it has also created these problems, or challenges. Space does not permit an elaboration of each individual challenge, but each must be dealt with realistically by those charged with educating America's black children and youth.

Virginia educator J. Rupert Picott, discussing tests, cites the controversy between blacks regarding the validity of standardized tests. He relates this incident:

> The major use of tests, including National Assessment for Educational Progress became so controversial during the past fifteen years that in August 1974, Barbara Sizemore, Superintendent, threatened to drop testing in the public schools of the District of Columbia. William Raspberry, a Washington Post Columnist and Black, in an obvious answer to Mrs. Sizemore, insisted that blacks operate in a "white world" and must be taught to pass tests in advance. Raspberry did not doubt that educational tests are biased and need to be changed.[54]

The resegregation of black and white youth in the public schools resulted from the rise of white-only academics, "white flight" from the cities, and the suburbanization process. Far too often the black schools were poor learning centers. Their populace was disproportionately poor, classroom management became difficult, and even the middle-class minority parents took to "black flight" rather than subject their children to schools which were increasingly black and poor.

Black ghetto students are still academically and intellectually behind their suburban majority counterparts; short on skills, verbal self-expression, training, refinement, and all the other attributes which lend themshelves to learning. Cities have turned to busing to save the schools from becoming black or to achieve what is called "racial balance." However, cities like Atlanta, Richmond, and Washington, D.C., have experienced swelling populations of blacks as whites move to the suburbs.

The changes in central city racial balance have intensified, according to the U.S. Commission on Civil Rights. It reports that enrollment in the 100 largest city school districts dropped by 280,000 children. The U.S. Census Bureau reported that 66.6 percent of white school age children lived in the suburbs, according to the 1974 Census. These facts must be faced in the future in planning for the education of young black people.

54. J. Rupert Picott, "A Quarter Century of the Black Experience in Elementary and Secondary Education 1950–1975" (Washington, D.C.: Art Litho Co., 1976), pp. 68–69.

A LOOK TO THE FUTURE

The future for blacks education in America is a positive one with the potential for real progress. In the past black people have survived on hope, and it is with hope and self-determination that blacks must face the future. The history and heritage, the culture and identity of the black people must be maintained. The future must not, however, merely be a return to the past, but should nourish those traditional and valued elements which persist into the present. Developing a black awareness does not mean wholesale rejection of contemporary values or the Hebrew-Christian ethic. Blacks must recommit themselves to traditional moral values by reinforcing those which stress commitment to the well-being of the group, care for fellow humans, and pride in the individual. Schools can not be expected to do the whole job; the black community must offer its support. Jobs for young people that develop skills and responsibility are essential. Programs to nourish the cognitive, affective, and psychomotor needs of black youth should be available from youth centers and churches. Black leaders, politicians, and the middle class must become more responsive. The federal government must also be more responsive to the educational needs of blacks and the poor; however, there can be no substitute for self-help and self-determination.

The Kennedy and Johnson presidencies offered great hope for the equal education of blacks in America, hope which has since diminished. The sympathetic effort by all levels of government, business, and industry can restore that hope, and the education of black Americans can be the means to the restoration of the "American Dream."

BIBLIOGRAPHY

Adams, Russell L. *Great Negroes Past and Present.* Chicago: Afro-American Publishing Company, 1954.

Alvord, J. W. *Semi-Annual Reports on Schools for Freedmen,* no. 10, Washington, D.C.: Government Printing Office, 1866–70.

Andrews, C. C. *The History of the New York African Free Schools from Their Establishment in 1787 to the Present Time.* New York, 1830.

Aptheker, Herbert. *A Documentary History of the Negro People in the United States.* New York: Citadel Press, 1951.

———. *The Negro in the Civil War.* New York: Citadel Press, 1951.

Bennett, Lerone, Jr. *Before the Mayflower: A History of the American Negro.* Chicago: Johnson Publishing Co., 1962.

Boese, Thomas. *Public Education in the City of New York, Its History, Condition, and Statistics. An Official Report of the Board of Education.* New York, 1869.

Bond, Horace Mann. *The Education of the Negro in the American Social Order.* New York: Prentice-Hall, Inc., 1934.

Bontemps, Arna. *We Have Tomorrow*. Boston: Houghton, Mifflin Co., 1945.

Brawley, Benjamin. *A Short History of the American Negro*. New York: Macmillan Co., 1931.

————. *Dr. Dillard of the Jeanes Fund*. New York: Fleming H. Revel Co., 1930.

Brooks, George S. *Friend Anthony Benezet*. Philadelphia: University of Pennsylvania Press, 1937.

Bullock, Henry Allen. *A History of Negro Education in the South*. Cambridge, Mass.: Harvard University Press, 1967.

Burns, W. Haywood. *The Voices of Negro Protest in America*. New York: New American Library, 1957.

Butcher, Margaret Just. *The Negro in American Culture*. New York: New American Library, 1957.

Clement, Rufus F. "The Present and Future Role of Private Colleges for Negroes." *Phylon*, 10, no. 4 (1949): 323–27.

Clift, Virgil A.; Anderson, Archibald; and Hullfish, H. Gordon. *Negro Education in America*. New York: Harper Brothers Publishers, 1962.

Coleman, James S. *Equality of Educational Opportunity*. Washington, D.C.: U.S. Government Printing Office, 1966.

Cromwell, John Wesley. *The Negro in American History*. Washington, D.C.: American Negro Academy, 1914.

Daniels, W. A. *The Education of Negro Ministers*. New York: George H. Doran, 1925.

Davis, John W. "Problems in Collegiate Education of Negroes," *West Virginia State College Bulletin*, June, 1937.

Douglass, Frederick. *Life and Times of Frederick Douglass*. Boston: DeWolfe, Fiske and Co., 1892.

Drake, Thomas E. *Quakers and Slavery in America*. New Haven, Conn.: Yale University Press, 1950.

DuBois, W. E. B. *The Common School and the Negro American*. Atlanta, Ga.: Atlanta University Press, 1911.

————. *Dusk of Dawn*. New York: Harcourt, Brace and Co., 1940.

————. "The Negro Common School." *Atlantic University Publications*, no. 6. Atlanta, Ga.: Atlanta University Press, 1901.

————. *The Souls of Black Folk*. Chicago: A. C. McClung and Co., 1904.

Franklin, John Hope. *From Slavery to Freedom: A History of American Negroes*. 2d ed. New York: Alfred A. Knopf, 1961.

Frazier, E. Franklin. *The Negro in the United States*. New York: Macmillan Co., 1957.

Goodwin, M. B. "History of Schools for the Colored Population in the District of Columbia," *Report of the United States Commissioner of Education*. Washington, D.C.: U.S. Government Printing Office, 1871.

Greene, Lorenzo, and Woodson, Carter G. *The Negro Wage Earner*. Washington, D.C.: Association for the Study of Negro Life and History, 1930.

Harlan, Louis R. *Separate and Unequal*. Chapel Hill: University of North Carolina Press, 1958.

Hastie, William H. "Some Pains of Progress." *Journal of Negro Education* 27: (Spring 1958): 151–58.

————. Speech delivered at the Special Convocation commemorating the 125th Anniversary of the American Baptist Home Missionary Society, 12 and 13, November 1957 at Virginia Union University, Richmond, Va.

Jernegan, Marcus W. *Laboring and Dependent Classes in Colonial America 1607–1783*. Chicago: University of Chicago Press, 1931.

Johnson, Charles S. *Patterns of Negro Segregation*. New York: Harper Brothers, Publishers, 1943.

Jones, Thomas Jesse, and associates. "Negro Education: A Study of the Private and Higher Schools for Colored People in the United States." *U. S. Bureau of Education, Bulletins, 1916* nos. 38 and 39. Washington, D.C.: U. S. Government Printing Office, 1917.

Knight, Edgar W. *Public Education in the South*. Boston: Ginn and Co., 1922.

Lincoln, C. Eric. "The Strategy of a Sit-in." *The Reporter*. 5 January 1961.

Locke, Alain L. *The Negro in Art*. Washington, D.C.: Associates in Negro Folk Education, 1940.

Lomax, Louis E. *The Negro Revolt*. New York: Harper and Row Publishers, 1962.

Mangus, Charles S. *The Legal Status of the Negro*. Chapel Hill: University of North Carolina Press, 1940.

McCluistion, Fred. *The South's Negro Teaching Force*. Chicago: Julius Rosenwald Fund, 1932.

McMillan, George, "The South's New Time Bomb." *Look*, 5 July 1960, pp. 21–25.

Miller, Kelly. *The Education of the Negro: Report of the United States Commissioner of Education*, chap. 16. Washington, D.C.: U.S. Government Printing Office, 1901.

Murray, Florence. *Negro Handbook*. New York: W. Malliet and Co., 1949.

Nabrit, James M., Sr. "Legal Inventions and the Desegregation Process." *The Annals of the American Academy of Political and Social Science* 304 (March 1956): 36.

Nabrit, S. M. "Desegregation and the Future of the Graduate and Professional Education in Negro Institutions." *Journal of Negro Education* 27 (Summer 1958): 415.

National Scholarship Service and Fund for Negro Students. *Interim Report—Southern Project*. New York: The Fund, November, 1954.

Nicolay, John G., and Hay, John. *Abraham Lincoln, A History*. New York: Century Co., 1904.

Noble, Stuart G. *A History of American Education*. New York: Farrar and Rinehart, Inc., 1938.

Puryear, Bennet [Civis]. "The Public School and Its Relation to the Negro." *Southern Planter and Farmer*. Richmond, Va.: Clemmitt and Jones, printers, 1877.

Quarles, Benjamin, ed. *Narrative of the Life of Frederick Douglass*. Cambridge, Mass.: Belknap Press, 1960.

Range, Willard. *The Rise of Progress of Negro Colleges in Georgia: 1855–1949*. Athens: University of Georgia Press, 1951.

Rollins, Charlemae Hill. *They Showed the Way: Forty American Negro Leaders*. New York: Crowell, 1964.

Sawyer, F. A. "The Common Schools—What They Can Do for a State." *Proceedings*. National Teachers' Association, 1870.

Silberman, Charles E. *Crisis in Black and White*. New York: Random House, 1964.

Smuts, Robert W. "The Negro Community and the Development of Negro Potential." *Journal of Negro Education* 26 (Fall 1957): 458.

Taylor, Julius H., ed. *The Negro in Science*. Baltimore: Morgan State College Press, 1955.

Toppin, Edgar A. *A Biographical History of Blacks in America Since 1528*. New York: David McKay Company, Inc., 1971.

Washington, Booker T. "The Educational Outlook in the South." *Proceedings*. National Educational Association, 1884.

———. *Up from Slavery*. New York: A. L. Burt Co., 1901.

Wells, Guy H., and Constable, John. "The Supreme Court Decision and Its Aftermath." *Negro Education in America*. Edited by Virgil A. Clift and others. New York: Harper Brothers Publishers, 1962.

Wickersham, J. P. "Education as an Element in Reconstruction." *Proceedings*. National Teachers' Association. 1865.

Woodson, Carter Godwin. *The Education of the Negro Prior to 1861*. Washington, D.C.: Associated Publishers, Inc., 1919.

———. *The Negro in Our History*. Washington, D.C.: Associated Publishers, 1922.

Work, Monroe N. *Negro Year Book, 1931–32*. Tuskegee, Ala.: Negro Year Book Publishing Co.

Harold Cruse

The Creative and Performing Arts and the Struggle for Identity and Credibility

Whether viewed historically or from a contemporary perspective, the black creative artist is, first of all, an individual member of a group which produces an inordinately large number of artists. (For purposes of conceptual simplification, the "creative arts", and the "performing arts" are used interchangeably when necessary, although there are of course manifest differences in the "art" of creative "practice.") In the United States, observers from the revolutionary era such as Thomas Jefferson[1] down through W. E. B. DuBois[2] and his twentieth-century contemporaries have emphasized the fact that the Negro is highly endowed artistically.[3] Hence, the creative and artistic proclivities of Afro-Americans, due to their oppressed, underclass social position, have revealed an amazingly large number of fascinating variations and styles on the theme of artistic creativity. The social factors that influence and generate these variations are many; for example, race, class, economics, educational levels, psychology, aesthetic responses and judgments (both

1. Thomas Jefferson, *Notes on the State of Virginia* (New York: Harper Torchbook Ed., 1964) , p. 135. Despite his biases, Jefferson recognized the Negro's superiority over the whites in musical gifts.
2. W. E. B. DuBois, *Gift of Black Folk* (New York: Washington Square Press, 1970), pp. 150–90.
3. Morgan Smith, *The Radical* 2: 39–41 (1867) . Morgan Smith (thought to be a former Union Army officer) , wrote: "Many years of familiar knowledge of negroes [sic] has convinced me that they are born orators, painters, sculptors, musicians, actors, though for the present dwarfed by the spell of the wicked magician Opression, whose hideous skill is still at work in many parts of the world transforming princes into beasts."

Professor Cruse is in the Department of History and Afro-American Studies, University of Michigan, Ann Arbor.

a priori and spontaneous, or traditional or adaptively attitudinal), skin color, sex, and so forth.

Due to the Afro-American's special group molding, the black creative artist, out of social necessity, appears under different guises at different times and circumstances. The Afro-American creative artist might appear also as a student, a worker, a juvenile delinquent, a teacher or college professor, or a civil rights leader. An actor, singer, painter, or poet might also be an organizer of social protest action; a writer might be a porter or an expatriate in Paris or Rome; the dramatist might also be an actor or director; the poet might also be a lawyer or a foreign service diplomat; a composer might have been a pullman porter in 1935 and a composer-in-residence at a university in 1970. Was James Weldon Johnson a better poet and novelist than he was a lawyer, diplomat, lyricist, or NAACP official? Was W. E. B. DuBois a better literary essayist and poet than he was a social philosopher and civil rights radical? Was Paul Robeson's artistic career on the stage more important than his later role as Negro rights spokesman on the civil rights fronts? By what criteria do we assess the creative artists' struggle for identity and credibility, and what *ought* to be some of our conclusions in the light of the social imperatives of today?

Because of the complexity and delicacy of this problem, little has been said about it from a standpoint of definitive criticism that is also creative, for criticism is an art that ought to be as creative as the creative product or function the critic is confronting. One of the more serious flaws in the black creative and artistic tradition is not so much in the quantity or quality of creative output as in the thinness of the accompanying tradition of criticism. But the absence of a mature critical tradition in the creative arts signifies the absence of, or at least the insufficiency of, the Afro-American's school of cultural history. As "black history" goes, a school of Afro-American cultural history hardly exists, but the limitations and superficiality of what passes for black cultural history in America is rooted in the fact that the Afro-American lacks that all-important adjunct or division necessary to the credibility and viability of anybody's historical traditions (written or oral) and that, in the case of Afro-Americans, is a black intellectual history.

Such assertions as these immediately arouse a number of instantaneous questions and even objections, such as: What does "history" (cultural, intellectual, or otherwise) have to do with the struggle of the Afro-American for identity and credibility, especially in the creative and performing arts? Moreover, after the literary deluge on the meaning of "blackness" that flooded bookshelves in the 1960s, is there not enough black history to suffice until at least the 1980s? Perhaps, but the problem here is not one of quantity but quality. In addition, the historical "black experience" remains an experience in search of a more explanatory methodology. Black historical methodology cannot as yet provide us with a consensus on the meaning and impact of the black experience on America, although we suffer no lack of political and social histories dealing with the social, political, economic, religious, and other aspects of the black experience.

In the main, black history writing is at present that of a subject people struggling for social justice, as defined by a number of stated American ideals. At this new stage of black development, it is open to justifiable criticism for its lack of both depth and conceptual scope. What is required is a black historiography that attempts to transcend the conceptual limitations of the history of "race struggles," or the generalized "slavery to freedom" panoramic view that somehow blends in the general black "freedom march" with the forced pace of America moving towards its Manifest Destiny—whatever that is supposed to be. One recent critic called this approach to history writing the "intrinsic approach to ideas." This technique, he says, "gets around the mind-environment dilemma by in effect ignoring environment. It approaches ideas where scholars readily find them—ordinarily in printed text—and it tends not to ask how they got there. . . . It is not much interested in connecting ideas to things in the world outside."[4]

However, the same critic identifies the opposite approach to the dilemma inherent in history writing, the "extrinsic approach, which is more after the utility of ideas."

> This approach is not much concerned with the idea itself, but rather what's behind and around the idea. It interprets ideas not as causes but as effects or symptoms, and its focus usually strains outward from the individual mind to the collective experience. . . . Where intrinsic scholars pretty much ignore environment to focus on the individual, extrinsic scholars see the individual pretty much determined by the environment surrounding him.[5]

This critic, like many others, is aware of the methodological and interpretive crisis in American historiography and sets out to challenge a number of basic assumptions adhered to by most of the leading American historians. No doubt black American historiography does inherit many of the assumptions of its white American counterpart. What American history writing needs, says this critic, is better intellec-

4. Gene Wise, *American Historical Explanations* (Homewood, Ill.: Dorsey Press, 1973), p. 142.
5. Ibid.

tual history in which "we can also repicture history, or intellectual
history, as an ongoing series of problems or dilemmas which people
must confront."[6] And, he concludes,

> Thus, history, and especially the history of ideas, becomes not the story of
> finished things, but the analysis of problematic things. And we're not after
> ideas wholly as ideas—as "isms" or broad, floating "currents." Rather, we're
> after ideas coming hard up against the substance of things, in situations.
> By connecting these ideas back to their generating situations, and to other
> situations which they must confront through time, we concern ourselves
> not only with their logic, but their life history too. That's one reason to
> call ideas "strategies" here—to give them a living, experiential character.[7]

An application of this "extrinsic" methodology to a problem in black
history, such as that of the creative and performing arts and the struggle for identity and credibility, would provide a clearer perception of
the methodological implications. For, in our historical view of things,
the struggle for this kind of identity and credibility has traditionally
not been as crucial nor important as, for instance, the struggle for the
identification and credibility of Negro leaders such as Booker T. Washington, W. E. B. DuBois, or Marcus Garvey. Such attempts for identification are the mainstay of written Negro history, representative of
a limited view of the black past that has prevented the achievement
of any meaningful conceptual advance towards a valid black intellectual history.

An intellectual history has to be predicated upon a cultural history;
that is, a history of *ideas*. Without such a historical methodology, Afro-
Americans lack the means to find their identity and credibility in the
creative and performing arts. Thus the decade of the 1890s saw the
emergence of a new class among black Americans—the creative artists
and performers, writers, poets, actors, singers, dancers, comedians, composers, theatrical experimenters and pioneers, scholars, and educators.
A further indicator of the increasing "intellectual" resources of Afro-
Americans was the establishment in 1897 of the American Negro Academy, inspired by Alexander Crummell, who was called "an apostle of
Negro Culture."[8] The interesting and unique aspect of this burst of
creativity was its occurrence during the darkest decade of racial oppression that American blacks had suffered since the political eclipse of
Reconstruction in 1877. Rayford W. Logan dismally described this
period as the "lowest and lowliest position" that the Negro had occu-

6. Ibid., p. 146.
7. Ibid., p. 147.
8. William H. Ferris, *Alexander Crummell—An Apostle of Negro Culture*, Occasional Papers, no. 20 (Washington, D.C.: American Negro Academy, 1920).

pied since emancipation, culminating in what he termed "the nadir under McKinley."[9] This was the decade of *Plessy* v. *Ferguson* and the "separate but equal" doctrine of 1896, which saw the complete disfranchisement of blacks in the South, wholesale terrorization and lynchings, and the complete banishment of blacks from the political life of the southern states. Even so, out of the trials and tribulations of the Afro-American during post-Reconstruction, "the muses were heard."

But to most historians, black or white, the voice of the black muse was not included in their accounts. Whites usually include their own cultural achievements as part of their history, and convincingly detail the evolution of the manifold achievements of "Western culture" especially in the creative arts, philosophy, and aesthetics; Western society's intellectual history is traced back to ancient Greece, specifically Athens. But, since the 1890s, black historiography has had problems dealing with the unique intellectual and cultural aspects of the black experience. One of the first black historians to recognize this problem was Benjamin Brawley (1882–1939). Brawley was a historian, clergyman, and professor of English during his career as an educator at black universities. In the opening lines of the preface to his scholarly *A Social History of the American Negro* (1921), Brawley stated that it was his aim to "give fresh treatment to the history of the Negro people in the United States, and to present this from a distinct point of view, the social."[10] In point of fact, Brawley's social history was the first comprehensively conceived work on Negro history since George Washington Williams's pioneering *History of the Negro Race in America from 1619 to 1880* (1883). Brawley differentiated his methodology from that of Williams's and other "studies of periods or episodes since [Williams's] work appeared" on the basis that his own approach was "social," as opposed to being strictly "political."

Despite the fact that the Negro problem was just as "political" in 1921 as it had been prior to the Civil War and during and after Reconstruction, Brawley considered the purely political approach to history writing as somewhat deficient, lacking in its ability to reveal social facts and truth and to provide edification. To correct this deficiency, Brawley asserted that "it is necessary accordingly to study the actual life of the Negro people in itself and in connection with that of the nation, and something like this the present work endeavors to do."[11]

9. Rayford W. Logan, *The Negro in American Life and Thought* (New York: Dial Press, 1954) , pp. 79–96.
10. Benjamin Brawley, *A Social History of the American Negro* (New York: Macmillan, 1921, 1970), p. ix.
11. Ibid.

Brawley's "social history" was undoubtedly superior to the highly formalized workmanship of Williams's historical method, but not because Brawley's work avoided anything political. Brawley was simply the superior scholar, had access to a greater number of primary sources, and benefited from improved academic methods in the training of historians and social scientists. Williams, who was sometimes referred to as the "Black Bancroft," published his major work before the 1884 founding of the American Historical Association. The writing of history in America before 1884 was primarily a literary pastime, usually reserved for wealthy or self-supporting, self-made scholars and gentlemen of leisure. George Washington Williams had been trained as a lawyer, rather than a historian or social scientist. No doubt Williams, who for a number of years led an active political career on both state and federal levels, was politically motivated to undertake the arduous challenge of writing a history of the Negro race, and his study was completed simultaneously with the development of new methods of historical studies in America.

A careful study of Brawley's *A Social History of the American Negro* is in order. One of the major problems evident in Brawley's 1921 study is that it was not social enough; and, in terms of the critical thrust of our theme, it therefore was also not cultural enough in light of the thirty years of black experience preceding its publication. As a result, his study could not contribute very much to the kind of black intellectual history that should have been forthcoming. Despite Brawley's magnificent efforts, his social history barely escapes being the kind of political history he criticized.

A Social History of the American Negro is essentially a political history on another scholarly and literary level. Brawley, a true academic product of his era, had absorbed the contemporary methodology that the German school of history writing had passed on to American universities, including Leopold Von Ranke's technique of weaving research results into a fluent and readable narrative. As a writer Brawley was not much better than Williams, except in his mastery of narrative. Williams had lived in Civil War America, and that trauma informed his writing; Brawley witnessed the equally traumatic post-Reconstruction encounter of blacks being pushed down to the nadir of racial ostracism and denigration, and their slow rise to the precarious position they held in the 1920s.

In Brawley's social history we catch vivid glimpses and revealing flashes of the cultural ferment taking place from the 1890s to the 1920s, but the manner in which he treats these developments betrays his subjective, intellectual, class and even aesthetic responses. This is shown in his selectivity. At the outset, he declares that "in view of the enormous amount of material, we have found it necessary to confine ourselves within very definite limits."[12] He also states that "there are some topics . . . that have already been studied so thoroughly that no great modification is now likely to be made of the results obtained."[13] But, even within the limits of Brawley's selectivity, his method of emphasis and deemphasis of both older and newer trends—particularly cultural trends—is open to question. Brawley was not blind or myopic; he thoroughly scanned the panorama of black experience up to the 1920s, and was well aware of the cultural aspects. In his summary chapter he even stated:

> If we study the real quality of the Negro we shall find that two things are observable. One is that any distinction won so far by a member of the race in America has been almost always in some one of the arts; and the other is that any influence so far exerted by the Negro on American civilization has been primarily in the field of aesthetics.[14]

Illustrations of this fact were abundant, Brawley wrote; he then proceeded to a brief summary of the American Negro's performance in the arts, mentioning, in passing, "a long line of singers and musicians." Brawley thus clearly recognized the impact of the Afro-American on the arts; why then could he not find space in a study of over 400 pages for at least a modest chapter on the Negro in the arts? Instead, he referred to only sixteen black artists, mentioning them in scattered places in his study. The names included are: Ira Aldridge, William Wells Brown, Harry T. Burleigh, Cole and Johnson Company, Paul Lawrence Dunbar, Fisk Jubilee Singers, Meta Warwick Fuller, Sissieretta Jones, Charles W. Chesnutt, Williams and Walker Company, Frances E. W. Harper, Claude McKay, Madame Marie Selika, Henry O. Tanner, and Phyllis Wheatley. He also mentioned Paul Robeson, but not as an artist. Robeson had not arrived as an actor-singer in 1921, but was known for his athletic prowess as "Robeson of Rutgers," the great football end in 1918.

Of the sixteen creative and performing artists mentioned by Brawley, only nine were really products of the cultural flowering of the 1890s which led to the Harlem Renaissance of the 1920s: Burleigh, Cole and

12. Ibid.
13. Ibid., p. x. In this regard, Brawley included slavery as being in this category: "Such are many of the questions revolving around the general subject of slavery" (p. x).
14. Ibid., p. 381.

Johnson, Fuller, Jones, Chesnutt, Williams and Walker, McKay, and Tanner. The others, such as Ira Aldridge, had made their mark long before Brawley was born, and even some of the moderns of the 1890s were, perhaps, older than he was. In 1920 these artistic personalities were assessed by Brawley as success symbols, those who had somehow "made it" in the hostile white environment that blacks had come to view as inevitable. In mentioning them, Brawley cited them as Negroes who had achieved something, in the same manner as his references to black athletes who had won distinction in boxing, baseball and football.

The main thematic weakness in Brawley's approach to social history, however, appears to have been a bias rooted both in his class outlook and also in his aesthetic responses. The remarkable achievements in music by such individuals as Will Marion Cook and James Reese Europe were not mentioned by Brawley; their names do not even appear. W. C. Handy and Scott Joplin, black music pioneers, do not receive even honorable mention. Despite the unique versatility displayed by James Weldon Johnson and his brother J. Rosamond from 1899 to 1920 in the fields of law, education, literature, music, theater, diplomacy, and the NAACP, neither are mentioned.

Nothing reveals Brawley's limited and superficial perceptions regarding the social roles of creative and performing artists more than this selectivity in citing examples, combined with his very conventional assessments of their achievements. "Mme. Sissieretta Jones" and "Mme. Marie Selika" are pictured as singing artists and "cultured vocalists" of the "first rank." According to Brawley, Harry T. Burleigh won his musical medals by "competing against sixty candidates"; he further mentions that Burleigh "became baritone soloist at St. George's Episcopal Church, New York, and . . . also at Temple Emanu-El, the Fifth Avenue Jewish Synagogue."[15] Not a hint is given here concerning the implications of both Burleigh's and Will Marion Cook's study under the Bohemian composer Anton Dvořak during the 1890s at the National Conservatory of Music, founded by Mrs. Jeannette Thurber. Dvořak was one of the first symphonic composers to demonstrate that Negro folk music could be rendered harmonically and orchestrally into the "classical" symphony with his no. 5 *(New World)*.

Thurber and Dvořak, the two directors of the National Conservatory, had insisted that the student body be composed of equal numbers of blacks, whites, and Indians, much to the consternation of racists in the New York musical hierarchies of that time. The short life of this insti-

15. Ibid., p. 308.

tution has been attributed to lack of financial support due to its racial policies. Historical facts such as these provide information as to the real nature of the struggle of Afro-American creative and performing artists for identity and credibility; they form the important ingredients in a cultural history, and Brawley's lack of attention to these developments weakened his study as a valid social history. His lack of vision here was exceptionally curious, since he was certainly no stranger to these men and events, even if he was a full-time academic.

In addition, how could a historian with Brawley's training and broad contacts refer to Alexander Crummell only twice and then very briefly— as a clergyman and a missionary in Africa—while ignoring the important fact that Crummell was the guiding spirit and intellectual force behind the founding of the American Negro Academy in 1897? Crummell's motivation for creating the academy was to convene a community of forty scholars "whose purpose should be to foster scholarship in the Negro race and encourage budding Negro genius."[16] Was it because Brawley did not consider this development very important as social history? The record reveals that the academy did not really accomplish very much beyond its intramural deliberations. The group floundered about precariously for almost twenty-five years before disbanding, but it was a genuine outgrowth of the cultural and intellectual ferment occurring among the Negro elites of the time. It is, therefore, a legitimate development in the intellectual history of the Afro-American, despite its failures, and it is a characteristic flaw in Brawley's social history that nowhere does he mention it.

During the years from 1890 to 1920, a conservative estimate indicates that thousands of blacks were either personally involved in, or related in some fashion to what constituted a genuine movement of creative and artistic energy in a struggle for identity and credibility in the creative and performing arts. Although this movement was perhaps of interest to Brawley, he apparently thought it was of minor importance when compared to other trends of a social, political, or racial nature. His lack of vision may also be attributed to his class outlook, which defined his aesthetic judgments. In view of the prevailing aesthetic tastes of the era, it was not accidental that Brawley's historical selectivity led him to cite mainly those creative and artistic personalities whose achievements had won recognition in the aesthetic realm of the established and accepted "classical" criteria. This outlook was, of course, legitimate in view of Brawley's training at Harvard and elsewhere. The flaws in his assessments lay in the fact that he could not cope

16. Ferris, p. 9.

critically with the new criteria in artistic creativity being generated within the mass movements of blacks (and their elites) to the large northern urban centers.

This black creative ferment was destined to challenge the supremacy, if not the legitimacy, of many facets of the established aesthetic criteria in artistic form and content that were previously accepted as a basic part of the American psychological makeup. How did Americans, black or white, react to these aesthetic confrontations? How did these black creative impulses impact on American white ideals, and vice versa? These were the social implications of the Harlem Renaissance that set the tone and established the framework for the arguments that followed the publication of *A Social History of the American Negro*. Brawley, curiously enough, had reacted to the problems of "the Negro in litera-ture and the arts" as early as 1910, in a number of articles that were issued in book form in three editions between 1918 and 1929. These were minor critical efforts and indicated his essentially conventional aesthetic judgments. Brawley did not attempt to overcome the limita-tions of those early efforts until 1937, when he published *The Negro Genius—A New Appraisal of the Achievement of the American Negro in Literature and the Fine Arts* (note the imposing title and the em-phasis on "fine arts"). Actually, his aesthetic outlook had remained the same during the intervening years. His "new appraisal" was, in fact, a revision of *A Social History* . . . enlarged to include new advances in achievement.

Brawley's critical evaluations were consistently conventional, de-scriptive, biographical, bland, and informed by the same aesthetic judg-ments he displayed in 1921; he apparently had learned very little from the Harlem Renaissance. His aesthetics could be called purely atti-tudinal, in the sense that they are of the "nonpractical" type, judgments divorced from the impact of the prevailing social fabric within which the creativity occurs. Such aesthetic judgments were distillations of nineteenth-century ideas on the meaning of art as "expression," and the subjective responses as they are conditioned to art either from moral ideals or a priori standards for what is aesthetically traditional. Such a philosophy has trouble coping with rapidly changing social contexts, the economic impact or influence on creativity, and the political conse-quences which follow. In addition, the 1920s experienced, for the first time in modern society, the ingredients of race differences and ethnic consciousness impinging in a new way on the idea of a "national cul-ture." Brawley could not depart from the aesthetic standards of judg-ment that were current both in Europe and America, in the universities, in the press, and all the institutional forms established by the ruling American cultural elites. In fact, most of Brawley's contemporaries found the challenge a hard one. But the essential challenge of the Harlem Renaissance demanded that new criteria in aesthetic judgments be established. It was this problem, one of a racial, social, urban, ethnic, and political nature, that greatly influenced the manner in which the Afro-American creative artist and performer struggled for identity and credibility in the creative and performing arts.

The need for new criteria is, at the same time, a specific theme in the writing of cultural history. The superficial manner in which cultural and creative problems have been approached in black historiography blocks the way toward the cultivation of black intellectual history. As critic Gene Wise has suggested, a cultural or intellectual history is not simply the history of "isms" like "civil rights-ism" or "Garveyism" or "Pan-Africanism" or "black-ism." Nor is it simply the charting of currents or trends as they arise, only to wither away to make room for the next "ism." Rather, we are after the ideas representing these "isms." To quote Wise:

> By connecting these ideas back to their generating situations, and to other situations which they must confront through time, we concern ourselves not only with their logic, but their life history too. That's one reason to call ideas "strategies" here—to give them a living, experiential character.[17]

Let us, then, investigate a number of ideas emerging out of the Harlem Renaissance.

FROM MINSTRELSY TO MAINSTREAM

The cultural movement known as the Harlem Renaissance produced numerous black creative artists who endeavored to express themselves in a variety of art forms. These artists were followed by critical writers who attempted to judge, criticize, or otherwise interpret the expressions in terms of meanings, aesthetic content, and creative forms. Two outstanding personalities were produced by the Harlem Renaissance: Alain Locke, a critic, and Paul Robeson, a creative artist or, to be more precise, an actor-singer-performer.

Although the Harlem Renaissance had a number of chroniclers, a number of years, even decades, had to elapse before valid historical perspective could be brought to bear on the 1920s by a competent historian. Such a historian, out of necessity, would have to possess more insights into the ingredients of cultural history than Benjamin Brawley exhib-

17. Wise, p. 147.

ited in 1921. For our purposes, the intervening years between 1930 and
the 1960s did produce such a historian in Nathan I. Huggins, whose
study of the Harlem Renaissance is by far the best that has appeared
to date. Although the critical, historical, social, and cultural continuity
between Locke, Robeson, and Huggins represents a lengthy and somewhat attenuated linkage, the three personalities are related by a tradition that has had to struggle simply because it was stigmatized at birth,
and the stigma was slavery. When Huggins's study, *Harlem Renaissance,*
appeared in 1971, the ghosts of slavery still hovered in the background
of black consciousness, while the black militant movements of the 1960s
were entering the period of a "second" post-Reconstruction. Although
most black militants would deny it, it is a fact that all of the "evil
spirits" of the ordeal of slavery have not as yet been exorcised from the
black psyche. Many historical facts can be conveniently forgotten, but
the unconscious has a way of retaining the memories of an unhappy
past.

Americans, both black and white, are still aware of the former slave
status of blacks, to such a degree that the aura of a white "superior"
race holding a dominant position to "inferior" blacks lingers on in the
psychological etiquette of interracial and even intraracial experiences.
American whites do not have to verbalize racial attitudes toward blacks
as individuals or as people; neither do blacks have to verbalize their
self-concepts. In both cases, the essential substances of internalized be-
liefs on race are revealed in unconscious ways. For example, in the
writing of history scholars and students still engage in analyses and
reassessments of the slave experience in the Western hemisphere. There
are even those who view the slave experience as the *main* priority in
black historical research today. While I do not agree with this view, I
also do not consider that the slave experience was an unimportant fact
of history that ought to be forgotten. On the contrary, my differences
with the slavery experts are based on methodological premises. It is my
contention that twentieth-century black movements such as the Harlem
Renaissance are the developmental outcome of black social trends
which occurred *after* slavery and Reconstruction, and I believe that
the 1890s are especially crucial to the methodology I am proposing.

In the main, written black history, as exemplified by Brawley, is
social and political history. It is the history of a subject people struggling to break shackles, to be "elevated"; it is the history of "from
slavery to freedom." In other words, black history writing has, of
necessity, been the scholarly handmaiden of the struggle against slavery,
and later on, the academic counterpart of the civil rights movements.
But this approach has its limitations. For one thing, such a standard

approach to historiography cannot produce the kind of cultural history which will establish the groundwork for the all-important intellectual history still to appear.

More to the point, conventional approaches to black history cannot deal effectively with the theme of the creative and performing arts and the Afro-American's struggle with identity and credibility. This, as previously mentioned, is because, in our historical view, the cultural approach to the black struggle was not (and still is not) as crucial or important in our historical experience as, say, the struggle for identity and credibility on the part of black leaders such as Booker T. Washington, W. E. B. DuBois, Marcus Garvey, or Malcolm X. Our writers, artists, and cultural heroes may indeed be important as individuals, but their individual experiences are not to be precisely equated with the civil rights struggles of the "people" or the "masses." Although the struggle of the creative artist is, in some sense, unique, it cannot wholly be divorced from the main thrusts of the civil rights movement. Yet, at times, the activities of the creative artist appear peripheral to the essentials of the social, economic, and political aspects of the *real* movement. The seemingly ambivalent stance toward creative artists as a group in regard to the social protest movements results from the fact that the creative artists represent other important social (i.e., "cultural") dimensions which conventional history writing fails to encompass. Herein lies the importance of Nathan I. Huggins's *Harlem Renaissance.*

In this study, Huggins transcends the conventional limitations of social or political history and accomplishes an excellent critical survey of black cultural history. In his study, the Harlem Renaissance is not passed over or only recalled now and then in the onrush of social history. Yet he too evinced some of the conventional historian's lingering doubts about the exaggerated claims of the Harlem Renaissance. Huggins indicates his belief that even the optimistic hopes of many of the renaissance participants were rather questionable in view of the "real" position of blacks in the Harlem ghetto or those in other major northern cities:

> All of the ingredients for ghetto-making were in evidence in the 1920s. Yet, in those years few Harlem intellectuals addressed themselves to issues related to tenements, crime, violence and poverty. Even *Opportunity*, the magazine of the Urban League and social work among Negroes, did not discuss urban problems as much as it announced the Negro's coming of age.[18]

18. Nathan I. Huggins, *Harlem Renaissance* (New York: Oxford Press, 1971), pp. 4–5.

He went on to assert that "present-day readers are likely to be annoyed with what they will see to be the naiveté of men like [James Weldon] Johnson. Some would call them elitists when it comes to culture. With notable exceptions, like Langston Hughes, most Harlem intellectuals aspired to *high* culture as opposed to that of the common man, which they hoped to mine for novels, poems, plays and symphonies."[19] What Huggins implies here, in the true conventional attitude, is that "real" black history, as *history*, and those individuals who were part of the 1920s' scene, ought to have been more concerned with the social and political implications of poor housing, crime, poverty, and violence, and so forth. Even so, Huggins had to qualify his assertions and modify the conventional historian's views to justify his own foray into cultural history: "Our problem, here, as in any problem in history, is to see men and women of another era in their own terms and not our own. And that will require of us a humanism that will modulate our egos and self-consciousness enough to perceive theirs. Their world was different from ours. We must start there."[20]

The first personality mentioned in Huggins's introduction is James Weldon Johnson, essentially a product of the 1890s who became one of the elder statesmen of the Harlem Renaissance, rather than a product of the era. James Weldon Johnson and his brother, J. Rosamond, arrived in New York in 1899 from their home in Jacksonville, Florida, full of hope for success in the creative fields of music, poetry, and the theater. Many other creative blacks came to New York before and after the Johnson brothers with the same high aspirations. Huggins gives an interesting account of this black creative assemblage—Bert Williams, George Walker, Tom Fletcher, Paul Lawrence Dunbar, Ernest Hogan, Bob Cole, Sissieretta Jones, Jesse Shipp, Will Marion Cook, and others. His account of the theatrical achievements of this group from the 1890s to the early 1900s is especially important as a latter-day supplement to what James Weldon Johnson achieved in his *Black Manhattan* (1930), which explains the origins of "Negro theater." But it was in Huggins's treatment of Negro theater that he ran up against a century-old issue—the problem of "Negro minstrelsy."

One of the most persistent ghosts from the desolate graveyard of the old slave plantation era is the "evil spirit" of Negro minstrelsy. In the United States, the real birthplace of Afro-American creative inspirations in their most unique and distinctive forms derives from the slavery experience—thus the stigma. Huggins's subjective responses to this

19. Ibid., p. 5.
20. Ibid., p. 6.

stigma was an attempt to banish it by a denial of its cultural legitimacy as a genuine black art form. Apart from the detrimental influence of this bias, he undermined the legitimacy of his own basic thesis for the proper critical study of the Negro theater. He wrote: "The theatrical stage itself, more than any other cultural phenomenon, opens a perspective into the pathology of American race relations. It exposes the white-black dependency which has defined race relations in the United States and which persists despite all reform."[21] The idea of the theater as a form and also a paradigmatic cultural model for a proper study of black cultural problems and paradoxes is not original with Huggins, but Huggins proceeded to negate the positive use of the model by a fruitless attempt to debate away the real origins of Negro minstrelsy which, historically, has to be a factor in his model. Thus his analysis of black theater is marred. If Huggins had begun his analysis of black theater with the 1890s, when black reforms were actually in progress, his critical treatment of the Harlem Renaissance might have been more enlightening, inasmuch as the Harlem 1920s were the direct cultural and creative outcome of the 1890s.

Negro minstrelsy and its interpretation as a theatrical form has been handed down to us by historians as an institutionalized "distortion" or "stereotype" of the Negro personality. The majority of educated blacks appear to have despised and rejected the minstrel in the 1890s. However, Negro minstrelsy has been projected into the twentieth century, in the words of C. Eric Lincoln, as a "distortion or the modification of a distortion."[22] As the black past recedes, Negro minstrelsy becomes the distortion of a distortion of a modification; it becomes an evil ghost from the slave past that, in the imagination, has become more hideous than it actually was. So objectionable does Huggins find the image of black minstrelsy that he even attempts to deny what was and has been general knowledge among both laymen and experts: that Negro minstrelsy was, originally of black origin. He differs with James Weldon Johnson, Hans Nathan, Carl Wittke, and others, including Benjamin Brawley, on the real origins of what came to be called "Negro minstrelsy." James Weldon Johnson wrote:

> Negro mintrelsy, everyone ought to know, had its origins among the slaves of the old South. Every plantation had its talented band that could crack

21. Ibid., p. 245.
22. C. Eric Lincoln, in his introduction to 1970 edition of Brawley's *Social History* ..., wrote: "The socio-historical image of the Blackamerican is always either a distortion or the modification of a distortion. It is never prototypical in the sense that Brawley wanted his book to be" (p. xviii).

Negro jokes, and sing and dance to the accompaniment of the banjo and the bones. . . .[23]

Carl Wittke, an early historian on minstrelsy, wrote:

Without the large Negro population of the southern states, the one purely native form of entertainment and the only distinctively American contribution to the theater—the Negro Minstrel—would have been equally impossible.[24]

Huggins, however, not only refutes writers like Johnson, Wittke, and many others on the origins of minstrelsy; he even disagrees with actors, such as the old Tom Fletcher whose short biography, *100 Years of the Negro in Show Business,* tells the story of Fletcher's own personal role as a youthful entertainer in real minstrel shows. Here is how Huggins refutes Johnson and the rest:

Of course it will be said that Negroes were only incidentally related to the origins of blackface minstrelsy. That is true. It developed out of early nineteenth-century circus performances by white men who blacked their faces, and it was formalized in the 1840s by white performers. . . . Despite standard explanations that these white showmen were mimics of southern plantation Negroes, there is very little evidence to support the claim. Close analysis of the minstrel shows reveal very little Afro-American influence in the music, dance or inspiration.[25]

In this fashion, Huggins is able to banish the hated ghost; he was further able to claim that the "Negro theatrical tradition" which "black performers encountered in the late nineteenth century was of white creation [which] made it, in many ways, all the more formidable. This very popular cultural phenomenon pervaded the American imagination and served important emotional needs."[26] Huggins cites the formidable cultural barriers encountered by black performers in the late nineteenth century, but his notions concerning the origins of the Negro theatrical tradition are refutable on nearly all counts. In fact, to accept his thesis on origins is to eliminate, at the outset, any possibility of clarifying the creative and cultural role of the Afro-American's struggle for identity and credibility in the creative and performing arts, either in terms of the nineteenth-century experience or in terms of present-day cultural conditions.

23. James Weldon Johnson, *Black Manhattan* (New York: Alfred Knopf, 1930; reissued by Atheneum Press, 1968) , p. 87.
24. Carl Wittke, *Tambo and Bones* (Durham, N.C.: Duke University Press, 1930), p. 3.
25. Huggins, p. 248.
26. Ibid., p. 249.

Huggins's claim that early nineteenth-century minstrel shows had "very little Afro-American influence in the music, dance, or inspiration" is palpably inaccurate. Reliable sources reveal that John Durang, a popular white actor and dancer, imitated Negro dance patterns as early as 1790.[27] It is also worth noting that the use of Negro song and dance motifs predates the American institution of the traveling circus, mentioned by Huggins, which did not appear until 1826.[28] Marshall and Jean Stearns mention that the influence of Afro-American dance forms were evident in colonial America as early as 1706 in references by "Protestant ministers who objected especially to dancing on Sunday."[29] They add that, "spurred by the example of Durang and others, various imitations of the Negro gradually become popular on the American stage. In 1799 a 'Song of the Negro Boy' was presented between the acts in a Boston theater."[30] Marian Hannah Winter, a dance critic, observed that "the juba dance (simplified from [African] giouba) was an African step-dance which somewhat resembled a jig with elaborate variations, and occurred wherever the Negro settled, whether in the West Indies or South Carolina."[31] G. W. Cable also observed the same dance in Georgia—"The guiouba [sic] was probably the famed Juba of Georgia and the Carolinas."[32] Note that all of these early cultural diffusions of Afro-American music, song, and dance were before the rise of Negro minstrelsy as an institutionalized theatrical form. The diffusion and aesthetic internalization of these African ingredients by whites were so pronounced that a completely new form was established using white imitations of black content. Thus the Stearns could write with historical accuracy that "by 1820, white dancers in blackface imitating Negroes—accompanied by banjo, tambourine, and clappers—were all the rage and beginning to create a new blend."[33] This new blend came to be known as Negro (or blackface) minstrelsy. It serves very little purpose, here, to argue with Huggins over whose "emotional needs" were being served—black or white. In art forms, emotional needs are usually translated into the deep need for expression, and it is probably safe to conclude that *both* blacks and whites had a profound need for

27. Marshall Stearns and Jean Stearns, *Jazz Dance—The Story of American Vernacular Dance* (New York: Macmillan, 1968), p. 38.
28. George L. Chindahl, *A History of the Circus in America* (Caldwell, Ohio: Caxton Printers, 1959), pp. 17–80 passim. Author states that American form of circus originated "circa 1820." *Encyclopedia Americana* gives date as 1826 (vol. 6, p. 737).
29. Stearns, p. 21.
30. Ibid., p. 39.
31. Marian Hannah Winter, "Juba and American Minstrelsy," *Dance Index* 6, no. 2:29 (February 1947).
32. Stearns, pp. 27–28.
33. Ibid., p. 39.

such expression; this need obviously led blacks and whites into a self-induced psychic syndrome of imitating each other. In social psychology and anthropology today, this phenomenon is recognized as a rather universal human trait called "acculturation."

Huggins's problems are confounded when dealing with early nine-teenth-century minstrel beginnings. In the early history of American theatrical developments, Huggins does not explain how there could be "white-black dependency" without white-black imitation both in life styles and especially in the art forms then prevalent. In the cursory fashion in which he banishes Negro minstrelsy into the obscurity of long-forgotten circus fads and the pathological antics of whites, he does violence to the *real* history of one of the personalities with whom we are most concerned—the Afro-American performer.

In his preoccupation with the early minstrel period, Huggins curiously did not mention the "nonminstrel" African Grove Theater, established in New York City in 1821; nor did he cite the famous Shakespearean actor Ira Aldridge, described by some historians as a product of this Negro theater group. We are evidently to assume that since these per-formers established no firm theatrical tradition in the face of the over-whelming appeal of Negro minstrelsy, Huggins could overlook their existence. But no serious writer of American theater history can write about Negro minstrelsy from any perspective without reference to Wil-liam Henry Lane (c. 1825–52), the famous Negro dancer known as Master Juba. Winter, the dance history authority, wrote of Master Juba:

> This most influential single performer of nineteenth-century American dance was a prodigy of our entire theatre history. Almost legendary among his contemporary colleagues, the Juba epic dwindled into oblivion, Negro historians intent on apotheosizing Ira Aldridge, the African Roscius, ig-nored him. Yet this is equivalent to writing a twentieth-century theatrical history of the Negro mentioning only Paul Robeson and omitting Bill Robinson, the great Bojangles. It is more outrageous in that Robinson has embellished an already established form, whereas Juba was actually an ini-tiator and determinant of the form itself. The repertoire of any current tap-dancer contains elements which were established theatrically by him. Herein is the cornerstone of his memorial.[34]

But Negro historians have, to an inexcusable degree, done a disser-vice to Afro-American cultural history by perpetuating distortions and omissions by the method of biased selectivity and the apotheosizing of those trends and personalities which approximate conventional stand-ards of either high culture, moral uplift, or positive achievement. It is

34. Winter, p. 28.

ironic that the dance historian and critic is called upon to single out the flawed professionalism of the social and political historians. And it is here, also, that we come to closer grips with Huggins's flawed analysis of Negro minstrelsy. For Huggins, Negro minstrelsy "became a place for Negro achievement and thus siphoned off black talent that might have developed an authentic ethnic theater."[35] Huggins refers, of course, to the late nineteenth century, the post-Civil War period, and here begins to talk in vague terms about "ethnic theater"; he does not provide any clues as to the ingredients necessary for the establishment of such a theater, one which never emerged.

Dance critic Marian Hannah Winter, among others, has pointed out that the very survival of Negro music in America during the years of the 1740 slave laws was miraculous. The laws, put into effect after slave uprisings in South Carolina during 1739 (the Stono Insurrection), prohibited "beating drums, blowing horns or the like which might on occasion be used to arouse slaves to insurrectionary activity." Winter remarks that, "since most states patterned their slave laws after those of South Carolina and Virginia, the effect of these prohibitions would have discouraged any people inherently less musical."[36] But how did the slaves react to these restrictions?

Substitutions for the forbidden drum were accomplished with facility— bone clappers in the manner of castanets, jawbones, scrap iron such as blacksmith's rasps, hand-clapping and footbeats. Virtuosity of foot-work, with heel beats and toe-beats, became a simulacrum of the drum. In modern tap-dancing the "conversation" tapped out by two performers is a survival of African telegraphy by drums. Since African dance had already developed rhythms stamped or beat out by dancers as counterpoint to antiphonal musical accompaniment, and solo dances set against the communal ring-shout, the formal source material surmounted any restrictions. The slave created the bonja (banjo) too, made from a hollow gourd without a resonance board, slack strung, which developed into the banjo of minstrelsy and jazz.

The Juba dance (simplified from giouba) was an African step-dance which somewhat resembled a jig with elaborate variations and occurs wherever the Negro settled, whether in the West Indies or South Carolina. One variation—crossing and uncrossing the hands against the kneecaps which fanned back and forth—was incorporated in the Charleston of the 1920s. Juba and Jube are recurrent slave names with particular association to dancers and musicians. Juba also occurs as the name of a supernatural being in some American Negro folklore, and became the popular name for an expansive weed, the Juba's bush or Juba's brush.[37]

35. Huggins, p. 251.
36. Winter, p. 28.
37. Ibid., pp. 28-30.

Thus there was a genuine folk element in Negro minstrelsy, and not only was it genuinely black, it was also a genuine Negro recreation of ingredients that were genuinely African in origin; in short, original African music and dance remolded for survival purposes in the Western hemisphere. Small wonder then, that the dance creativity of a Master Juba made him appear amazing to critics.

To be historically accurate, we must admit that Huggins *is* partially correct is his total rejection of Negro minstrelsy as a white creation. As Winter points out, the Negro dancer on the American stage was originally an exotic. But what other role could the Negro dancer adopt in an Anglo-Saxon, Puritan, cultivated society which, despite its occasional departures from Puritan norms of social behavior, still upheld the strictures of New England's Increase Mather's publication *An Arrow Against Profane and Promiscuous Dancing?* I, for one, do not believe that Huggins's allusions to the "Protestant ethic" and its collective emotional needs to fashion a black-faced persona through which to vent psychological inhibitions through emotional release fully explains the minstrel tradition. A society creates its cultural forms and institutions out of the ingredients that are either borrowed, on hand, or inherited. How and why societies do these things are always intriguing questions. Winter and Huggins agree on one important aspect of the Negro minstrel tradition: Winter writes, "by the 1870s there was a relentless, and impalpable, pressure to stereotype the stage Negro completely." She continues: "The Negro performer found that unless he fitted himself into the mold cast for him as typical he could get no work."[38] While agreeing, Huggins dissents; in his opinion the minstrel tradition was a complete stereotype from the outset, containing nothing genuinely black and legitimate. Winter differs:

> In America it was Juba's influence primarily which kept the minstrel dance, in contrast to the body of minstrel show music, in touch with the integrity of Negro source material. There was almost a "School after Juba."[39]

It was only after the passing of the Juba school, Winter writes, that "unquestionably the Negro qualities of minstrel music dwindled, and even the adapted Negro techniques of performance which had been taken over, grew vague and sloppy, save in rare instances. Yet because of the vast influence of one Negro performer, the minstrel show dance retained more integrity as a Negro art form than any other theatrical derivative of Negro culture."[40] Evidence unmistakably indicates that

38. Ibid., p. 40.
39. Ibid., p. 38.
40. Ibid., p. 31.

Huggins is historically inaccurate when he describes the Negro's relationship to minstrelsy in this fashion:

> It was this highly stylized variety show with which Negroes made their first appearance in the commercial theater. Afro-Americans were thus faced with a "Stage Negro" who had become a dominant type for more than forty years. Black entertainers played this white creation rather than themselves.[41]

Apart from the fact that this is an awkwardly exaggerated assessment, Huggins insists on the more negative conclusion, that Negroes were both inhibited from and also incapable of bringing anything original to the American theater in the late nineteenth century. If black performers had made their first appearance in Shakespearean drama or English operetta, they would also have been playing white, rather than black, creations. Ira Aldridge, in fact did just this until 1867 and won accolades for dramatic universality. During the 1890s, when Afro-Americans ushered in their new phase in the Negro theatrical tradition, however, they did, in fact, reestablish their own legitimate originality, even within the old minstrel form. James Weldon Johnson claims that "in the professional theater the first successful departure made by the Negro from strict minstrelsy was in 1890."[42] Winter writes that: "in 1897 a brilliant period for Negro entertainment, lasting something more than a decade, was inaugurated. It produced musical comedies and extravaganzas. . . . The titles of many of these shows . . . have a close relationship to the minstrel show stereotype, and the comedians wore the burnt cork . . . but the music and dances were unfettered by past conventions, and the raw elements of twentieth-century popular music acquired a style which would supersede the schottisches, waltzes and cotillions of the nineteenth."[43] Even the conventional and venerable social historian Benjamin Brawley admitted that the Negro musical comedy of the 1890s was "intermediate between the old Negro minstrelsy and a genuine Negro drama."[44] Only grudgingly, however, will Huggins concede that any artistic advances were made in the Negro theatrical tradition of the 1890s. At one point he states that "comedy and blackface remained, but the form and some part of the content of the minstrel was giving away to innovative Negro talent."[45] He later qualifies this assessment by claiming that "these changes, notable as they were, remained essentially formal; the stage characterization—the theatrical Negro—

41. Huggins, p. 250.
42. Johnson, p. 95.
43. Winter, p. 46.
44. Brawley, p. 308.
45. Huggins, p. 275.

improved only slightly."[46] He then continues on to demonstrate how "black performers helped to perpetuate the 'darky' tradition in other ways."[47] Huggins cites the staging of an 1896 show in Brooklyn, New York, called *In Black America*. This show featured an attempt "to exploit the idea of the sentimental South 'before the war.' " The white producer, writes Huggins,

> reproduced a southern plantation into which he worked a Negro show. In the end he used five hundred people. Cotton plants (with buds) were transplanted, bales of cotton and a real cotton gin were set up. There was livestock and cabins for the "field workers"; some of the cast actually lived in the cabins for the summer. This property was arranged throughout the park to provide "atmosphere," and the patrons could wander through, watching the black actors pretend to be slaves in the South. . . . *In Black America* was just an extreme example of a rather general phenomenon: black performers perpetuating rather than changing the theatrical stereotype.[48]

Contemporary critics reveal that Huggins did not fully enter into the spirit of that age, and so did not realize that he was not, in this instance, dealing with black professional theatrical talent perpetuating stereotypes, but instead with the exploitation of unsophisticated pawns in the soulless game of amusement promotion. Luring blacks from the southern states primarily for diverse economic reasons has long continued in America. The American theater, like American labor which once imported southern Negroes for strike-breaking purposes, depends on expediency and follows what some observers have called a "prosperity-policy."[49] But to agree with Huggins that "the theatrical stage itself, more than any other cultural phenomenon, opens a perspective into the pathology of American race relations,"[50] the observer must insist that this pathology, while psychologically complex, was not theatrically as morbid as Huggins's post-Freudian analysis suggests. Whites and blacks were interdependent in all essential areas of the broader society—political, economic, and cultural. Even in the institution of slavery—the breeder of minstrelsy and the folk expressions of the Afro-American—blacks and whites were interdependent. In this case, the whites happened to be more self-revelatory in theatrical culture than in other institutional forms in which their dominance and cultural ego

46. Ibid., p. 276.
47. Ibid., pp. 277–78.
48. Ibid., pp. 278–79.
49. Harold E. Adams, "Minority Caricatures on the American Stage," in *Studies in the Science of Society* (New Haven, Conn.: Yale University Press, 1937) . Excerpted in *When Peoples Meet,* ed. Alain Locke (New York: Progressive Education, 1942) , pp. 351–52.
50. Huggins, p. 245.

prevailed, and in which their self-esteem would not allow them to admit how much they needed the Afro-American, upon whose backs they built their monuments of Anglo-Saxon preeminence.

Yet, while it is extremely important that we be critical of the Afro-American's cultural response to this interdependence, let us also be realistic. Huggins is to be applauded for applying to this cultural development a literary level of insightful perceptions that has been sadly lacking in the black cultural tradition. But in his rejection of the Negro minstrel bugaboo, he has simply dressed up an age-old bias peculiar to a certain traditional attitude that has been almost as negative to genuine black creativity as the original exploitative use of the black image by white imitators.

To censure the theatrical 1890s because it did not represent a clean break with Negro minstrelsy also further complicates the problem of dealing critically with the Harlem Renaissance. The problems of the renaissance were, in fact, a continuation of the problems of the 1890s in a new, urban, national and international context.

Even the 1970s has not witnessed a clear break with minstrelsy, if for no other reason than that jazz itself is an outgrowth of the continuous stream of minstrelsy. Even Huggins perceived the reappearance of the minstrel tradition in such white comics as Jack Benny, Rowan and Martin, and the Smothers Brothers, and such black comics as Pigmeat Markham and Moms Mabely. Huggins should have also added that when the young blacks of the 1960s and 1970s create new dance patterns and cavort en masse in TV extravaganzas such as "Soul Train," or combine theatrical antics with the singing and dancing of "soul music" singles, doubles, trios and quartets a la James Brown before student audiences, they are continuing Negro minstrelsy in modern dress. Negroes sing and dance, mimic and clown as avidly now as they did in 1873 or 1893 or 1920. This fact provided the "high priest" of black literary and cultural criticism, Alain Locke, his problems with the Negro theatrical tradition in the 1920s. Locke could not come to terms with the minstrel tradition, and thereby contributed additional disorientation to an already compromised and poorly oriented Harlem Renaissance movement.

In 1925 Alain Leroy Locke, the first Negro Rhodes Scholar, edited and presented his original, ground-breaking anthology of black literary, musical, sociological, theatrical, artistic, historical, social, and academic representations of the American Negroes' manifest achievements toward what was judged as their rightful place in the American cultural mainstream. The imposing publication was titled *The New Negro,* and it remains an impressive exposition of the general mood and expectations of the Harlem Renaissance period.

The New Negro attempted, essentially, to interpret a social, intellectual, creative, and aesthetic ferment already in evidence—especially in and about Harlem, New York City. The book did not inspire or create the renaissance movement, but was a self-conscious product of a sociocultural phenomenon already apparent as the culmination of a new quality of racial acculturation versus racial assertiveness, via the societal process of rapid urbanization.

The eclectic array of individual inputs into this interpretive symposium on the Harlem Renaissance was exciting. Practically the entire range of the potential and kinetic content of Afro-American cultural possibilities was surveyed with striking perceptions. Every facet of the black cultural persona was appraised and exhibited by both critics and creators in conjunction with connoisseurs of Negro (African) art, poetry, drama, music and the "new jazz," dance, and fiction. In addition, an anthropological interpretation of "blackness," the ideological imperatives of Pan-Africanism, the sociology of urbanization, the advocacy of the ideals of new Negro youth, and the outcome of educational philosophies then some sixty years in the making were, among other issues, assessed, including an essay on black feminism.

In addition to editing *The New Negro,* Alain Locke contributed not only the foreword, but also an introductory profile-essay on the group personality of the "new Negro"; a paean to Negro youth; a deification of Negro spirituals; and a veneration of "The Legacy of the Ancestral Arts" (by which he meant African plastic and craft arts). The anthology itself was timely, relevant, and a pioneering achievement in the fallow field of black cultural history. Even now few critics could argue with the cultural avant-garde optimism that was exuded in its forward-looking perspectives. Alain Locke thus emerged as the foremost dean and critic of the Harlem Renaissance, which he admitted at the time was not a clearly delineated movement but "more of a consensus of feeling than of opinion, of attitude rather than of program. Still some points seem to have crystallized."[51]

At that moment (1925), Locke's general assessment of the renaissance was doubtless accurate. Blacks of all classes, both plebian and elitist, were experiencing varying degrees of adjustment to the new northern urban environment. "Harlem, I grant you, isn't typical—but it is significant, it is prophetic," Locke wrote. And to show how atypical Harlem was, he said:

51. Alain Locke, ed., *The New Negro* (New York: Atheneum, 1968) , p. 10.

Here in Manhattan is not merely the largest Negro community in the world, but the first concentration in history of so many diverse elements of Negro life. It has attracted the African, the West Indian, the Negro American; has brought together the Negro of the North and the Negro of the South; the man from the city and the man from the town and the village; the peasant, the student, the business man, the professional man, artist, poet, musician, adventurer and worker, preacher and criminal, exploiter and social outcast. Each group has come with its own separate motives and for its own special ends, but their greatest experience has been the finding of one another.[52]

Sociologically, Locke possessed a keen eye for the colorful variety of "colored peoples" whose influx had contributed the atypical qualities of black Harlem. However, a year later, in 1926, Locke published an article that not only further exposed his personal, aesthetic, and unadulterated canons of critical faith; it also revealed that Locke was not aesthetically conditioned to accept every creative style exhibited by that multihued mass of Harlem humanity whose "greatest experience had been the finding of one another." The article was called "The Negro and the American Stage," and it served to bring out in bold relief some barely visible inadequacies in the overall critical thrust of *The New Negro*. Apparently Locke had a number of reservations about the Negro theater which he did not wish to discuss in his grand opus; he left that matter to Montgomery Gregory, an organizer of the Howard University Players. Gregory's contribution on that touchy question was "The Drama of Negro Life," a rather uninspired but historically informative survey. Knowing Locke's intimate sensibilities on the matter of Negro theater, perhaps Gregory's views inspired him to set the matter straight, as it were, and the sooner the better. Thus, eight months after publication of "The Negro and the American Stage," Locke published "The Drama of Negro Life." Both articles revealed a questionable flaw in his assessment of the "new Negro" in the theater. Locke could not or would not accommodate his aesthetic sensibilities and his critical range to include the totality of the creative imperatives of the Harlem Renaissance. Historically and critically, this fact is crucial to our theme.

In 1927 Nathan I. Huggins was born; forty years later he wrote the most definitive reassessment of Locke and the Harlem Renaissance. Huggins was perhaps too kind to Locke, even in view of Locke's immense contributions to the art of criticism and cultural history. His kindness probably stems from the fact that, despite Huggins's gentle differences with Locke on such problems as defining "normative models for Negro art" in the face of the "fundamental dilemma of creative

52. Ibid., pp. 6–7.

work" (i.e., individual versus group expression), Huggins's aesthetic and critical perceptions were really quite similar to Locke's. At one point Huggins writes:

> Alain Locke and others were correct in saying that there was a new Negro: an artistic self-consciousness of the Negro's human and cultural worth, the sense of an urgent need for self-assertion and militancy, and the belief in a culturally enriched past in America and Africa; these themes were real enough in the works of Negroes of talent. It was not merely Locke's imagination, although like an anxious parent he nurtured every suspicion of talent as if it were the bloom of genius. If the American context forced it to be artificial and contrived, it should not be thought Alain Locke's fault.[53]

Something is out of historical and sociological focus here. To imply that only "Negroes of talent" represented the sole content of the renaissance is a distortion. Who, indeed, comprised the "audience"? One can see why Huggins, early in his book, stresses the "cultural elitism" he detects in the minds of the "elites." The American context forced the creative output to be "artificial and contrived," he says, but "distorted" would have been a more accurate description. Something that is artificial and contrived bespeaks an absence of a germinal genuineness at the outset; this is unfair. This, naturally, leads Huggins to declare that the Harlem intellectual leadership was "epiphenomenal . . . it had no grass roots attachments."[54] In many respects this idea was valid, depending on the individual's view of the renaissance. In this connection, Huggins allows a fleeting political judgment of the Harlem elites' contacts with the "masses": "Neither DuBois nor Johnson could have affected the political machine that in those years had been winning minor concessions for immigrant masses in the cities. They were not involved in block or precinct work that would have given them the kind of political leverage that the American political system understood."[55] This fact may indeed be valid, but why single out men like DuBois and Johnson for political insolvency at that moment in history, when even grass roots street-corner radicals like Randolph and Owens could hardly galvanize a mass demonstration from a single block between Lenox and Seventh Avenues in 1925, or make the *Messenger* magazine a self-supporting radical publication?

Huggins, sharing the same intellectual and critical tradition as Locke, could not avoid bringing up the problem of art versus politics under the critical stress of dealing with the renaissance. Yet Huggins, further

53. Huggins, p. 65.
54. Ibid., p. 48.
55. Ibid.

on in his critique, chides Locke for being unwittingly and casually contradictory in demanding that at one moment the black artist choose the "role of group expression," and at the next turn pursue a creativity that is a "deeply individual and personal expression."[56] Elsewhere he upholds Wallace Thurman for satirizing Locke as Dr. Parkes in his novel *Infants of the Spring*, for insisting that "art should come before propaganda," which was, says Huggins, also a criticism of "the very self-conscious promotion of art and culture typified by Locke and the 'New Negro.'" Thurman knew, writes Huggins, "that artistic production was an extremely personal, individualistic thing, not to be turned on or off by nationalism of any kind."[57] In other words, art that ceases to be individual, free expression, might possibly become group expression, which begins to border dangerously on propaganda; this propaganda in black art can become nationalist in its content. In fact, art then becomes political, to such an extent that the artist might even submerge his artistic impulses to the extent of becoming a politician. This phenomenon, which will be discussed in detail, has occurred in a number of extremely critical cases.

Huggins is on sure ground when he points out that Locke's contradictory vacillations between individual expression versus group expression did not allow much of a middle ground in the definition of the artist's role. Thus, in view of Locke's inability to solve this ongoing dilemma in black creativity by way of a critical methodology, it was rather gauche of Huggins to cite the DuBoises and the Johnsons, et al., as Harlem intellectuals without a political following among the masses. At least DuBois and Johnson considered themselves politically *accountable* to the masses, even from their lofty "traditional middle class reform" position, as Huggins terms it. From the standpoint of cultural history, it is more significant that Alain Locke's articles on Negro theater had very little cultural contacts with what the Harlem masses preferred in the way of theatrical entertainment, and, moreover, he was *not* accountable to them. Locke was, aesthetically, an aristocrat who haughtily dismissed the highly visible vestiges of Negro minstrelsy found in most theaters. Thus, in spite of Huggins's commendable critical foray into the many sided evolution of the Harlem Renaissance and its multicolored facets and fashions, one feature is shared by both Locke and Huggins—an excessive disdain and resentment of that reminder of the slave past—Negro minstrelsy.

In 1934 LeRoi Jones—one of the more celebrated "new Negroes" of

56. Ibid., pp. 201–202.
57. Ibid., p. 241.

the 1960s—was born in Newark, New Jersey. Like one of Alain Locke's original favorites, Jones emerged on the scene of the new black renaissance bearing a cornucopia of scintillating creative gifts in poetry, fiction, drama, criticism, and assorted belles lettres. In fact, Jones was so "new" that he eventually changed his name to Imamu Amiri Baraka (un nom de guerre politique Africaine-Arabe). While still called LeRoi Jones, this gifted writer, who could hardly have experienced the impact of the 1930s even vicariously, wrote about Alain Locke and the 1920s:

> It was the beginning of what was called the "Negro Renaissance," and the emergence of what Alain Locke called the "new Negro." . . . Even the term *new Negro,* for all its optimistic and rebellious sound, still assumes that it is a different kind of Negro who is asking for equality—not old Rastus the slave. There is still, for all the "race pride" and "race consciousness" that these spokesmen for the Negro Renaissance claimed, the smell of the dry rot of the middle class Negro mind: the idea that, somehow, Negroes must *deserve* equality.[58]

Thus did the "new Negro" representative of the 1960s view Alain Locke's renaissance brood. At that moment in his young life LeRoi Jones, as avant-garde as he thought he was, probably had not the slightest notion of how much he personified both a continuation of the cultural faith of the Harlem Renaissance and a manifestation of the unsolved problems of that Lockean decade. In 1973 the career of Baraka summed up in a new persona the ongoing black creative dilemma of art versus politics or, better, the unsolved problem of the interconnectedness of black culture, politics, and economics within the context of movements and social methodology. Unlike Alain Locke in 1925, the black cultural movements of the 1960s could not state that: "the new psychology at present is more of a consensus of feeling than of opinion, of attitude rather than of program."[59] Between 1963 and 1970 LeRoi Jones, the creative artist, became Baraka the black politician with an organized program for social action. This single individual career exemplifies the unsolved problems of the Harlem Renaissance, which culminated in a unique convergence on another inconclusive level. In short, the crisis in culture is not solved when the creative artist turns politician; it only intensifies.

The year before *The New Negro* appeared, Paul Robeson made his debut in a revival of Eugene O'Neill's *The Emperor Jones,* and later appeared in O'Neill's *All God's Chillun Got Wings.* The Negro actor

58. LeRoi Jones, *Blues People—Negro Music in White America* (New York: William Morrow & Co., 1963) , pp. 133–34.
    59. Locke, p. 10.

Charles Gilpin had already created the role of Brutus Jones in the first production of *The Emperor Jones* back in 1920–21. However, the re-creation of Brutus Jones through the gifted acting of Paul Robeson, plus Robeson's subsequent role in the racially controversial *All God's Chillun Got Wings,* launched him as the most publicized, lionized, glamorized, and, in time, most immortalized actor-performer to emerge from the Harlem Renaissance. *The Emperor Jones* represented a revolutionary departure in theater craftsmanship, aside from its racial implications in terms of dramatic characterizations. It became something of an off-Broadway hit, and was revived in 1924 and again in 1926, this time with Charles Gilpin, whose great talents did not insure his immortality (some critics claimed that Gilpin was a better actor than Robeson). In the meantime, Robeson was scoring further successes as a gifted singer. Theater records relate that "the Provincetown Playhouse introduced Paul Robeson as a singer in 1925" in a program of Negro spirituals. Thus, by the appearance of Locke's *The New Negro,* Robeson was considered to be an artist with an unusual range and quality of physical, intellectual, artistic, and interpretive abilities.

Robeson became a legend, one that still lingers in the consciousness of many Afro-Americans who were born in the late 1940s and early 1950s. While this generation comprehends very little about the career of this remarkable man, they remember him. For the purposes of this critique, it is enough to point out that Robeson's artistic and political career epitomizes, more than that of any other Afro-American actor-performer-singer, past or present, the struggle for identity and credibility in the creative and performing arts.

When Alain Locke published his aesthetic thesis on "The Negro and the American Stage," the performances of Paul Robeson, Charles Gilpin, and a few other talents were the ones that had fired his dramatic imagination and reinforced the substance of his theatrical doctrine. At the same time, however, Negro musical shows like the famous *Shuffle Along,* among other musical renditions of "neo-minstrelsy," had also made a tremendous impact on the theater-going public, both black and white. Locke did not warm up to these Negro musicals at all, despite their popularity. An endemic duality in Negro theater practice was developing at this point, featuring the trend toward legitimate drama, transplanted in America from the European tradition, as opposed to the evolution of the more authentic Negro musical tradition in the theater, a refinement of the ingredients of Negro minstrelsy handed down from the nineteenth century. Locke wanted no part of these Negro musical hand-me-downs. This was, of course, a matter of "taste," but Locke proceeded to confound the matter by his inability to separate personal taste in art from the more enduring and prevalent problem of form and content, the actuality of *existing* theatrical ingredients, plus the exigencies of theater craftsmanship which demand the masterful use of those ingredients already possessed in abundance. What the Afro-American did possess in abundance was the folk resources of music, song, dance, and pantomime (read "mimicry"); these were the essential ingredients so exploited by whites in Negro minstrelsy (whether in white/blackface, black/blackface, or during the musical comedy "reformation" of Cole and Johnson or Williams and Walker of the late 1890s). Locke could not help but agree that these ingredients existed; hence he wrote:

> One would well to imagine, therefore, what might happen if the art of the Negro actor should really become artistically lifted and liberated. Transpose the possible resources of Negro song and dance and pantomime to the serious stage, envisage an American drama under the galvanizing stimulus of a rich transfusion of essential folk-arts and you may anticipate what I mean.[60]

What Locke meant by "liberated" was a deliverance from the "handicaps of second-hand exploitation and restriction to the popular amusement stage."[61] To be more precise, Locke stated that "the art of the Negro actor has had to struggle up out of the shambles of minstrelsy and make slow headway against very fixed limitations of popular taste."[62] But this was easier said by Alain Locke, the critic, than achieved in theatrical practice, given the real and persistent folk substance of Afro-American music, song, dance, and pantomime. Locke, in rejecting minstrelsy in *any* form (as practiced during the 1920s), set up a creative roadblock, confounded theatrical reality, and helped to discourage, on the part of blacks themselves, any real and consistent attempts to creatively refine Negro folk elements. The musical *Shuffle Along*, written, composed, and produced by blacks—Noble Sissle and Eubie Blake—was, according to all critical assessments, an artistic improvement and creative refinement over the Negro musicals of the 1890s, and certainly over the Negro minstrels of the 1870s and 1880s. This was also true of other Negro musicals such as *Eliza* and *Runnin' Wild*, despite their evolutionary imperfections. Yet Locke intolerantly rejected the genuine seeds of creativity in these shows. It was a demean-

60. Alain Locke, "The Negro and the American Stage," *Theatre Arts Monthly* 10, no. 2, 112–20 (February 1926).
61. Ibid.
62. Ibid.

ing misfortune, thought Locke, that great talents such as Bert Williams, Florence Mills, Bill Robinson (Bojangles), Josephine Baker, Abbie Mitchell, and Ethel Waters had been consigned to the theatrical purgatory of having nothing but Negro musicals through which to exhibit their talents. "The real mine of Negro dramatic art and talent," wrote Locke, "is still in the subsoil of the vaudeville stage, gleaming through its slag and dross. . . ."[63] "What Negro," he asked, "who stands for culture with the hectic stress of a social problem weighing on the minds of an over-serious minority could be expected to enthuse" over the "tawdry trappings" of Negro musicals? In response to a white critic and director who had perceived tremendous artistic possibilities in these Negro musicals, Locke said with characteristic hauteur: "We had come to discuss the possibilities of serious Negro drama, of the art-drama, if you please."[64] And did Locke see the glimmer of a possibility for "art-drama" anywhere on the theatrical horizon? Most certainly! He wrote:

From the vantage point of advanced theatre, there is already a significant arc to be seen. In the sensational successes of *The Emperor Jones* and *All God's Chillun Got Wings* there have been two components, the fine craftsmanship and clairvoyant genius of [Eugene] O'Neill and the unique acting gifts of Charles Gilpin and Paul Robeson. From the earlier revelation of the emotional power of the Negro actor by Opal Cooper and Inez Clough in the Ridgely Torrence plays of 1916 to the recent half successful experiments of Raymond O'Neill's Ethiopian Art Theatre and the National Ethiopian Art Players of New York . . . an advanced section of the American public has become acquainted with the possibilities of the Negro in serious dramatic interpretation.[65]

Critically speaking, Locke's purview on the emergence of Negro art-drama reveals a number of contradictions, inconsistencies, and conceptual flaws which were crucial in any evaluation of the theatrical possibilities of the "new Negro": (1) The black art-drama acceptable to Locke was written by white dramatists; (2) this art-drama contained no music, song, and dance which Locke, himself, had emphasized were the basic ingredients of the Negro folk gifts which admittedly had "considerably influenced our stage and its arts" (even though he thought that the Negro influence on American drama had been negligible); (3) the Negro dramatist, per se, was not accepted by Locke as a factor "from the vantage point of advanced theatre." In fact, he veritably

63. Ibid.
64. Ibid.
65. Ibid. For an account of the Ridgely Torrence "Negro plays"—*The Rider of Dreams, Granny Maumee* and *Simon the Cyrenian,* see Johnson, *Black Manhattan,* pp. 175–78.)

eliminated the black playwright as a necessary factor in the evolution of Negro art-drama. He justified this negation of the black playwright in this way:

> Primarily, the Negro brings to the drama the gift of temperament, not the gift of a tradition. Time out of mind he has been rated as a "natural born actor" without any appreciation of what that statement, if true, really means. . . . Welcome then as is the emergence of the Negro playwright and the drama of Negro life, the promise of the most vital contribution of the Negro to the theater lies, in my opinion, in the deep and unemancipated resources of the Negro actor, and the folk arts of which he is as yet only a blind and hampered exponent.[66]

The critical and creative philosophy of Alain Locke with regard to the Negro on the American stage can be summed up as: Although Negro folk expressions in music, song, dance, and pantomime have considerably influenced the American stage and its arts, the Negro has no tradition in drama (since Negro minstrelsy is not a tradition). However, the Negro folk resources of music, song, dance, and pantomime can be transposed to the serious stage, provided they can manage not to be transposed in company with the "tawdry trappings" found in such crude Negro musicals as *Eliza, Shuffle Along,* and *Runnin' Wild.* However, serious drama of Negro life can dispense with such folk gifts as song, dance, and so forth, because the Negro, a natural born actor, can perform satisfactorily *without* singing and dancing (as in crude musicals). This level of artistic performance is made possible by the energies of the "advanced theater" through the superior craftsmanship of white dramatists, which renders the black dramatist unnecessary and superfluous.

Forty years later Nathan Huggins, reviewing the nineteenth century, judged Negro minstrelsy as nothing but a white creation which produced the "stage negro"; he stated that "black entertainers played this creation rather than themselves."[67] Huggins, in keeping with his aesthetic and critical affinities with the Lockean tradition, accepted the validity of the white creations of Negro art-drama in the 1920s in this way:

> Whatever the intention and quality of the white plays in the 1920s, the remarkable thing was that Negro performers were getting an unprecedented chance to do respectable, serious drama in downtown theaters. . . . However much one might regret the failure of an authentic ethnic theater, it is

66. Ibid.
67. Huggins, p. 250.

impossible to challenge their right to grasp the chance to contribute to the American stage.[68]

Respectable for whom? That is, and was, the question. Huggins clearly illustrates the continuation of the dichotomized Negro theatrical tradition legitimized and encouraged by Locke. This dichotomization of the tradition was present before Locke; it was a reflection of the dual tendencies operative since the days of Ira Aldridge and the African Grove Theater during the 1820s. However, the Lockean view contains a reification of an aesthetic concept of Negro theater which favors and encourages the perfection of what is culturally, for blacks, a nontraditional trend—European dramatic forms (i.e., respectable forms). Involved here are a number of biases, conceptual flaws, aesthetic tastes, and criteria which have less to do with class differences and "cultural elitism" (as Huggins says) than with miscomprehension of what the Negro theatrical tradition was all about. The *real* Negro theater tradition involved the collaboration of actors, dancers, musicians, composers, librettists, lyricists, poets, and painters, or at least designers, including those unregenerate and disreputable mimics and clowns. Once the Negro theater trend swings toward legitimate or respectable drama, the black group character of theatrical collaboration is weakened, because the legitimate drama requires only actors. What then happens to the dancers, musicians, composers, librettists, lyricists, poets, and painters? These members of the Negro theatrical traditions, necessary since the 1890s, are counted out.

Disregarded also was the question of the audience—that is, the black audience. The majority of Negroes during the 1920s and the 1930s preferred the musical theater. Both Locke and Huggins disregard this important aesthetic response. Like Locke, Huggins provided preferential treatment for Negro actors; he thought it was justifiable for the actors to "grasp the chance to contribute to the American stage" (they lacked the "gift of a tradition," according to Locke), even if they had to make this respectable contribution through drama of white creation. On the other hand, Huggins refused to justify the historical right of Negro performers to "do their own thing" from 1820 to 1920, because Negro minstrelsy, unlike *Emperor Jones,* was a white creation that was not at all respectable.

Huggins's assessment of the situation might be accepted on the grounds that there were good and respectable, as well as bad and disreputable, white creations for Negro actors. But Huggins was forced to

68. Ibid., p. 298.

hedge a bit on their ethnic authenticity; he was forced to qualify his acceptance of these white creations as authentic, because he was unable to accept (or did not recognize) the fact that Locke's original concept of a genuine ethnic theater was a theater based on the black folk arts of music, song, dance, and pantomime.[69] In the hectic cultural arts hassle and confrontation of the 1920s, this concept of black theater became misplaced, pushed aside, lost, banalized, commercialized, ostracized, and, finally, forgotten. This creatively and aesthetically refined fusion of the fundamental elements of the black theater tradition has thus never been achieved.

The Lockean critical tradition left a creative void which was soon filled by another white creation—*Porgy and Bess*—a theatrical phenomenon that has left in its trail a deep and lasting malaise of black guilt and well-camouflaged resentment, plus a creative frustration of deferred hopes and aspirations. Trapped in Lockean logic and aesthetics, Huggins could do no more with *Porgy and Bess* than label it another stereotype, which was hardly original (Hall Johnson had said everything that needed to be said about the stereotype back in 1936, plus a lot more).[70] For Huggins, as well as for other young blacks in later generations, *Porgy and Bess* had become nothing less than a reincarnation of Negro minstrelsy.

Claude McKay pointed out the actual story of the outcome of the Negro musical. *Shuffle Along* established a new musical model that was immediately imitated by white producers and commercialized in the same manner that nineteenth-century whites had imitated and commercialized the black idiom in the pristine age of Negro minstrelsy. But McKay also revealed that in the commercializing process, which Huggins termed a "vogue," the Negro actors succumbed to the blandishments of white commercialism. They were, of course, doing the same thing that black performers did during that calamitous period of Negro minstrelsy in the 1890s (and before), except that Huggins was not as critically hard on Locke's favorite actors of the 1920s as he was on the irresponsible black performers in *In Black America* of 1896 who, for the most part, were not even professional actors.

Thus, a continuation of the time-honored white commercialized imitation, plus the dire need of actors seeking work, fame, and (some) fortune, further degraded the Negro musical. But instead of fighting for the integrity of the Negro musical and its development, Locke abdi-

69. See Locke, "The Negro and the American Stage."
70. Hall Johnson, "Porgy and Bess—A Folk Opera?," *Opportunity Magazine* 24–28 (January 1936). Reprinted in *Anthology of the American Negro in the Theater,* ed., Lindsay Patterson (International Library of Negro Life and History, 1969) , p. 196.

cated; hence, his original projection, that Negro music, song, dance, and pantomime would be elevated into a genuine art form, did not materialize in the creation of what Huggins later vaguely projected as genuine ethnic theater. This occurred because the flaws in Locke's assessments were further confounded and the basic issues lost in the social confusion of the 1930s, particularly after the advent of *Porgy and Bess* in 1935.

A number of renaissance figures believed that Locke never really understood or appreciated black jazz. This allegation is not unconnected with Locke's disdain for both Negro vaudeville and musical comedies such as *Shuffle Along*. During the 1920s and 1930s, Harlem Negroes went to vaudeville in droves because of an attachment to their traditional, musical theater. Moreover, this vaudeville was *in* Harlem. The exact number of Harlem vaudeville devotees who went to see *Shuffle Along* is open to question since it played on Broadway, but it is absolutely certain that the native Harlemite enjoyed *Shuffle Along* as well as Langston Hughes's work and that of others. Harlemites became addicted to vaudeville because their theater writers, composers, and choreographers seldom gave them anything else more aesthetically uplifting. But when *The Emperor Jones,* Locke's and Robeson's symbol of the elevated Negro art-drama, was brought to Harlem, the Harlem audience turned thumbs down on it. Hughes recalled that *The Emperor Jones* was staged at the old Lincoln Theater, a theater previously devoted to "ribald, but highly entertaining vaudeville. And when the Emperor started running naked through the forest, hearing the little Frightened Fears, naturally they howled with laughter. 'Them ain't no ghosts, fool!' the spectators cried from the orchestra. 'Why don't you come on out o' that jungle—back to Harlem where you belong?' . . . In those days Ethel Waters was the girl who could thrill Harlem . . . Louis Armstrong a killer! . . . But who wanted *The Emperor Jones* running through the jungle? Not Harlem!"[71]

Thus, for all of Huggins's valuable new critical insights into the novels, poetry, and graphic arts of the 1920s, he was caught up in Locke's aesthetic constructs on Negro theater and did not transcend the latter's faulty critical approach. This is why, at the very end of his study, Huggins, still enmeshed in the toils of renaissance dilemmas still operative in the 1960s, could manage only a vague, poetic conclusion concerning the Negro's place in the American cultural complex. After explaining why the art of the Harlem Renaissance was so "problematic, feckless, not fresh, not real," he stated that the lesson it taught is "that

71. Langston Hughes, *The Big Sea* (New York: Alfred A. Knopf, 1945) , pp. 258–59.

the true Negro renaissance awaits Afro-Americans' claiming their *patria,* their nativity."[72] This conclusion sounds like a benediction after a powerful sermon on some hard truths of cultural experience or, more precisely, like a musical coda to a tragic symphony, a revelation whose meaning, while comforting, is meant to be unclear because—well, what *is* the meaning of it all? What "patria" does Huggins mean? Today, some of the latter-day descendants of Locke's renaissance proteges, such as Imamu Amiri Baraka, claim that the real patria is Africa, not their cultural conditioning as per the American experience. But this was certainly not what Huggins intended: "The truth was (and is) that black men and American culture have been one—such a seamless web that it is impossible to calibrate the Negro within it or to ravel him from it."[73]

Alain Locke, during his flights of critical contemplations on Negro theater, often spoke of the importance of the Negro moving back "over the trail of his group tradition to an interest in things African."[74] Locke's interest in things African was, of course, symbolic and thematic rather than racial and ideological, like the Garvey movement. The contrast was unique, because Garvey's ideology was basically economic in motivation rather than aesthetic or cultural; there is no evidence that Garvey had any aesthetic appreciation for African art or symbols, —and none are present in his pageantry, regalia, costumes, or heraldry. Unlike the 1960s' Pan-Africanist revival, the Garvey movement did not inspire its followers to adopt African names (in the manner of LeRoi Jones). In his preface to *The New Negro,* Locke conceded that "Garveyism may be a transient, if spectacular, phenomenon, but the possible role of the American Negro in the future development of Africa is one of the most constructive and universally helpful missions that any modern people can lay claim to."[75] As movements go, there could have been very little rapport between the Harlem Renaissance and the Garvey movement, because the politics of the latter was that of separation, withdrawal, and a rebuttal of everything social or cultural that had emerged from the Afro-American's historical encounter with whites in the Western hemisphere. (At least this is what Garvey's "political" position implied.) However, the precise nature of the subterranean attitudes between Garvey and the Harlem intellectuals has been obscured by the bitter polemics between Garvey and the Harlem intellectual "elders"—DuBois, Johnson, and A. Philip Randolph. The only well-known writer of the renaissance who apparently supported

72. Huggins, p. 309.
73. Ibid.
74. Locke, "The Negro and the American Stage," pp. 112–120.
75. Ibid.

Garveyism was Eric Walrond, the journalist and short story writer from British Guiana, and even Walrond never completely severed his ties with such writer's outlets as the Urban League's *Opportunity* magazine and the radical left's *New Masses*. Claude McKay seems to have flirted with Garvey's *Negro World* for a spell before calling Garvey a "charlatan." Alain Locke managed to keep clear of involvement in the Garvey-DuBois controversy. This can possibly be explained by the fact that Locke had no political or other commitment to any movement or institution but the cultural aspects of the renaissance and Howard University.

Theodore G. Vincent, the historian of Garveyism, claimed that "Garveyites played an important role in the Harlem Renaissance of the 1920s."[76] This claim is dubious on the grounds that if Garvey, himself, had any concern for the cultural aspects of the renaissance, it is not reflected in his available writings, nor in those of his wife, Amy Jacques Garvey. While a number of individuals who were identified with the Harlem Renaissance might have also sympathized with the Garvey movement, no such visible collaboration was manifested between the prominent spokesmen for either Garveyism or the Harlem Renaissance. The Pan-Africanist influence of the 1920s was exhibited on different levels in both the cultural renaissance and the Garvey movement. However, the origins of the Harlem Renaissance and Pan-Africanism *both* precede the Garvey movement. The literary, musical, and theatrical aspects of the Harlem Renaissance were the outgrowth of the 1890s as also, for that matter, was the rise of Africa consciousness and Pan-Africanism reflected in the involvement of DuBois in Pan-African congresses beginning in 1900. However, during the 1920s the Pan-Africanist temper rose sharply following the international and colonial impact of World War I. Thus Africa consciousness was reflected in the thinking of Harlem intellectuals representing a variety of ideological positions, from the extreme black radical left to the NAACP to the extreme black nationalist content of Garveyism. Harlem poets such as Hughes and Cullen both reflected African sentiments; Randolph's *Messenger* and DuBois's *Crisis* both dealt extensively with the African question. Paul Robeson, the epitome of the Afro-American actor's struggle for identity and credibility in the performing arts, even during his apolitical period, revealed his Africa consciousness through his study of African languages. Although he was a genuine product of the 1920s, however, Robeson was (or later became) critically opposed to

76. Theodore G. Vincent, *Black Power and the Garvey Movement* (Berkeley, Calif.: Rampart Press, n.d.) , p. 159.

certain aspects of the Garvey philosophy.[77] Like Garvey, he never visited Black Africa, although his wife, Eslanda, took an extensive African tour in 1936 in pursuit of her anthropological studies; in the same year, Paul Robeson travelled as far as Egypt.

The career of Paul Robeson graphically revealed that the theatrical issues stemming from the Harlem Renaissance were not simply creative or aesthetic matters of taste in art. The roots of the problem were variegated, and lay deeper in the psychocultural manifestations that emerged out of the sociology of the urbanized black and white racial encounter.

Following his initial successes in the plays of Eugene O'Neill and other white dramatists, and his publicly acclaimed concert program of Negro spirituals, Robeson and his wife Eslanda went to England, where he opened a run of *The Emperor Jones*. Robeson had already played in *Taboo* (a "white creation") in London in 1922. However, it was during his 1925 London sojourn that Robeson decided he preferred England to the United States. He returned to America for a concert tour in 1926, then went back to London in 1928 to play a role in the musical *Showboat,* a stage success that further augmented his London popularity. The Robesons finally decided to settle permanently in England. He toured the European continent, where he became a concert sensation in capitols such as Prague, Budapest, and Vienna.

Between 1928 and 1939 Paul Robeson was, for all intents, an expatriated Afro-American living in England and on the continent. He had no intentions of ever residing in the United States again. He had experienced a dozen years of perhaps the rarest successes ever offered an Afro-American of his generation, including contacts with the cream of English, European, Russian, African, West Indian, Chinese, and Indian political, artistic, intellectual, and social life. Robeson also made a great deal of money during this emigre career; in short, he had received the fullest measure of artistic fulfillment. Yet as an artist, Robeson carried within him the seeds of bitter resentment against the racial slurs and scars associated with his life and experiences in his native United States; this reason caused the Robesons' emigration.

When Robeson finally decided to sever his ties with America, his decision was not that of a political thinker, but of a Negro artist whose race and color was a handicap in the United States. In England and Europe Robeson discovered that he was accepted both as a man and an artist. In America he had to be concerned about racial discrimination,

77. Paul Robeson, *Here I Stand* (New York: Othello Associates, 1958; reissued by Beacon Press, Boston, 1971) , pp. 111–112.

but he was not concerned about race politics; he was actually apolitical during the 1920s and early 1930s. Towards the latter half of the 1930s, however, he become more and more politicized in his thinking. Many events brought about this change, not the least of which was his growing dissatisfaction with his essential role as a Negro artist. In 1935 he was quoted as stating that "all Negroes are exhibitionists, and I say this with no intent to slight myself or my race. Rather I mean that we have a natural ebullience. And this, too, stems from Africa and not from Harlem. Thus I have no call to the law, challenging the white man. I have a definite call to delineate the Negro and to dispense, so far as my talent may permit, his art."[78] This statement was made in an answer to certain criticisms by members of his family in Philadelphia, who wanted him to give up the theater and concert halls and practice law. Robeson explained: "My mother's people, who are in Philadelphia, and who were educated, the intellectuals of my family, think that I am just playing some game when I tour as a concert singer or appear in plays abroad and here."[79] This was an artist speaking, but a black artist—an actor who had real cause to complain about the dire lack of decent roles for Negro actors. Despite his permanent address in London, however, Robeson never gave up his U.S. citizenship, and seldom turned down an American engagement. He spent a good part of his emigre years shuttling back and forth between London and New York. His adventurous experiences during the 1930s inevitably led him to make statements that were increasingly political and to take stands that eventually drew him into the politics of race and civil rights.

In the process of this transformation from his individual stance as a Negro artist to that of civil rights leader and protest spokesman, two events were crucial. First was Robeson's experience in the Soviet Union, and second was his involvement in an ill-fated film on Africa, *Sanders of the River*, made in England. The first experience radically altered Robeson's political orientation and steered him into studying, and eventually embracing, Marxism. The second experience forced him to seriously examine his role and function as a Negro artist. Robeson was given a rude shock on discovering how easily films could be used to distort an actor's image and intentions when the actor had no control over the film's editing, production, and reshooting. *Sanders of the River*, with Robeson playing the role of an African chief, was a disaster from the black or the African point of view. Africans and West Indians in

78. *New York World Telegram*, 15 October 1935. Quoted in Edwin P. Hoyt, *Paul Robeson—The American Othello* (Cleveland, Ohio: World Publishing Co., 1967), pp. 80–81.
79. Hoyt, pp. 80–81.

London protested against the raw procolonialist propaganda in the film, and Robeson was called upon to explain himself both in London and America. As his biographer Edwin P. Hoyt wrote, "Paul's interest in Africa kept raising its head, even on the American tours of 1935 and 1936. He was called on to defend his leopard-skin role in *Sanders of the River,* and he did defend it in those years, even though he was ashamed of it and later said he had been misused."[80]

When the Robesons returned to America in 1939, they did not come intentionally to stay. The object of the trip was Robeson's scheduled appearance in the play *John Henry,* by Roark Bradford, the story of the legendary giant Negro folk hero. But Robeson did a few concerts in New York and discovered that, as a result of the Great Depression and Roosevelt's New Deal administration, things had changed and were changing in America. The American and international events of 1939–40 induced him to remain. And, the longer he stayed in America, the more political he became. His biographer stated:

> The political man was not complete. Deep inside Paul lay the old yearnings and the old turn of mind. Essie [Eslanda] and others had worked on Paul for a long time to bring him around to the Marxist point of view about freedom and the Western democracies, and they were still working on him, but Paul was conscious much more of his Negro heritage as a colored man than of his heritage as brother of all the oppressed workers in the world. The change to political man was fermenting within him, but it was not yet a complete change.[81]

In the winter of 1940, Robeson's new play, *John Henry,* opened on Broadway. It lasted only five performances and closed as a dismal failure. The dean of drama critics, Brooks Atkinson, then made the following observation: "It is something to see Paul Robeson again and to hear the cavernous roar of his voice. . . . It serves chiefly to remind us that someone ought to write a musical drama that would rouse Paul Robeson and keep him on the stage."[82] Robeson next appeared in a New York production of *Othello* for nearly a year, 1943–44, a record run; during this period he reached the peak of his fame in the United States. From that point on he became more political, more outspokenly pro-Soviet Russia while moving consistently left in politics until he arrived into an openly pro-Communist party position. By 1947–48 Robeson had become a completely political man, and the theaters, concert stages, and mass media were closed to him because of his increas-

80. Ibid., p. 80.
81. Ibid., p. 99.
82. Quoted in ibid., p. 107.

ingly unpopular and vocal views. This new image marked the end of Robeson's career as a Negro artist. He had, in truth, gained identity and credibility, but not in the way he really wanted it. For a while, Robeson had achieved a measure of political credibility which was soon dissipated in the wave of political reaction that moved through America in the post-World War II era. From that point on, Paul Robeson became frustrated and beleaguered, a man whose profound idealism had been steered into dubious channels where it was projected to the world at large through the verbiage of ill-fitted political dialogue and awkward stratagems. As his biographer noted, "the fact was that Paul Robeson did not know his own country very well. He had not lived in that country in its hour of trial—the years between 1929 and 1939, years in which the hates and fears of the past were tempered, and in which the old capitalistic economy was tempered. Paul had been living 'high on the hog' in Europe while millions of his fellow Americans, black and white, struggled to achieve the social changes that he now demanded so vociferously."[83] This explanation, while partially valid, does not explain everything. One must go back beyond the years 1929–39 into the 1920s to find the roots of Robeson's problem.

Alain Locke stated at that time that "a change in the Negro had occurred far beyond the measurement of the sociologists,"[84] and he was quite right. Hence, since no sociology existed at that time in America to encompass Negro developments, Robeson, like many others of the 1930s, chose the Russian Marxist sociology as a guide for fighting the American racial problem. Unfortunately, this led him into a cruel trap from which he could not escape in time to recover. In 1959 the Robesons went to London in the hopes of appearing in a new *Othello*. "He did so, but this was a dismal performance; the old Paul was gone, and only the shadow of him remained. . . . The 'presence' had disappeared. The voice was shaky. The career was over."[85] Paul Robeson *had* to return to *Othello* because there was simply nothing else written that was worthy of him. And we must note that the theater tradition that created Paul Robeson in the 1920s had not produced the kind of musical drama that Atkinson clearly saw was needed if Robeson were to be kept on the stage.

This inevitably brings us back to Alain Locke's seminal ideas in

83. Ibid., p. 134.
84. Locke carried on a running argument about the inability of sociologists to embrace the full range of black social and cultural factors during the 1920s. See, e.g., Locke's articles "Who and What Is Negro?" and "It is useless to throw the question back at the sociologists or the anthropologists, for they scarcely know themselves," *Opportunity Magazine* (February-March, 1942), pp. 36–41 and pp. 83–87.
85. Hoyt, p. 224.

theater criticism during 1926 for a reexamination of the kind of atti-
tudinal response this criticism both reflected and encountered. Objec-
tively, the Negro theater tradition had real and pressing needs which
only a very strong and imaginative guiding philosophy could hope to
meet. Obviously there were not hundreds, but thousands of blacks in
New York trying to get into show business, and most of them were like
Paul Robeson—untrained, but theatrically gifted in one degree or another. Many, like Robeson, didn't know where they were going or how—
they simply, like Robeson, "had an urge." In 1925, Robeson wrote:
"Fate, however, was still conspiring to draw me away from the learned
profession. . . . In the middle of the year I was offered a part in Miss M.
Hoyt Wiborg's *Taboo,* a play of 'Voodooism.' . . . It's been most thrill-
ing this acting. So much so, that I'm going to keep on trying to do it.
What are the opportunities? Just what I will make them. . . . We who
start on this rather untrodden way need all the support and encouragement we can get. I approach the future in a happy and rather adven-
turesome spirit. For it is within my power to make this unknown trail
a somewhat beaten path."[86]

Robeson entered a field in which he needed only to be gifted to survive the challenges, because the path to success had been charted and
paved by others. But intellectually and critically, Robeson was unpre-
pared at that moment to grasp the intricate implications of this theatrical fate as they unfolded. Paul Robeson probably never seriously felt
the absence of what Huggins described as a genuine ethnic theater, or
what the continued lack of such a theater would mean in his future.
But if the transcendent critical mind of Alain Locke also did not see
this absence as crucial, why should Robeson?

When Paul Robeson first indicated that he was moving toward politics, Locke was expressing doubts about his cultural position. By this
time, 1935, the Harlem Renaissance was over, the scattered remains
were being absorbed into the New Deal, and Locke said of himself:

> Verily paradox has followed me the rest of my days: At Harvard, cling-
> ing to the genteel tradition of Palmer, Royce, and Munsterberg, yet at-
> tracted by the disillusion of Santayana and the radical protest of James.
> . . . At Oxford, once more intrigued by the twilight of aestheticism, but
> dimly aware of the new realism. . . . Finally a cultural cosmopolitan, but
> perforce an advocate of cultural racialism as a defensive counter-move for
> the American Negro, and accordingly more of a philosophical mid-wife to a
> generation of younger Negro poets, writers, artists than a professional
> philosopher.

86. Paul Robeson, "An Actor's Wanderings and Hopes," *The Messenger Magazine*
32 (January 1925).

Small wonder, then, with this psychograph, that I project my personal history into its inevitable rationalization as cultural pluralism and value relativism, with a not too orthodox reaction to the American way of life.[87]

In the 1920s, even before the appearance of *The New Negro,* composers and musicians were already reacting to the visible threat of mass communications media to their creative legitimacy. A critic complained: "It will hardly be denied that without composers there could be no music, yet [phonograph record] corporations keep on growing rich and the creators of the music that they sell either receive a mere pittance for it or are paid nothing at all. The vendors of canned music get the money; the actual makers of their merchandise receive the alms."[88] The critic went on to relate how the tangled net of composer-corporation relations exploited the creator with the backing of the copyright law.

The critic was white and speaking primarily on behalf of white authors and composers experiencing the threat of radio broadcasting. But, if this development was a threat for whites, it created a crisis for Alain Locke's "new Negroes." These new artists were temporarily spared only because the liberal intelligentsia of white patrons and backers celebrated and nurtured them. The crisis of the "new Negro" quickly became entwined with the evolution of a larger crisis in American culture, however:

> The United States is still referred to as young. Cynical critics, foreign ones especially, say we have no art. Some even deride our literature. A London critic not long ago expressed serious doubts that *any* American could write a good play. If that is true, then it is certainly not due to lack of effort. If we ever *are* to have a sound native art we must recognize that effort—we must give it fair play, an equal chance with trade.[89]

The "new Negro" authors and composers entering the 1930s did not get fair play or an equal chance with trade. For instance, by 1920 record companies had discovered and exploited the "race record" market of the black community, especially in the new northern urban communities. The "blues" became the most popular musical idiom with a mass audience in the black community. Dozens of blues artists such as Mamie

---

87. Alain Locke, quoted in Horace M. Kallen, "Alain Locke and Cultural Pluralism," in *What I Believe, and Why Maybe Essays for the Modern World,* ed. Alfred J. Marrow (New York: Horizon Press, 1971), p. 131.

88. Harry B. Smith, "Canned Music and the Composer," *American Mercury* 406–410 (August, 1924).

89. Ibid.

Smith, Ethel Waters, and Lucille Hegamin were recorded under such labels as "Paramount," "Columbia," "Vocalion," "Decca," "Okeh," "Victor," and so on. By 1928–29, the output of blues and gospel records reached over 500,000 (if corporation figures are to be believed), but by 1933–34, the figure had dropped to approximately 150,000 as a result of the economic depression. Obviously, for the race record market to have been so effectively exploited, the black community had to be a high-rate consumer of phonograph record players. From the complaints of the white critic previously quoted, the cash exploitation of the black blues and gospel singers and musicians of the 1920s must have been criminal. But during this decade, the Harlem Renaissance had produced a new generation of black musicians who had cultivated the new jazz into a tradition of jazz "classics" which they carried on into the 1930s. This was the development in jazz that produced Ellington, Henderson, Redman, Webb, Calloway, Waller, Hopkins, Russell, Hines, Lunceford, Hawkins, Tatum, Wilson, and others. From the point of view of the aesthetics of jazz, this period, which ended with the coming of World War II, was truly the golden age of jazz creativity. However, only written data could reveal the true scope of the racial exploitation of this jazz age in cash terms, and to date such data has been lacking. During this transitional period, the white composer and musician quickly adjusted to canned music and radio broadcasting as new techniques in mass communication. Thus the white jazz trend was able to establish economic hegemony over jazz music while attempting to rival black jazz supremacy on the aesthetic front. In this effort, white jazz performers were aided and abetted by record companies, booking agencies, theater owners, radio broadcasters, and Hollywood film producers. It was against this discriminatory coalition that the black composers and musicians had to wage a many sided struggle.

The terms, exigencies, and imperatives of this uniquely American intergroup cultural and economic struggle were formed during the 1920s. Herbert Schiller, in his *Mass Communications and the American Empire,* states,

> The impact of broadcasting on economic development has been obscured by historical circumstance. Radio was one of the accompaniments of successful industrialization in Western Europe and the United States. Its utilization and expansion in the North Atlantic area occurred *after,* not alongside of, initial national economic growth. Its applicability to developmental needs remained unrealized. Broadcasting came to populations already largely literate and to states well-launched on their developmental paths. Other natural resource conservation was of slight concern. The United States in 1920, despite frequent warnings by concerned individuals, con-

tinued to consider North America a rich and inexhaustible continent. . . .
In the United States, radio quickly became an adjunct to the mass production way of life, accommodating itself quite easily to the requirements and
priorities of its developers and promoters.[90]

And, "since radio is essentially a *means of communication* and only
incidentally a manufacturing activity," Schiller continues, "the development of the industry in the United States completely reversed what
might be considered rational priorities and subordinated communications objectives (whatever they might be regarded to be) to the
manufacturing and sales of receiving sets." In response to this manufacturing boom in radio sets, plus the expanding allocations of radio
transmitter licenses, the "popular enthusiasm rose spectacularly." Thus,
from 1922 to 1925, "the number of families with radios increased from
.2 percent to 10.1 percent of the population. The value of sets produced
grew from $5 million in 1922 to $100 million in 1926 and even more
rapidly thereafter."[91] In 1933, President Roosevelt inaugurated the
"Fireside Chat" and, for the first time in U.S. history, a president was
able, through radio, to speak to the entire nation at one stroke. Thus
mass communications and the political process were effectively combined to facilitate the governing and the administration and the reform
of an economic system in the shambles of collapse.

Given Alain Locke's intellectual and academic background and his
ability to perceive, during the 1920s, that American sociology could not
encompass changes in the Negro, it is difficult to understand why Locke
did not see that the vast economic, political, governmental, and technological alterations in this country could not fail to impose fundamental changes in the theories, practices, conceptions, and analyses of
sociology itself. And if this happened in sociology, it would also affect
Locke's own field of cultural criticism. Even George Santayana, who
greatly influenced Locke at Harvard, did not consider aesthetic judgments to be concerned only with form, content, expression, taste, or
philosophy on the nature of beauty and separated from economic fact
or influence.

Locke's book *The Negro and His Music* (1936) was a reflection of
his essentially fixed and passive aesthetic view of reality. But artistic
creations, especially in music, dance, song, acting, pantomime, or theater, must relate to an audience response in order to have empathetic
resonance and experiential meaning. Projected into this creative am-

90. Herbert I. Schiller, *Mass Communications and the American Empire* (Boston:
Beacon Press, 1971) , p. 21.
    91. Ibid., p. 24.

bience, in addition to racial values, judgments, and taste, are other
psychological, sexual, economic, intellectual, and educational values
and influences. All of these factors in the creative experience were
fundamentally qualified by mass communication's impact on the already existing economic determinants that frame creativity, distribution, and audience response.

The social upheaval of the 1930s also had profound political rami-
fications for the creative artist, as seen later on in the politicizing of
Paul Robeson, even though the seeds of such racial discontent had
already been planted deeply into Robeson's consciousness as a result
of his memories of racism's abrasive rub during his Rutgers and post-
university period. But even so, his biographers tell us, Robeson's first
mature responses to all of this was purely emotional. It was not, in the
end, America that politicized Robeson—it was his European experiences, especially the Russian; personal pressures from intimate associates, including his highly political wife, were also responsible. Away
from home most of the time, Robeson was able to maintain a distant,
objective view of America without the deadening daily grind of racial
obsession wearing on his psyche. But as he learned more of the world,
he was able to make comparisons between what America professed to
be, and was not, and how other parts of the world and other peoples
lived. To most Americans at that time, such comparisons were down-
right invidious, but Robeson was a man of conscience. During his years
of European successes, Robeson was never completely at ease. For instance, during the 1930s Hitler was gaining power, and Robeson had
had a dangerous if momentary brush with some Nazis in Berlin.
During the 1920s he had become deeply attached to England, but
later questioned his personal ties to the English upper classes who
lionized him and, moreover, England *was* the leading colonialist power
at the time. Thus when Robeson visited Russia, what he saw there
made him change loyalties. As one biographer put it, Paul Robeson
saw the Russians as "a friendly people. . . . Even less than the English
did the Russians have familiar relations with black peoples, for Russia
had never ventured in African colonization. The Russians had no racial
prejudice, and greater Russia was such an amalgam of racial varieties
that any kind of prejudice could not be tolerated. Of course, speaking
politically, it was absolutely essential that the Soviet State wipe out
any vestige of racism, in order to hold the Union together."[92] Robeson
was deeply impressed with the Russian experiment and became "emo-
tionally bound to the Soviet Union with such strong ties that they

92. Hoyt, pp. 69–70.

would be hard to sever." His biographer quoted Robeson as saying about Russia, "All I can say is that the moment I came there I realized that I had found what I had been seeking all my life."[93]

Although Robeson's dissatisfactions with his essential role as Negro artist continued to increase, there is no evidence that he ever connected the problem of his individual artistic role with the larger imperfections of the Harlem Renaissance of which he was, personally, the prize ornament on world display. Whatever his thoughts might have been concerning the fate of the renaissance, he did not verbalize much sentimental interest in how the movement fared in the 1920s. In Europe, he was remote from it all and his artistic fate was not dependent upon the good will of American patrons. Moreover, when Robeson began to turn "political" in the 1930s, the 1929 economic crash had all but scattered the blooms of the Harlem Renaissance like so many petals in a whirlwind. In his autobiography he makes only one fast, apologetic mention of the 1920s: "In the early days of my career as an actor, I shared what was then the prevailing attitude of Negro performers—that the content and form of a play or film scenario was of little or no importance to us. What mattered was the opportunity, which came so seldom to our folks."[94]

That Robeson's existential thrust toward a political role was a gaudy mixture of Marxism, free will and idealism indicates that he did not fully grasp the implications of what he was doing in the 1930s. In effect, he was misled by what he perceived as the true substance of a political role for blacks. In keeping with the dominant trends in white political thought, Robeson separated *politics* as politics from *creativity* as creativity. In so doing, it was not understood that, in American culture, *black creativity* as creativity has its own politics, if properly applied. If the cultural thinkers of the Harlem Renaissance had been able to get their true bearings, Robeson could have been forewarned that a politics that destroys black creativity is not good politics for blacks. But in America, this was a difficult thing for black militants to see. If, in the 1920s, either a Robeson or a Locke had considered the implications of why Harlem blacks who liked Negro musicals did not like O'Neill's *Emperor Jones,* their answers could have been the beginning of cultural wisdom. And, while these answers would not have solved all the intricate problems of the Negro theatrical tradition, they might have hinted to someone like Robeson that something might be a little "off" in black politics. Robeson sang spirituals and folksongs for his

93. Ibid., p. 72.
94. Robeson, "The Actor's Wanderings and Hopes," p. 39.

people and played *Othello* for the cultural uplift of his educated black
elites; they loved it, and Robeson became a great cultural hero. However, this black adulation could not have been translated into the mass
political following that Robeson foresaw awaiting his belated arrival.
In his thrust for a political role, Robeson overlooked the fact that his
own cultural, creative, and aesthetic tastes had never been in full con-
sonance with that of the Harlem masses (Harlem being Robeson's
political base). Another biographer quoted Robeson's views on folk
music in 1935, when in Moscow: "The Negro love song is the rough-
house Blues," he said, "but the tenderness of the love song finds expression in the Spirituals."[95] Here Robeson's affinities agreed with Locke
who also worshipped the spirituals; this fact revealed the difficulty
many educated black elites faced when attempting to sort out the rich
store of ingredients in the Negro musical tradition and deal with them
in a creative manner. The question of taste is always at the forefront
of aesthetic judgments, and in 1935 Robeson seemed to be unaware
that, as far back as 1920, the musical taste of the masses that he proposed to lead was centered in the blues and gospels as the race records
industry was quick to discover. In short, Robeson's taste in folk music
separated him from the very theatrical music that the masses preferred.
In 1935 Robeson's tastes were, like his politics, going through a quiet
transformation; so, too, were Alain Locke's aesthetic judgments in the
field of music. Of the thirty-six contributors to Locke's *The New Negro,*
not one was a musician, composer, or professional music critic. Although the new jazz was by far the most popular trend to emerge from
the Harlem Renaissance, jazz music received only nine pages of treatment, and that from J. A. Rogers, a journalist, free-lance writer, and
correspondent. Apparently Locke, like many erudite scholars of the
time, was a little embarrassed by the unorthodoxy of jazz, music which
was part and parcel of that "tawdry" paraphernalia of Negro musicals
with all their "dross and slag." But by 1934 Locke had reconsidered:

> Jazz has already prepared us for new things: it may create them. Already it
> has educated the general musical ear to subtler rhythms, unfinished and
> closer harmonies, and unusual cadences—indeed it has been a conquering
> advance-guard of the modern type of music in general. It has also introduced
> new principles of harmony, of instrumental technique and instrumental
> combinations, and promises to lead to a new type of orchestra and orches-
> tration. Yet it must completely break through the shell of folk provincialism
> as only the spirituals have as yet done, and completely lift itself from the
> plane of cheap popular music. The academic musicians must look to their
> laurels.[96]

95. Marie Seton, *Paul Robeson* (London: Dennis Dobson, 1958), p. 87.
96. Alain Locke, "Toward a Critique of Negro Music," *Opportunity Magazine* 365
(November-December 1934).

What Locke thought he meant by all of this is difficult to say. But, with the benefit of hindsight, we can say that Locke's views had little influence on the evolution of jazz. As music, jazz was born into a network of institutional, economic, and technological strangulation which Locke was unable to clarify in terms of sociology. In the meantime, his personal and intimate musical tastes were satisfied by his yearly attendance at the Salzburg Music Festivals.

Politically, Locke's imagination did not transcend the external social goals of Roosevelt's New Deal, to which he became a staunch adherent. He was not alone in this, since he was merely following the sentiments of blacks everywhere during the Great Depression. But to many college graduates in the 1930s, the New Deal was not enough:

> One result may be seen in the "muffing" of the greatest chance which has come to the Negro in America since the World War. The chance to swing upward under the shout and echo of the New Deal. Society was shaken. For a moment, people, terror-stricken by the complete crash which threatened, forgot their petty prejudices. If the Negro had had the definite leaders able to comprehend the situation, drive down and cement a program, all of us should be now emerging on a higher plateau. However, there were no such captains speaking the language of the day. The colleges had not given us the intelligent, sagacious and fearless men needed. Accordingly, it seems that if and when the nation does issue from the economic shadows, the Negro shall come forth but little improved over his previous status. . . . The stark fact remains, we just do not have the scholars, the bold thinkers, the men. . . . Before our very eyes the spirituals are wrested from us. Roark Bradford and others appropriate and ruin our best themes . . . the generation which comes to college contain our best minds. . . . If through ignorance or error we destroy these—what then?[97]

This statement, by Lawrence D. Reddick, a graduate of Fisk University in 1934, is similar to those of black students in 1964. And it was to such a chafing mood of growing discontent that Paul Robeson returned to the United States in 1939. That he returned poorly prepared to assume the political role that he did was obvious; the fact that he returned to star in the Roark Bradford play *John Henry* revealed how far he was removed from the category of leadership thinking cited by Reddick. With all of his European successes, the role of John Henry was one Robeson did not need; his acceptance of the role was a continuation of that fatal flaw in all the so-called political thinking indulged in by black leadership. This fatal flaw was then, and remains, the cultural flaw.

During the thirties, Robeson complained continuously that he was

97. Lawrence D. Reddick, "The Younger Negro Looks at His College," *Opportunity Magazine* 210–11, 22 (July 1934).

not being offered the kind of black acting roles that befitted his stature and abilities. In 1936 when such a role was offered to him in the play *Toussaint L'Ouverture,* by a black author, C. L. R. James, Robeson was presented with the opportunity to strike out independently and produce the James drama himself. This he did not do; the free will choice was there, but Robeson did not accept that challenge. Edwin R. Hoyt reported that in 1936 Robeson was about to give serious thought to establishing his own repertory theater for and by Negroes. Such a move would have been a crucial step toward black cultural autonomy in the cultural arts, a step that only a Robeson was in the strategic position to take and legitimate. Instead of responding to his own native instincts toward the imperatives of black culture, Robeson was led, ultimately, to sacrifice his black cultural arts role in favor of a civil rights leadership role, a role for which he was awkwardly unsuited. The irony was that Robeson never made a major appearance in a dramatic role written by a black author. Instead, he became a rival protest spokesman in a civil rights age he played no role in bringing about—the Age of A. Philip Randolph. Fighting Randolph was, of course, a prime objective in Communist party strategy in 1940.

The cultural flaw in black political thinking leads to a misconception as to what black politics as politics ought to consist of. Black political thinking that does not attempt to explain to blacks the nature of their cultural status in the United States, that fails to educate blacks as to what they must themselves do theoretically, programmatically, conceptually, critically, educationally, and technically on the cultural front is not the politics of what Reddick called, in 1934, "bold thinkers." In 1939, Robeson did not have the kind of bold thinking that would have allowed him to refuse to play in *John Henry* and also explain why it was necessary for him to refuse.

Paul Robeson, the idealist, had been led to believe that Russian Marxist sociology was the answer to the Afro-American's predicament in the United States. His biographer reveals that, while in Moscow, a leading American Negro Communist had advised him to return to the United States because the struggle there needed him. Robeson's view of Russian society apparently ignored the 1935 Soviet decree to artists and writers concerning "Socialist Realism," which declared that all literature and art had to become identified with the Communist party's ideological and political objectives. Or perhaps it was of no importance to Robeson that all the creative experimentation that followed the Russian Revolution during the age of Mayakovski was exterminated. At any rate, the fact that the American Communists successfully drew Robeson into political alliance with them was the result of the politics of expedient opportunism. The Robeson image, allied with the Communist left, was intended to demonstrate what Robeson had already come to believe—that Russian Marxist sociology was applicable to the United States. He apparently did not face the fact that the New Deal had effectively nullified the Marxian program with Roosevelt's economic and social reforms while simultaneously coopting the best Communist thinkers into support of the New Deal bureaucracy. By the beginning of World War II, the Communist party was already weakened in a process of disintegration that continued into the 1940s and 1950s. Robeson was not the only one deceived.

The 1920s and 1930s had created a political vacuum for blacks, a poor political status exacerbated by the depression. Blacks were forced into the Democratic party in growing numbers for reasons of morale and physical and political survival. Since the cultural analysis necessary for black solvency had not been achieved in the 1920s, no other political alternative was viable for blacks and their leaders but to embrace Roosevelt's Agricultural Adjustment Administration (AAA), National Youth Administration (NYA), Civilian Conservation Corps (CCC), National Labor Relations Board (NLRB), and especially the Works Progress Administration (WPA). The WPA did marvelous things for black writers, artists, and actors, much to the satisfaction and relief, no doubt, of Alain Locke. But for Robeson, who had not been hit by the ravages of the economic slump, such New Deal reforms were not enough. From his lofty international perspective as a world figure, Robeson imagined a grander role than that of second fiddle to the savior of American capitalism. From 1939 until the end of World War II, while the United States and the Soviet Union were military allies, Robeson's political ideas were tolerated. But in 1946, as his biographer relates, "Robeson and white America parted company."[98] His criticisms and complaints against the system were justified and generally correct; it was his inept manner of expounding his views that was questionable, since he hurt and destroyed nothing and no one but himself. "Paul never pretended to understand the American political system nor to worry about its inner workings,"[99] one biographer noted. Having accepted the tenets of Russian Marxism, Robeson wanted revolutionary changes, "but he failed to differentiate between an independent social revolution, brought about from within a country, and a foreign-sponsored political and social revolution brought about from the outside."[100]

The purpose here is not to enter into a detailed analysis of Robeson's

98. Hoyt, p. 136.
99. Ibid., p. 142.
100. Ibid., p. 134.

political career as black spokesman and pro-Communist sympathizer. However, there is strong evidence that after the Peekskill Riots of 1949, the shock of this bloody and shameful event brought Robeson face to face with the fact that he had to pursue an independent line as a black spokesman. Although his political ineptitude had gotten him into an almost untenable position, this independent move was the beginning of his political wisdom. So much was clear at that time because, although the Communist party did not "own" Robeson, it attempted to control him. Robeson's independent phase, his *Freedom Newspaper* political phase, was his last; curiously enough neither of his two major biographers even mentions it in passing. This journalistic phase lasted from 1951–55, and the contents of *Freedom* indicated that Robeson, and those around him, had become prisoners of a political philosophy that had evolved into a theology.

The newspaper also revealed that Robeson did not know how to establish an independent black political line. Such an independent black political program did not need Marxist legitimacy. It would, first of all, require a grounding in a cultural theory, which the Harlem Renaissance had failed to provide. Such a cultural theory, in turn, should have been premised on the renaissance experience, incorporating Locke's essentially nineteenth-century aesthetics with a new analysis of the racial, economic, technological, and structural (i.e., sociological) developments of the 1920s.

Locke blamed American sociology for not accepting his aesthetic judgments as relevant. To better understand the sociological and historical implications of these problems from the 1920s requires the examination of the findings of a writer such as Schiller on mass communications. In his chapter on the "Democratic Reconstruction of Mass Communications," Schiller confronts a number of challenges posed by the contemporary status of mass communications to countermovements for social change. He says:

> Linking the mass media with what Gunnar Myrdal calls the "underclass" and other unaffiliated underdogs is not suggested out of sentimentality. The Establishment is top dog and its outlook, its methodologies, and its behavior have demonstrated their total incapability of extricating us from onrushing disasters, much less of perceiving incipient crises in advance.
>
> Are there centers of dynamism in the American community with which the mass media, set free of their current ties, might identify and, in doing so, lead the way to popular acceptance of social change? . . .
>
> The most explosive element in contemporary American society is the developing *black social movement.* Emerging from the city ghettoes and the rural slums, thousands of young, articulate militants are questioning the

fundamental assumptions of American life that have gone unchallenged for three hundred years. The black rebellion cannot be contained, and each new outbreak produces new layers of involvement.[101]

The Afro-American is therefore crucial in this matter; just as blacks were crucial to the matter of mass communications when canned music and radio broadcasting became controversial technological innovations in 1924. The problem is, and was, that American sociology never identified them. Neither did Alain Locke enlighten his "new Negro" brood as to what their strategical cultural role had to be in the politics of cultural equality. While what C. Wright Mills was later to call the "cultural apparatus" was rapidly changing and qualifying the societal and structural ground rules for American cultural developments in the 1920s, Locke was worrying about the aesthetically inimical carry-overs of Negro minstrelsy in musical comedies. Mass communications, rapidly emerging in the 1920s, were destined to expand beyond the limits of public control for the public good, and would, as a result, become a powerful weapon to be used *against* all the American social trends for progressive social change. If the leading black cultural critic, Alain Locke, did not grasp the meaning of this, what could be expected of the culture hero, Paul Robeson?

In 1951, when Paul Robeson initiated *Freedom Newspaper* as the standard-bearer for his independent political phase, Alain Locke also signed a contract with Alfred A. Knopf for the publication of *The Negro in American Culture*. In 1952, because of illness, Locke confided to Margaret Just Butcher that he would not be able to complete this book. Butcher relates:

> This book was to have been his *magnum opus*. For years he had written articles, collaborated with other authors, and delivered lectures. . . . Yet he had never written a comprehensive book summing up his broad interest in Negro art and culture as related to and intertwined with American culture as a whole.[102]

Two years after his death in 1954, Butcher completed the editing of Locke's intended project. Thus *The Negro in American Culture* appeared in 1956, written according to Locke's conception of its format: "To trace in historical sequence—but topical fashion—both the folk and formal contributions of the American Negro to American Culture." It is no injustice to Locke to say that the book is not a "great" work,

101. Schiller, pp. 155–156.
102. Margaret Just Butcher, *The Negro in American Culture* (New York: Alfred A. Knopf, 1956) , p. viii.

but a creditable representation of the essential aesthetic and cultural views of the man. Locke was never a facile nor engaging writer; writing seemed to come hard to him. Thus it is doubtful that *The Negro in American Culture,* if completed by Locke, would have offered much beyond certain intimate touches of the Lockean flavor. An ironic fact about this book is that nowhere in its entirety is the name of Paul Robeson and his over thirty years of activity in the theater, concert hall, and film even mentioned. Thirty years after Robeson impressed Alain Locke with his performances in the O'Neill plays and became the gem among the "new Negroes," Paul Robeson had become, in the Lockean tradition of cultural criticism, *a nonperson* in a manner reminiscent of the way Communist historians were known to have written important individuals completely out of the historical record for their political transgressions. Why Locke and/or Butcher refused to deal with Robeson in this book is not known.

That such a glaring omission of popular fact and personal history could be tolerated by a major publishing company in a book published, supposedly, to posthumously represent the mature thinking of a major scholar and critic is deplorable. Such an omission could only happen in a cultural tradition that is not taken seriously enough for critics, black or white, to expend the necessary time and analytic attention to vital evolutionary details. As a result Paul Robeson, through his unique and tragic transformation from Negro artist to idealistic black spokesman, remains an unsolved problem in critical understanding. In an unseemly transfiguration, Robeson's role as a recognized Negro artist recedes into a kind of cultural anonymity, while his protest or political image is highlighted and praised well beyond its essential importance. This transfiguration indicates why Sterling Stuckey, reviewing the reissue of Robeson's book *Here I Stand,* only discusses Robeson the political activist, not Robeson the artist and culture hero; Stuckey's review was, of course, in keeping with the established conventions of black history writing as the history of race struggles or the handmaiden of the civil rights movement.

During the 1960s LeRoi Jones, a more recent "new Negro" in the creative arts tradition, traveled the route from pure creative artist to "pure" politician as Imamu Amiri Baraka, thus repeating, on another level, the Robeson model. Like Robeson, Baraka's creative qualities declined in the process; also like Robeson, whose political mutation led into the quagmire of Communist politics, Baraka's transformation led him into the blind alley of the politics of black separatism. Baraka, too, became ultracontroversial in the process of changing images. However, Baraka would almost certainly deny that he had inherited another version of Robeson's political dilemma.

Black history, like all histories, is one of "problematic issues," of "ideas"—an ongoing series of problems or dilemmas which historians, or people generally, must confront. The same issues or ideas keep recurring in black history from one stage or era to the next, whether they are political, economic, cultural, Pan-Africanist, integrationist, separatist, or whatever. To cope incisively with such ideas today they must, in the manner suggested by certain critical schools, be traced back to their generating situations, so that their life history can be better understood.

In the United States, the Afro-American creative and performing artist has had a unique set of ideas and problematic issues revolving around the struggle for identity and credibility. Thus, the role of the creative artist and/or performer is related to purely political or economic struggles in ways that are so unique that conventional history writing has been unable to clarify them. And, because of this inability of conventional history writing to conceptually accommodate the cultural and creative factors of the black experience, the scattered, disparate, and marginal phases of the black cultural tradition appear peripheral, tending either to get lost or obscured in the conventional rendering of social or political history. In this manner the creative and artistic issues of a Robeson's identity and credibility problem become lost in the final summation of the critical and aesthetic tradition of an Alain Locke. In one way or another, this becomes the fate of *all* black creative artists in *all* creative fields, whether in the 1920s or the 1970s. That a Paul Robeson's contemporary image is an undecipherable blending of culture hero and political ideologue (who was, at one and the same time, an actor, singer, Pan-Africanist, pro-Communist, pro-Marxist, and civil rights leader spokesman) suggests the reason why Locke and/or Butcher could not depict Robeson's role even in a cultural history.

In this regard, the transformation of LeRoi Jones to Imamu Amiri Baraka—from pure creative artist to Pan-Africanist political ideologue—bears a certain resemblance to the Robeson saga, but on another plane and under different circumstances. In both cases, however, the assumption of political roles led, inevitably, to problematic dead ends—pro-American Marxism and its extreme black opposite, black separatism. The endemic conflict between black cultural creativity and black protest politics has a peculiar character, the uniqueness of which is seldom divined as a problem in criticism, social analysis, and history writing.

Poor cultural analysis leads, on the one hand, to a flawed and inadequate political response to social reality; on the other hand, a black political analysis that is not predicated on the insights of the clarifications of cultural analysis leads to political incompetence. What remains, therefore, is a problem in the craft of black history writing—an unrealized potential for intellectual excellence which conceals the outlines of a cultural history awaiting its legitimate recognition.

Lawrence Jones

The Organized Church: Its Historic Significance and Changing Role in Contemporary Black Experience

FROM EARLIEST BEGINNINGS TO THE CIVIL WAR

Over a century and a half passed between the first importation of blacks into America and the establishment of any institution which they controlled and which could be called an organized church. It was nearly two centuries before a black denomination came into being. All of this is to suggest that to fully understand the religious experience of blacks in America necessitates an investigation which is not restricted to the history of conventional ecclesiastical organizations. This statement remains valid even to the present day. The religious experience of the minority of blacks who were involved in Christian institutions before emancipation was so closely intertwined with their total life experience that the beginning point in any effort to understand its meaning must be that total life experience.

Paradoxically, this nation, founded initially by persons who had left their own homeland to escape religious, political, and economic oppression introduced, almost immediately, one of the most oppressive systems of slavery that the world has witnessed. This paradox, in one way or another, has been both a source of guilt for whites, and a goad to reforming action throughout American history. The first efforts at Christianizing blacks had its source in this paradox.

Christianity had not taken root in Africa when the first slaves were

Lawrence Jones is dean of the School of Religion, Howard University, Washington, D.C.

103

brought from those shores.[1] Nevertheless, though blacks were not Christians when they came to America (this was later to be a rationalization for their enslavement), they were a religious people, since in their native land the totality of their lives was informed by what in western Europe was defined as "religion," but which in Africa was a basic part of life. Thus they brought "religion" with them; some had been exposed to the Moslem faith before their capture.[2]

The earliest efforts to convert the slaves were made within the context of family life, where master and mistress sought to share the liberating message of salvation. The irony of seeking to win converts to Christianity, with its emphasis upon freedom, was only overcome by teaching that the freedom which the Gospel promises is primarily spiritual in nature. This clear rationalization was given legal basis in the enactments of several of the colonial legislatures and later came under the spiritual benediction of the bishops of London.[3] Later in the Colonial period, individual clergymen felt called to preach the Gospel to the slaves and did so with some vigor but minimal results.[4]

The first organized efforts to Christianize the slaves and Indians undertaken by the religious establishment was the creation, in 1701, of the Society for the Propagation of the Gospel, by the Anglican Church. The S.P.G. worked with indifferent success and frequently against considerable opposition but endured till the coming of the Revolution.[5] The decades immediately preceding and those following the revolutionary struggle were not distinguished as times of high religious fervor. By the end of the eighteenth century only about 4 or 5 percent of blacks were enrolled on the rosters of the churches. The impact of religion upon blacks should not, however, be measured exclusively in terms of church statistics.

The delicate accommodation of slavery and Christianity which some

1. Christianity in Africa was restricted mainly to the coastal areas around the forts during the period of the slave trade; it penetrated the interior, from which most slaves were collected for export, only very superficially. Christopher Fyfe, "Peoples of the Windward Coast A.D. 1000–1800" in J. F. Ade Ajayi and Ian Espie, *A Thousand Years of West African History* (Ibadan, Nigeria: Ibadan University Press, 1965), pp. 161–62; and, in the same volume, A. C. F. Ryder, "Portuguese and Dutch in West Africa before 1800," pp. 225–26.

2. J. O. Hunwick, "Islam in West Africa," in Ajayi and Espie, pp. 113–31.

3. See John C. Hurd, *The Law of Freedom and Bondage in the United States*, 2 vols. (New York: Negro Universities Press, 1968). See also Edmund Gibson, "Two Letters of the Bishop of London" (London, 1727), as quoted in Winthrop D. Hudson, *White over Black* (Chapel Hill: University of North Carolina Press, 1968), p. 191.

4. Marcus J. Jernegan, "Slavery and Conversion in the Colonies," *American Historical Review* 21: 504–37 (April 1916).

5. Frank J. Klingberg, *Anglican Humanitarianism in Colonial New York* (Philadelphia: 1940); and his *An Appraisal of the Negro in Colonial South Carolina* (Washington, D.C.: Associated Publishers, 1941).

white Christians were able to achieve was not acceptable to many others, who sensed that a deep contradiction existed between the Gospel and the practice of holding fellow human beings in thralldom. Persons in this latter group, whom I chose to call the "righteous remnant," initiated the first efforts designed to accomplish the abolition of the slave trade, organized the anti-slavery and abolition societies, and were intent to rid the church of the blight of slaveholding members. Individual Quakers such as Anthony Benezet and John Woolman led the way in this effort and as early as 1758 the Philadelphia Quaker Meeting passed legislation condemning the practice of trading in slaves.[6] A few other ministers and laymen, of whom the Congregationalists Samuel Hopkins of Newport and Samuel Sewall of Boston were typical, were in the vanguard of those who felt that Christianity and slavery were fundamentally incompatible.[7] They were not without their detractors. The relative success or failure of these efforts is not at issue here; their significance lies in the fact that these individuals were the first to contend that blacks and whites, slave and free, shared a common humanity, were creatures of a common Creator, and were the objects of the universal redemptive action of God in Christ. They were asserting that blacks, slave and free, were human beings.

Slaves were prohibited by custom and law from establishing organizations, or even from meeting for religious or other purposes without the inhibiting presence of their masters or representatives of that class. It was under these limitations that the first religious institution primarily controlled and administered by blacks was established at Silver Bluff, South Carolina, in the 1770s.[8] As might be expected, formal organizational activity was more frequent among free blacks in the urban North. These northern organizations were primarily mutual benefit societies which in effect sought to compensate for the neglect of blacks by white government and institutions. The earliest of these societies was the Free African Society of Philadelphia, which was established in 1778. Richard Allen and Absalom Jones, two exslaves who had been frustrated in their efforts to establish a religious society by opposition from within the black community, were the organizers.[9] The stated purpose of the society was that of supporting "one another in sickness,

6. Carter G. Woodson, *The History of the Negro Church* (Washington, D.C.: Associated Publishers, 1921), pp. 14–16.
7. Lorenzo J. Greene, *The Negro in Colonial New England* (New York: Atheneum, 1968), p. 288.
8. Woodson, pp. 35 ff.; Walter H. Brooks, "The Priority of the Silver Bluff Church and Its Promoters," *The Journal of Negro History* 7, no. 2: 172–96 (April 1922).
9. Richard Allen, *The Life Experience and Gospel Labors of the Rt. Rev. Richard Allen* (Philadelphia, n.d.).

and for the benefit of their [members'] widows and fatherless children."[10] A prime criterion for membership in all of these groups was
an "orderly and sober life." Most of them were, in fact, quasi-religious
bodies, and their memberships were heavily weighted with confessing
black Christians. Churches frequently came into existence out of the
memberships of these societies. The Free African Society of Philadelphia was the mother of two churches, St. Thomas Protestant Episcopal
Church, which was the first black congregation in that newly independent body, and the Bethel African Church, which was the first black
congregation in the Phladelphia Methodist Conference. In a profound
sense the benevolent, the educational, and the literary societies which
existed in great numbers in the first half of the nineteenth century were
part of a search for community. The Masonic Lodge, which the Reverend Mr. Prince Hall succeeded in establishing for blacks in 1787 with
the help of British Masons, was also part of this search.

During the antebellum period, organized black religion was literally
in its infancy: the ranks of its members were very thin and on the national level the bulk of black Christians belonged to predominantly
white Methodist and Baptist bodies. The basic disability from which
the organized black congregations suffered was a lack of qualified leadership. Few of the clergy were theologically trained and most of their
constituents possessed no formal educational background. Daniel A.
Payne reported that in the Bethel Church in Philadelphia fewer than
100 persons in a congregation of 1,500 "could be found with a hymn-
book in their hand."[11] In addition, the churches lacked the means of
communicating with their constituents, since their publication boards
were weak financially and had little prospect of developing in the light
of the small readership which they could hope to solicit. The management of organized institutions was a new thing for these northern
freedmen and they had a long apprenticeship to serve. Their structures
were weak and limited in effective power; their constituents existed on
the edge of poverty, and their real estate was heavily mortgaged. When
these disabilities were coupled to the overwhelming general welfare
needs of the community to which they were called to respond, their
accomplishments appear all the more remarkable.

Blacks were, more often than not, second-class citizens in the predominantly white churches to which they belonged. It was common

10. "A Minute to Be Handed to the Abolition Society for the Convention, Philadelphia, Nov. 3, 1794," as quoted in Benjamin T. Tanner, *An Apology for African Methodism* (Baltimore, 1867), pp. 144–45. Hereinafter referred to as "A Minute to Be
Handed."
11. Daniel A. Payne, *A History of the African Methodist Episcopal Church*, vol. 1
(Nashville: A.M.E. Sunday School Union, 1891), pp. 335 ff.

practice for pews to be provided for them in reserved sections of the churches. These benches were conventionally referred to as "nigger pews." In some churches blacks could only commune after the whites had done so; in others they could not vote or serve in any official capacity.[12] Segregated sections for blacks were provided in church cemeteries so that the moldering dust of blacks and whites might not become mingled, even after death. Not every congregation followed every one of these discriminatory practices, but no major Protestant body was free from some taint of racist thought and practice.

The reasons for the rise of separate black congregations and the eventual emergence of black denominations in the North are complex. Viewed from one perspective, the independent black congregations were responses to, and accommodative of, white racism and practice. The separating black brethren who formed the African Methodist Episcopal (A.M.E.) congregation in Philadelphia issued a public statement in which they asserted that they had taken this action to "obviate any offense our mixing with our white brethren might give them."[13] It is clear that the blacks, in addition to taking offense at the separate pews set aside for their use, were expressing their sensibility to the inhospitable reception their increasing numbers were receiving at the St. George's Methodist Church.

The ostensible reason for the withdrawal of black Christians from the John Street Methodist Church in New York City, which resulted in the formation of the first A.M.E. Zion congregation, was the failure of that church to adequately minister to the needs of its increasing number of black communicants.[14] Richard Allen, in Philadelphia, had offered a similar reason in partial explanation for the withdrawal of his group. There were other congregations which trace their origin to similar discontents.[15] Abyssinian Baptist Church in New York (1808) is a notable example. Its founders withdrew from the Gold Street Baptist Church in protest against the segregated practice of the church during worship services.[16]

Blacks also had reasons for separating from white congregations growing out of their concern for the souls of their fellows, which they felt were being insufficiently attended to by white churchmen. The African churchmen in Philadelphia offered as partial explanation for their withdrawal the felt need

12. Donald J. Matthews, *Slavery and Methodism* (Princeton: Princeton University Press, 1965) , pp. 64–65.
13. "A Minute to Be Handed," p. 145.
14. David H. Bradley, Sr., *A History of the A.M.E. Zion Church 1796–1872* (Nashville, Tenn.: Parthenon Press, 1956) , pp. 45 ff.
15. Allen, p. 25.
16. Adam Clayton Powell, Sr., *Upon This Rock* (New York, 1949) , p. 2.

to preserve, as much as possible, from the crafty wiles of the enemy [the devil] our weak-minded brethren, taking offense at such partiality [segregated practice] as they might be led to think contrary to the spirit of the Gospel, in which there is neither male nor female, barbarian nor Scythian, bond nor free, but all are one in Christ Jesus.[17]

In a similar vein they argued that their worship would be more efficacious if they were separated. These pioneer black evangelicals believed that if they were not worshipping with whites they could "more freely and fully hold the faith in unity of spirit and bonds of peace together, and build each other up in our most holy faith."[18]

To blacks, one of the most galling aspects of their bondage was the fact that they were not considered to be human. They very early perceived that part of the American conception of humanness included the exercise of control over one's property. To be human was to be free, to some extent, to deploy the resources one owned. In the light of this perception the rise of separate congregations must be seen as fundamentally an assertion by their founders of their own humanity. Separate congregations were the concretization of the desire to exert the power and control over some area of their lives which they understood was inherent in being human. Conversely, they were efforts to be free of the control of whites. The African congregations in New York and in Philadelphia included in their articles of organization stipulations which excluded whites from official membership and from the control of the churches' property.[19] These were crucial provisos, for during the first twenty years of the existence of each of these groups they were integral parts of the Methodist conferences within whose jurisdictions they were located. In point of fact, the Bethel Church withdrew from the Philadelphia conference when whites attempted to assert control over the pulpit and property of their black brethren.[20] An additional source of irritation to blacks in the Methodist Church was its failure to ordain blacks to the itinerant ministry. In New York this was the ostensible reason for the withdrawal of the Zion congregation from the Methodist Conference.[21]

In nearly every instance the separating congregations of blacks in the urban North were given financial assistance by benevolent whites. These benefactors frequently were not members of the congregations from which the blacks were withdrawing. The withdrawal of blacks

17. "A Minute to Be Handed."
18. Ibid.
19. *Articles of Association of the African Methodist Episcopal Church of the City of Philadelphia in the Commonwealth of Pennsylvania* art. 7 (Philadelphia, 1799), p. 7.
20. Bradley, pp. 52–53.
21. Payne, pp. 1–8. The Supreme Court of Pennsylvania affirmed the right of blacks to control these aspects of their church life in 1816.

from white churches did not result in their repudiation of the denomination as a denomination. The new congregations adopted virtually intact the polity, doctrine, and structures of the parent Methodist body, with few exceptions; the A.M.E. Zion group gave women the right to vote in their congregations and conference, and the A.M.E. Zion and the A.M.E. (Bethel) excluded whites from membership.

The survival of these congregations and the later denominations was remarkable. Though all the founders were individuals of deep religious faith, save for one or two who had financial resources in excess of their survival need, they were also of modest educational attainment and means. Of the nine men signing the A.M.E. Zion charter in 1801, four could not write their names and presumably could not read. Similarly, when the Philadelphia Bethel congregation was incorporated in 1796, three of the nine trustees signed the constituting document with an "x." Some indication of the limited academic achievements of the founders of the A.M.E. church as a denomination in 1816 is illustrated in the fact that Richard Allen's fourteen-year-old son served as secretary of the constituting conference.

In addition to those Methodist congregations which eventually became separate black denominations, nearly a score of independent non-Methodist local churches, mainly Baptist, were founded prior to 1820. Despite the appeal of the dissidents, a number of black members remained within the Methodist church. They formed the nucleus out of which separate black congregations were formed within white church structures.

At this time in the South, blacks were not free to establish separate congregations, and all those who were identified with institutionalized religion were affiliated with or supervised by white congregations. Whites were caught between their impulse to Christianize blacks and their need to exercise close control over the slaves and free blacks for reasons of security, and their distaste of being in the presence of too many blacks in a religious setting. Three patterns of congregational organization were employed which obviated the necessity of intimate association. Frequently separate meeting times for blacks and whites were initiated. Another stratagem was the organization of separate congregations supervised by a white minister. A third device was the creation of separate black congregations administered by blacks but with whites in attendance at all meetings. Black clergymen frequently were pastors of these churches and in some instances pastored white congregations as well for limited periods of time.[22] These means for dealing with the

22. Matthews, pp. 64–65.

problem of race in the southern community prevailed until after the end of the Civil War.

Though whites retained the reins of authority, blacks participated extensively in the ministry to the slaves. They were frequently deputized as "class leaders" in the Methodist church or as "watchmen" in the Baptist church and exercised oversight over the life and morals of the baptized Christians. They also preached the Gospel and won many of their brothers and sisters to the faith.[23]

The African Methodist Episcopal church, which was organized as a denomination in 1816 with an initial membership of 8 clergy and 5 churches, grew in thirty years to include 296 churches, 176 clergymen, and 17,375 members.[24] The African Methodist Episcopal Zion church did not grow as fast nor cover as wide a geographical area as did the A.M.E. church. It was organized in 1821 with 6 congregations, 1,410 members, and 22 clergymen. By 1864 it included 113 clergy, 132 church buildings, and 13,702 members, including 2,654 in the newly liberated state of North Carolina.[25]

Given the inexperienced leadership of these organizations, great amounts of time and energy were directed to strengthening their internal structures, vigorously seeking to train competent clergy for their increasing numbers of congregations, and striving to maintain the evangelical impulse. Because they were black, their concern for the slaves was axiomatic. The *Minutes* of the general and jurisdictional conferences are filled with references to the curse of slavery and the many disabilities that blacks labored under in the free territories. Like their counterparts in white denominations, they were concerned with temperance, moral reform, the care of superannuated clergy, and with initiating missions in foreign lands. In the free states the clergy waged a constant struggle to eradicate the residual effects of slavery upon newcomers. They deplored the absence of stable family life, the eroding effects of strong drink, and the indolence that characterized so many blacks recently freed from the enforced labor of slavery. Hardly a conference convened that did not consider these matters.[26]

23. Luther P. Jackson, "Religious Development of the Negro in Virginia from 1760–1860," *Journal of Negro History* 16, no. 2: 168–239 (April 1931). See also Woodson, pp. 34–60.

24. Tanner, p. 179.

25. Bradley, p. 146.

26. Few accessible records of the conferences of the A.M.E. Zion church are available covering this period. Their growth was relatively slow and they were beset by internal problems as well. Daniel A. Payne was the first official historian of the A.M.E. church and though his reports are abbreviated one gets a rather detailed insight into its history. His volume has already been cited. For a discussion of early Baptist history see Lewis G. Jordan, *Negro Baptist History U.S.A., 1750–1930* (Nashville, Tenn.: Sunday School Publishing Board, National Baptist Convention, n.d.) .

Black churchmen were also concerned for education, which they viewed almost with awe as the touchstone to acceptance into the American mainstream and as indispensable to personal and racial advancement. The Nineteenth Session of the Philadelphia Conference passed the following resolution which is typical of the concerns of the church:

Resolved: That it shall be the duty of all the preachers of this Conference strictly and perseveringly to recommend that "Temperance Cause," in their respective circuits or stations, both by example and precept; and should a complaint of default in this particular be made against any preacher, he shall be dealt with by the senior, according to the provisions made for all such cases of imprudence and neglect of duty in our form of discipline.

Resolved: That as the subject of education is one that highly interests all people, and especially the colored people of this country, it shall be the duty of every minister who has charge of circuits or stations, to use every exertion to establish schools wherever convenient, and to insist upon parents sending their children to school; and to preach occasionally a sermon on the subject of education; and it shall be the duty of all ministers to make returns yearly of the number of schools, the amount of scholars, the branches taught, and the places in which they are located; and that every minister neglecting so to do, be subject to the censure of the Conference.[27]

The slavery issue was also frequently deliberated by the A.M.E. church conferences. The *Discipline* approved in 1817 had included an article stating that "the buying and selling of men, women, and children with an intention to enslave them is prohibited by any member or members of this Church."[28] In the General Conference of 1856, the Committee on Slavery reported a resolution which would have forced the immediate expulsion of any slaveholding members, as well as that of any members who bought slaves and did not manumit them immediately.[29] It was frequently the practice of freedmen in the slaveholding states to buy their wives and children and then not grant them freedom legally, because some states required manumitted persons to leave their territories. Sometimes a freedman would act as agent for a slave and purchase the individual with the slave's own earnings. These persons, too, were often held in technical bondage. In the light of persuasive arguments in which these facts were highlighted, the conference affirmed its historic position of leaving it to the local clergymen to decide when the letter and the spirit of the church's regulations were being violated.

27. Tanner, p. 157.
28. *Discipline of the A.M.E. Church*, sec. 1, art. 3 (Nashville, Tenn.: Sunday School Union, 1948), p. 81.
29. For a full discussion of this historic issue see George A. Singleton, *The Romance of African Methodism* (New York: Exposition Press, 1952), pp. 45–46, and Payne, pp. 336ff.

During the decade before the Civil War, considerable agitation occurred among northern blacks concerning the desirability of emigrating to Africa, Haiti, Central America, or Canada.[30] Though the A.M.E. church was officially opposed to emigration, the Philadelphia Conference, in response to the passage of the Fugitive Slave Law of 1850, passed a resolution in 1851 which eulogized the British people and their queen for opening Canada to blacks. In the text of their resolution they took cognizance of the fact that, given the situation of blacks in America, sufficient reasons for emigration did exist:

> Resolved: That, under existing circumstance, in our judgment, it is unwise and disadvantageous, as well as impolitic, for us to resolve that we will not leave the United States, as every such resolve only goes to stamp us as being willing to suffer anything that may be imposed upon us, rather than remove or emigrate; thereby encouraging our enemies to greater aggressions, and emboldening them in their encroachment on our liberty, and discouraging our friends, who are willing to receive us as part and parcel of their people, free and untrammelled from the powers of wicked laws.[31]

As a matter of general practice, the churches refrained from making official pronouncements in political matters unrelated to slavery. Though conferences were cautious, their leaders were sometimes less restrained. Bishop Paul Quinn, in his closing address to the New York A.M.E. church conference of 1851, remarked with some bitterness: "Nine times out of ten when we look into the face of a white man, we see our enemy. A great many like to see us in the kitchen, but few in the parlor."[32]

But, above all, these early black Christians were "evangelicals" deeply concerned to share the gospel of salvation with their brethren. They came into existence as much for this reason as for any other. Though their growth was not phenomenal, it was steady. W. Paul Quinn was called in A.M.E. church circles the "Missionary to the West." If the white denominations had their "Yale Bands" and their great home missions agencies, the blacks had pioneer clergy who labored equally as valiantly as Peter Cartwright and Francis Asbury decades before. Quinn, as much as any, was responsible for the spread of the A.M.E. church into Western territories. He reported to the General Conference

---

30. Howard H. Bell gives a succinct account of this agitation in the introduction to the two volumes he edited dealing with proposals for emigration to Africa and to the Caribbean. James T. Holly and J. Dennis Harris, *Black Separatism and the Caribbean, 1860* (Ann Arbor: University of Michigan Press, 1970), pp. 1-16. Also M. R. Delaney and Robert Campbell, *Search for a Place: Black Separatism and Africa, 1860* (Ann Arbor: University of Michigan Press, 1969), pp. 1-22.

31. "Minutes of the Philadelphia Conference of the A.M.E. Church, 1851." Quoted in Payne, p. 251.

32. Ibid., p. 257.

of 1844 that in a four-year period he had helped establish 47 churches in the states of Indiana and Illinois, including 1,080 members, 54 clergymen, 70 congregations, 50 sabbath schools, and 40 temperance societies, and that he had conducted 17 camp meetings. In addition he had established congregations in St. Louis and Louisville, in the slaveholding states of Missouri and Kentucky, respectively. Commenting upon his new members, Quinn observed:

> . . . many of them within the last ten or fifteen years broke away from the fetters of slavery and settled with their families in those states, yet by dint of industry, they are not only supporting their families, schools and churches, but many of them are also acquiring wealth, amid opposing laws and chilling prejudice.[33]

Quinn was outstanding, but not unique. In these formative years virtually every pastor was a missionary and one could enumerate a long list of men in the A.M.E., A.M.E. Zion, and Baptist churches who did heroic pioneer work.

Despite the zeal of Quinn and others like him, the largest ingathering of blacks into the Christian fold occurred in the South under the aegis of white church bodies. In the period between the Nat Turner Rebellion of 1831 and the Civil War, Baptists, Presbyterians, Episcopalians, and Methodists expended considerable effort to win "black souls." After Turner's abortive attempt to exterminate Virginia whites, the slave states achieved what was virtually a monolithic defensive posture with respect to slavery, and proselytism of blacks received general public approval. Public antislavery agitation was muted and individuals and institutions alike sought to commend slavery as a "positive good," no less for blacks than for whites. Slavery was, some white churchmen argued, entirely consonant with the will and purpose of God for blacks and for America.[34] Southern churchmen organized to evangelize the slaves, in part to assuage their guilt for acquiescing in the slave system, in part to answer the charge of some abolitionists and anti-slavery forces that slaves were doomed to remain in their "paganism," in part in response to their honestly felt conviction that evangelization of all persons irrespective of color was integral to Christianity, and in part as a means of controlling the bondsmen. An article in the *Methodist Review* puts the case quite succinctly:

> . . . religious instruction administered by faithful and competent men lays the foundation of trustworthy morality; eradicates those tendencies to dis-

33. Tanner, p. 175.
34. A documentary summary of the arguments is contained in Eric L. McKittrick, *Slavery Defended: The View of the Old South* (Englewood Cliffs: Prentice Hall, 1963) .

sipation which destroy health and life: teaches principled contentment with the allotments of divine providence; puts into action a spring of industry and fidelity more powerful than the fear of corporeal punishment; and this, while it blesses the slave with the boon of that religion which is the poor man's chartered right, adds a thousand fold to the comfort and security of the master; and thus is largely instrumental in preserving and securing the public tranquility.[35]

Baptists and Methodists were most active in evangelizing the slaves and were the chief statistical beneficiaries. In relative terms the effort to Christianize the slaves could not be accounted an unqualified success, nor was the effort and money expended in any way sufficient to the task. The black population of the United States in 1860 was 4,444,830. Of this number, approximately 12 to 15 percent were enrolled as members of the churches—including men, women, and children with varying degrees of relationship to the congregations, and including also the more than 50,000 black Christians in the free states and territories.[36]

As has been indicated, the independent black churches adopted forms of polity identical in virtually every respect to those of the churches from which they had withdrawn. A similar statement may be made of the orders of service and the rituals observed in the congregations which had withdrawn from the white Methodist churches. On the other hand, because patterns of worship were not so uniformly prescribed in the free church tradition of the Baptist bodies, black Baptist congregations which derived from them exhibited wide variety in worship.

A distinctive characteristic of the interior life of black congregations was the spontaneous participation of individual worshipers in all aspects of the service. Frequently this participation was marked by a high degree of emotionalism, which in the period prior to the Civil War was more characteristic of the frontier revival services than of the formal worship of urban white churches. In addition, these churches frequently used spiritual folk songs drawn from the slave experience and the call-response style of congregational singing, neither of which were characteristic of worship life in most white congregations.

The differences of theological outlook observable in black churches in contrast with their white counterparts were related more to the life situations of the members than to deliberate choice. Blacks were an oppressed people, and while their traditional theology might be described as "evangelical" and their life style as pietistic, they balanced the "promise of heaven's reward" with expectations that God would

35. *The Methodist Review,* 1:321 (July 1847).
36. Exact figures are difficult to obtain. This educated estimate is based upon a compilation of statistics derived from numerous sources.

presently deliver their brethren from bondage and that He would liberate all blacks from social, political, and economic oppression.

Reference has previously been made to the relatively minimal inroads which the organized church bodies were able to make in their efforts to win "black souls." One caveat should be entered concerning the hazard of equating the influence of religious ideas with the statistics of ecclesiastical institutions. Christian ideas and teachings were carried among blacks far beyond the boundaries of the established churches. So pervasive were these teachings, and so extensive the quasi-religious groupings that developed around them, that one sociologist has referred to them as the "invisible institution."[37] Convinced black Christians carried the "good news" into areas inaccessible to the evangelizing efforts of the organized churches, and they gathered bands of worshipers who met together as circumstances permitted to praise God and to pray for their expected deliverance from bondage. In short, blacks themselves were doubtless the most effective evangelists among their own people—with and without official portfolio.[38]

Though the development of independent black Methodist bodies is more accessible to documentation, many independent northern black Baptist congregations trace their origins to the antebellum period as well. Most of these were located in the cities of the North and in the border states. Baptist polity permitted the organization of churches wherever the will existed among the people and wherever persons were available to assume pastoral leadership. Since in Baptist polity authority is vested in local congregations, and since these congregations were so widely scattered, black Baptists were slow to gather into associations for purposes of cooperative action and consultation. The first associations among black Baptists were the Provident Association, which was formed in Ohio in 1836, and the Wood River Association, organized two years later in Illinois.[39] Unlike the Methodists who met annually

37. E. Franklin Frazier, *The Negro Church in America* (New York: Schocken Books, 1963), p. 28.

38. This fact is documented in numerous slave narratives as well as in the literature dealing specifically with the religious instruction of the slaves. See the "Reports of the Association for the Religious Instruction of Negroes in Liberty County, Georgia, 1835–1847" where frequent allusion is made to "Watchmen" and "exhorters" among the blacks. Note also the legal restrictions imposed in several states against preaching to blacks in other than supervised situations.

39. The American Baptist Missionary Convention was organized in 1840 as a home missions body. It was incorporated in 1848 and had added a ministers Widow's Fund in 1845. Jordan contains the constitution of this body, pp. 66–70. The concerns of this body were later broadened to include foreign territories. They also declared themselves relative to temperance, education, and morals. "Report of the Nineteenth Anniversary of the American Baptist Missionary Convention" (New Bedford: 1959) cited in Jordan, p. 70.

in conferences under the leadership of bishops, and who could speak for the churches on important issues when such statement seemed warranted, the Baptists, without such structures, were local in influence and impact. The southern congregations remained under the close scrutiny of whites and were thereby effectually silenced.[40]

Like many U.S. benevolent institutions during the antebellum period, black Americans in the A.M.E. church began to look to British philanthropy and churches for financial assistance. The first such initiative was made in 1846, when the church designated two of its clergy to attend the General World's Convention of the Christian Church held in London. Daniel Payne, one of the delegates, did not attend because his ship was forced to turn back by a violent storm. His colleague, the Reverend Mr. M. M. Clark, did succeed in reaching London, participated in the convention, and remained in England after its conclusion soliciting funds for the A.M.E. congregation in Washington. Later, Bishop Payne was to combine attendance at the meeting of the Evangelical Alliance in Amsterdam with a fund-raising effort on the behalf of Wilberforce University.[41] Wilberforce was a successor institution to the short-lived Union Seminary which the Ohio Conference of the A.M.E. church had established in 1845. It was the first institution controlled exclusively by blacks devoted to higher education. Wilberforce had been begun in 1856 by white Methodists for the education of blacks and whites alike. By 1863 it was in danger of closing because its financial support had been eroded during the war. Payne, who had been a trustee of the institution since its opening, purchased the school for $10,000 "in the name of God, for the A.M.E. Church," in March of 1863. He offered his personal note. He became its first president and remained its chief advocate in the church until his death.[42]

When the Civil War began, the black churches could be encouraged by their achievements at organization. They had survived very tenuous beginnings. They had grown and expanded the territories within which they exercised jurisdiction. Schools had been established for the instruction of both adults and juveniles, and sabbath schools were integral to the programs of most congregations. They had erected church edifices, evangelized their fellow blacks, and established and maintained fraternal relations with white church bodies and with ecumenical groups. In most areas church buildings were the only available places where meetings could be held, and the congregations were generous in offering their facilities for all sorts of gatherings—cultural, political,

40. Woodson, p. 106.
41. Daniel A. Payne, *Recollecting Seventy Years* (New York: Arno Press and the New York Times, 1969) pp. 82–91, 166–181.
42. Payne, *History of A.M.E. Church*, pp. 151ff.

social, educational, and religious. As denominations or as congregations they made pronouncements and passed resolutions touching every pressing issue of the day. Even in this early period, the black churches were the most substantial institution and the largest owner of property in the black communities.

Though the institutions which black Christians had begun to develop represented a considerable achievement for persons of such limited organizational experience and material resources, the influence of Christianity beyond the churches was exerted primarily by individual Christians, particularly clergymen, rather than through the institutions which they had established. According to estimates, fully one-half of the black leadership in pre-Civil War days were clergymen. Then, as now, the problems which confronted these individuals transcended denominational differences and institutions sprang up outside the church looking to their resolution. Among the issues which engaged the attention of these men were such vital ones as "What does it mean to be human?" "How can we achieve the rights that accrue to a person just because he or she belongs to the human race?" "Do blacks have a stake in America or do we concur in the judgment of many whites and some blacks that we are aliens here?" "How do we change the conditions, and what strategies are appropriate to the effort?" "How can we be liberated from the oppression which afflicts us at every turn?" Without question the paramount sociopolitical issue was how an end could be brought to slavery and how the prejudice of whites could be overcome. In the North the question of access to the rights inherent in U.S. citizenship also claimed attention, including the right of access to the ballot box, the right to serve on juries, the right to public education, the right to service in public facilities and transportation, and the right to work.[43]

Clergy were in the vanguard of the anti-slavery and abolitionist movements.[44] They contributed greatly to the success of the "underground railroad"; they led the opposition to the American Colonization Society (A.C.S.) organized in 1817 for the purpose of transporting free blacks to Africa.[45] A few clergymen supported the A.C.S. as a poor but preferable alternative for free blacks to living in America.[46] Clergy and

43. Leon F. Litwack, *North of Slavery* (Chicago: University of Chicago Press, 1961), pp. 153–86.
44. Benjamin Quarles, *Black Abolitionists* (New York: Oxford University Press, 1969) .
45. Ibid., pp. 1–14.
46. The A.M.E. church was divided over this issue. Daniel Coker, for example, was among the first immigrants to Liberia in 1820. At the Philadelphia Conference of 1853 Dr. J. G. Bigs advised his associates not to go to Africa, but rather to go to Canada, Haiti or the British West Indies: Payne, *History of A.M.E. Church*, p. 28. At various times in the A.M.E. history Bishops James A. Handy, Willis Mazrey, Daniel Payne, and H. M. Turner endorsed emigrating schemes.

lay Christians alike fought for public education. They protested taxation without representation. They lobbied and petitioned for legislation to end slavery in the North. In the decade just prior to the Civil War some clergy were active in the political arena, particularly in New York State.[47]

Blacks did not share common opinions concerning the most appropriate strategies for dealing with their problems. At one extreme were those who advocated violent revolution as a means of ending slavery, including the alternative of "dying with honor rather than living in bondage." At the other extreme were those of whom Frederick Douglass was typical, the so-called "moral suasionists," who advocated various nonviolent strategies aimed at changing the attitudes and actions of the white oppressors. Even those blacks who affirmed the Bible to be the sole and authoritative source of guidance in all things were of divided minds. Denmark Vesey in South Carolina and Nat Turner in Virginia had found in their religion a mandate for violent revolution. The Reverend Henry Highland Garnet and David Walker took a similar position with careful qualifications. Douglass championed political means as a solution to the problem of slavery, though his position underwent some change in the decade before the war. The literature of the period reflects a variety of positions in between.[48] No black was unaware of his or her powerlessness, and the issue resolved itself into the question of whether blacks, in the assertion of their humanity, should give their lives in one violent, probably futile, battle for freedom, or, conversely, devote themselves to the tortuously slow process of appealing to the assumed innate sense of right in the oppressors. The question was unresolved then, and it has remained so.

COPING WITH REALITIES

Despite the vigorous efforts of black Christians and the spate of organizational activity,[49] when the Civil War began the great majority of

47. Quarles, pp. 183–96.
48. Howard H. Bell discusses these positions as they came to focus in national meetings in *A Survey of the Negro Convention Movement 1830–1861* (New York: Arno Press and the New York Times, 1964) See also Carleton Mabee, *Black Freedom: The Nonviolent Abolitionists from 1830 through the Civil War* (New York: Macmillan, 1970).
49. In addition to the Methodist and Baptist churches mentioned above there were several other groups which came into existence during the first half of the nineteenth century. One of these is the African Union Protestant church which is still in existence. Its founder in Wilmington, Delaware, the Rev. Peter Spencer, had been at the conference at which the A.M.E. church was constituted as a denomination but he chose not to maintain affiliation with that body because of a dispute over the discipline and polity. His congregation had withdrawn from the Methodist church in Wilmington for the sake of "religious liberty" in 1913. See Woodson, p. 93.

blacks in America were not Christian in any formal sense. The several black religious institutions, however, were on the brink of unparalleled expansion in the decade ahead. During the war, the churches wholeheartedly supported the Union cause, as did most blacks, and cooperated vigorously in raising troops. Later, they joined in pressuring President Lincoln to issue the Emancipation Proclamation. Freedom, the prize they long had sought, seemed within reach.

The decade between 1860 and 1870 was a period of accelerated growth for organized religion among blacks. The A.M.E. and A.M.E. Zion and Baptist churches sent missionaries into the South hard on the heels of the conquering Union armies and found among the recently freed slaves many who were anxious to affiliate with their black brethren. Most of these new members, though not all by any means, had previously been members of the churches of their masters. For example, the M.E. church (south) lost some 130,000 of its black members during the decade. The exodus from white Baptist churches was comparable. Of course, numerous black Baptist congregations were already in existence in the South, some of which were pastored by blacks and all of which were under the fairly strict control of white ecclesiastical bodies. These churches now became entirely free from white supervision.

The dimensions of the harvest of new members is evident in the following statistics: The A.M.E. church began the decade with less than 20,000 members and within six years had grown to include some 50,000 souls.[50] The A.M.E. Zion church had 46,000 members in 1860 and had achieved a membership of 125,000 by 1870.[51] This precipitous expansion created tremendous strains on the resources of the churches. The experience of Henry McNeal Turner, a presiding elder in Georgia and the first black chaplain in the U.S. Army, is instructive at this point. In his letter of resignation from the presiding eldership in 1872, he reported:

> I had to preach three times every Sunday and every night in the week, month after month, then come out of the pulpit and explain the history and character, purpose and object of our Church, for hours, to satisfy the colored and whites, who would often look at me as if I were a bear or a lion; sometimes just commencing the organization of the church about twelve or one at night. . . .
>
> Since I have been trying to preach the Gospel, I have had the inestimable pleasure of receiving into the Church on probation, fourteen thousand, three hundred and eighteen persons which I can account for, besides some

50. George W. Williams, *History of the Negro Race in America from 1619 to 1880* (New York: G. P. Putnams Sons, 1883), p. 454.
51. Bradley, p. 163.

three or four thousand I cannot give an account of. And I would guess . . . that I have received during and since the war about sixteen or seventeen thousand full members in the A.M.E. Church, by change of church relations, making in all nearly forty thousand souls that I have in some manner been instrumental in bringing to religious liberty.[52]

As Dr. Turner's report indicates, the churches grew through vigorous evangelistic campaigns as well as through the accession of members who were effecting a "change of church relations."

As might be supposed, the rapid expansion of these black denominations created immediate and pressing problems. Though new congregations were frequently granted permission by the Freedmen's Bureau or army commanders to take over buildings abandoned by whites, the problem of adequate housing persisted. Moreover, for all churches the supply of clergy was extremely limited. Turner often resorted to radical and irregular means to fill the pulpits:

> I have been accused of recklessly licensing preachers by the cargo, etc., because I had to license such a number. I admit that I did, on several occasions, exercise rather extraordinary powers in this respect, but in no instance where the emergency in the case would not justify such actions. I was for a longtime elder, superintendent and everything else, and sometimes had to make preachers of raw material at a moment's notice. I have licensed preachers while riding on the cars, but I always put [them] through an examination.[53]

While many other church leaders lacked the audacity and flamboyance of H. M. Turner, his activities with respect to filling pulpits was, without a doubt, duplicated in South Carolina, Alabama, and Mississippi. Turner's Georgia Conference, in its first session in 1871, admitted 41 men to the ranks of its clergy. The 1872 conference admitted an additional 48 men, with the list of those being admitted on trial being too long to include in the *Minutes*.[54]

The freedmen not only joined existing religious bodies, but in some instances, with the support and encouragement of the white brethren, created new ones. In 1865 the black members of the Primitive Baptist churches in the South withdrew and organized the Colored Primitive Baptists of America.[55] The black members of the M.E. church (south) were constituted as the Colored M.E. church, with some 70,000 mem-

52. Richard R. Wright, Jr., *The Bishops of the African Methodist Episcopal Church* (Nashville: A.M.E. Sunday School Union, 1963), pp. 333 ff.

53. Ibid., p. 334.

54. Charles S. Smith, *History of the A.M.E. Church 1856–1922* (Philadelphia: Book Concern of the A.M.E. Church, 1922), p. 94.

55. Woodson, p. 93.

bers in 1870. In 1869, the General Assembly of the Cumberland Presbyterian church organized its Negro membership as the Colored Cumberland Presbyterian church.[56]

The missionaries of white northern churches also followed the Union armies into the South and enjoyed some success in recruiting among the freedmen. But virtually every church body, North and South, in which whites were in the majority began to segregate blacks in separate judicatories and congregations, and at the national level agencies were established to oversee the "colored" work and to deal with the matters of race.[57] Even nondenominational agencies, such as the Young Men's Christian Association (Y.M.C.A.) and the Young Women's Christian Association (Y.W.C.A.), were no exception. The major energies of white northern Christians were expended initially, however, not in proselytizing but in developing and staffing educational institutions for the freedmen.[58] Black church bodies shared this concern for education and worked with equal vigor. By 1900 Baptist bodies were supporting some 80 schools and 18 academies and colleges. The A.M.E. church had raised over $1,100,000 for educational purposes between 1884 and 1900 and supported 22 institutions providing education above the elementary level. At the turn of the century, the A.M.E. Zion church was supporting, as a denomination, 8 colleges and/or institutes, while the Colored Methodist Episcopal church had established 5 schools during its 30-year history.[59]

Though far from being affluent themselves, black Christians in the North were actively involved in seeking to provide for the physical necessities of their recently liberated brethren.

Among the outstanding Negro freedman's aid societies were the Contraband Relief Association and the Union Relief Association of Israel Bethel Church (A.M.E.) in Washington; the Contraband Committee of Mother Bethel Church in Philadelphia. . . . Between 1862 and 1869 the African Methodist Episcopal Church contributed nearly $167,000 towards freedmen's relief.[60]

56. Andrew E. Murray, *Presbyterians and the Negro—A History* (Philadelphia: Presbyterian Historical Society, 1966), pp. 152–56.
57. For a full discussion of this phase of American church life see David M. Reimers, *White Protestantism and the Negro* (New York: Oxford University Press, 1965), pp. 25–83.
58. Henry A. Bullock, *A History of Negro Education in the South: From 1619 to the Present* (Cambridge, Mass.: Harvard University Press, 1967), pp. 25–35.
59. Lawrence N. Jones, "They Sought a City: Black Churches and Churchmen in the Nineteenth Century," *Union Seminary Quarterly Review* 26, n. 3:271 (Spring 1971).
60. August Meier and Elliott M. Rudwick, *From Plantation to Ghetto* (New York: Hill and Wang, 1966), p. 142.

The agenda of black churches has not only been mandated by the Gospel and by institutional considerations, but by the historical situation of their members. This was clearly the case in the years between the end of the Civil War and the dawning of the twentieth century. While the enactment of the Thirteenth, Fourteenth, and Fifteenth Amendments to the Constitution were supposed to guarantee the rights of the blacks as citizens and to assure their freedom, the historical reality was vastly different. In the years immediately following the war, blacks in the South picked up the agenda upon which their brothers had been working in the North—education, civil rights, economic equality, and the amelioration of the corrosive effect of prejudice and naked racism. Church meetings frequently addressed these questions, but by and large they were dealt with by clergy and laymen working on them as individuals or in secular organizations.

During the Reconstruction period, blacks began to develop alternative structures as means for dealing with their perennial problems. Involvement in political parties, particularly in the South, and the establishment of labor unions, commercial banks, and insurance companies, along with other types of voluntary associations, took some of the pressure off the churches. Moreover, for the first time the federal government began to develop agencies devoted to the welfare of the freedmen, and northern religious bodies were going all out to provide educational opportunities.[61] Though the black churches did not flag in their devotion to these concerns, they were liberated to a degree to attend to their own internal problems and to their "mission" as churches. And these internal problems were many. They included the assimilation of new members, the training of clergy, the provisions of houses of worship, the maintenance of discipline among clergy and lay persons alike, and the problem of developing structures appropriate to their new national status.

From the standpoint of ecclesiastical organization, no event was of more importance in the postwar decades than the gathering of the majority of black Baptists, the largest denominational grouping, under one roof. The congregational polity of Baptist bodies, historically, has made it extremely difficult for them to achieve unification. The Provident Baptist Association and the Wood River Association which were founded in the late 1830s began this process when they merged in 1853 to form the Western Colored Baptist Association, which included some, but not all, of the churches in Ohio, Illinois, Kentucky, Missouri, Indiana, Michigan, and Connecticut. Thirteen years earlier, in 1840, the

61. Bullock, pp. 25 ff.

American Baptist Missionary Convention had been established among the churches of New England and the Middle Atlantic states.[62]

In the interim between these early beginnings and 1895 when the National Baptist Convention (N.B.C.) was incorporated, several associations were organized mainly for the purpose of advancing foreign missions and education. In 1897 a large segment of Virginia Baptists seceded from the National Baptist Convention to form the Lott Carey Missionary Convention. Still another schism occurred in 1915, when a sizeable group led by R. H. Boyd seceded to form the National Baptist Convention, Unincorporated, the second largest black Baptist body in America. A third secession from the N.B.C. took place in 1961 when the Progressive National Convention was organized.[63]

As the nineteenth century drew to a close, black Christians had achieved a high degree of institutionalization. The Atlanta University census of black churches and churchmen, issued in 1906, reported that the A.M.E. church had expanded its rolls to include 494,777 persons, while the A.M.E. Zion church reported a membership of 184,542. The Colored Methodist Episcopal church had increased its membership two and one-half times, to 172,996. The National Baptist Convention was by far the largest denomination with 2,201,549 members, while 474,880 blacks retained membership in the predominantly white denominations.[64] Virtually every black group could count some of its missionaries in Africa and in the islands of the western hemisphere, and all had educational institutions to which they gave their support. Like their white counterparts, they were concerned with evangelization, with morality, and with the stability of family structures among their members and within the race. Unlike their white counterparts, they continued to be concerned with the oppression of blacks and the constraints placed upon them. The physical mark of this oppression was indicated in the escalating number of lynchings in the South and by state legislation and federal court decisions reflecting a climate of increasing hostility toward blacks.[65]

62. Jordan, pp. 63–112.
63. Ibid., 114–20. Edward A. Freeman, *The Epoch of Negro Baptists and the Foreign Missions Board* (Kansas City, Kans.: Central Seminary Press, 1953), pp. 81–99; R. H. Boyd, *A Story of the National Baptist Publishing Board* (Nashville: 1924); Lauris B. Whitman, ed., *1969 Yearbook of American Churches* (New York: National Council of Churches, 1969), p. 59.
64. See W. E. B. DuBois, *The Negro Church,* Atlanta University Report no. 8, 1903 (reprinted by Arno Press and the *New York Times,* 1969), for a compilation of statistics relative to these matters.
65. Constance Baker Motley, "The Legal Status of the Negro in the United States" in *The American Negro Reference Book,* John P. Davis, ed. (Englewood Cliffs, N.J.: Prentice-Hall, 1966), p. 516.

ORGANIZED RELIGION IN THE TWENTIETH CENTURY

The single most important factor bearing upon the organized church in the twentieth century has been the movement of blacks from the rural areas to the urban centers of the North and South.

At every census from 1790 to 1900, at least 90 percent of the Negro population of the United States lived in the South. In 1910, 89 percent of Negroes still lived in the South but the percentage fell succeeding decades, to 85 percent in 1920, 77 percent in 1940 and 60 percent in 1960.[66]

The greatest percentage of these immigrants moved into the cities of the eastern seaboard, the midwest, and the far west. By 1970 only 45 percent of all blacks remained in the old Confederacy states.[67] In 1969 70 percent of blacks lived in metropolitan areas, with 55 percent of them concentrated in the inner city, while 52 percent still lived in the South. The significance of these facts is that the ministry of the churches had increasingly to be addressed to persons for whom humane survival in the urban environment was problematic. The brutal fact is that the persons emigrating out of the South were, for the most part, inadequately prepared to survive in an urban environment. The legacy of discrimination and segregation in the United States has been most conspicuously and dramatically manifested in its cities. To compound the problems of the religious establishment, black emigrants settled in the inner cities which were already crowded and which blacks had come to after previous generations of immigrants had moved out. The churches, like the emigrants, had to move into previously occupied space, into buildings which white congregations had abandoned in their flight from blacks. In New York City, for example, the black community has twice been pushed out from the space it occupied before it settled in Harlem in the early decades of this century.[68] In many respects it was like trying to fit too many square pegs in an inadequate number of round holes. Since black communities are notable for the greater number of churches they support per capita compared to white communities, the number of church buildings available within the community were inadequate to the needs of its new inhabitants. The rise of the so-called "storefront" church is, in part, a function of the architecture of the urban conformation. In addition to being centers of community,

66. Karl E. Taeuber and Alma F. Taeuber, "The Negro Population in the United States," in Davis, p. 102.
67. *Britannica Book of the Year, 1972*, p. 22.
68. James Weldon Johnson, *Black Manhattan* (New York: Atheneum, 1968), pp. 59–159; Seth M. Scheiner, *Negro Mecca: The History of the Negro in New York City, 1865–1920* (New York: New York University Press, 1965), pp. 15–44.

these smaller churches are also outlets for the leadership ambitions of individuals who are denied access to other means by which to express them.

The city, too, as a sociological environment, was equally decisive insofar as worship and the structures of congregations are concerned. Persons moving from the intimacy of the rural South had greater need for supportive relationships in the matrix of the hostile city. Even today, city congregations are frequently transplanted rural southern churches in form of worship, in patterns of personal relationships, and in structures internal to congregational life.

A number of black churches made determined attempts to deal with the massive problems which mass emigration and urbanization thrust upon them in the twentieth century. They usually possessed the following characteristics: a sizeable middle class constituency, college-trained clergy leadership, and a much larger than average congregational size, frequently numbering as many as 12,000 members.[69] In comparison to conventional black churches, they included in their agenda many "secular" concerns. In Chicago, for example, Quinn Chapel A.M.E. Church, as early as 1902, operated a kindergarten, reading room and library, savings bank, and an employment bureau. In 1905 the Olivet Baptist Church in Chicago "had a complete roster of girls' clubs, boys' clubs, athletic activities and three years later, in 1908, sponsored a program for the relief of the unemployed."[70] Also in Chicago, Reverdy C. Ransom established the A.M.E. Institutional Church and Social Settlement in 1900. This innovative church operated a whole range of social services. "Institutional operated a day nursery, a kindergarten, a mothers' club, an employment bureau, a print shop, and a fully equipped gymnasium; it offered a complete slate of club activities and classes in sewing, cooking and music, its Forum featured lectures by leading white and Negro figures; and its facilities were always available for concerts, meetings, and other civic functions."[71]

In New York, Harlem was still "in the making" at the turn of the century and the movement of the churches to new locations "uptown" was incomplete. By 1930, however, the migration was complete and Harlem had become a Negro "Mecca."[72] There were several institutional churches which sought to minister to the community in other

69. Benjamin E. Mays and John W. Nicholson, *The Negro's Church* (New York: Institute of Social and Religious Research, 1933), pp. 119–23.

70. Allan H. Spear, *Black Chicago: The Making of a Negro Ghetto, 1890–1920* (Chicago: University of Chicago Press, 1969), p. 92.

71. Ibid., p. 99.

72. Scheiner, pp. 119–23.

than traditional ways. Notable among them were the Abyssinian Baptist, Salem Methodist, Mother A.M.E. Zion, St. Phillips Protestant Episcopal, and St. James Presbyterian churches. An innovative example of church participation in social change occurred in 1937 when A. Philip Randolph, Reverend Adam C. Powell, Arnold J. Johnson, and Reverend William Lloyd Imes joined together to form the Greater New York Coordinating Committee for the Employment of Negroes. For nearly a decade this coalition of clergy and secular leadership labored to improve the economic situation of blacks. They took on Consolidated Edison and other utilities in an effort to open up employment opportunities. The Reverend A. Lorenzo King, pastor of St. Mark's Methodist Episcopal Church, declared on one occasion during this period, "We're tired of religion that puts us to sleep. We've got to put religion to work for us!"[73]

The examples cited from Chicago and New York could be duplicated on a less grand scale in other areas, but it is clear that such churches were exceptions rather than the rule. That this should be the case is not difficult to understand. No matter how devoted the leadership or committed the membership, without training, financial resources, and sufficient "mass" no congregation can make a dint in the complex problems of the urban environment. In addition to its traditional ministries, perhaps the greatest service the black church rendered in the period following the Civil War was that it enabled some blacks to establish identities, to participate in stable institutions, and to develop a sense of self-worth guaranteed by the Creator of the universe. In the twentieth century it continues to serve in this way, but has served the additional function of being one means by which affiliated blacks have been enabled to preserve a sense of their individual uniqueness in the maelstrom of the city.

Historically the majority of blacks in the United States have been Protestant, though there have been black Catholics here from the earliest times. Since slaves tended to adopt the religious affiliation of their masters, the majority of these converts were to be found in the Catholic population centers of Louisiana and Maryland. Consistent with this pattern, the Archbishop of Baltimore reported that in 1785 there were 3,000 black Catholics in Maryland. Most of these had doubtlessly entered the church under the aegis of their masters, since the hierarchy did not encourage the aggressive proselytization of blacks. Nevertheless, when black concentrations developed, the church endorsed special min-

73. Roi Ottley and William J. Weatherby, eds., *The Negro in New York: An Informal Social History* (New York: New York Public Library, 1967), p. 289.

istries to and for them. The Oblate Sisters of Providence, established in Baltimore in 1829, had the specific mission of catechizing Maryland blacks whose population had been dramatically increased by an influx of some 500 slaves from San Domingo. These slaves accompanied their masters who were fleeing the slave uprising of 1793. This black order established several schools and performed works of charity among the blacks.

In Louisiana, the concern for the Christianization of blacks was somewhat more vigorously pursued. The *Code Noir* promulgated in 1724 by Governor M. Bienville specially provided that masters should take their slaves to church and have them instructed and baptized into the Catholic religion. As in Maryland, the political upheavals and slave revolts in San Domingo gave rise to a sudden increase in the slave population in 1801, when 2,000 black refugees arrived in the colony. In response to the growing number of slaves, the Christian Doctrine Society, an order of black women, was organized in 1818 in New Orleans to carry out a ministry of evangelism. Less well-organized initiatives occurred in Kentucky, South Carolina, and several other southern states with far fewer members of the Catholic faith in their populations. By the end of the Civil War there were approximately 100,000 black Catholics in the United States, of whom 16,000 were in Maryland and approximately 63,000 in Louisiana.[74]

Catholic race relations tended to duplicate those of other white religious groups. Like their Protestant neighbors, white Catholics established separate schools, segregated catechetical instruction, and other instrumentalities designed specifically to deal with the "Negro problem." In some parishes, though not in all, separate masses were said for black communicants. In the years following the Civil War the establishment of separate churches for blacks was accelerated.

There were three ordained black Catholic priests in America before Lee surrendered at Appomattox Court House. All were brothers, the sons of Michael Morris Healy, a wealthy Georgia Irish immigrant and a mulatto slave woman referred by Healy as his "Trusty Woman Eliza." Each of the Healy brothers carved out distinguished careers in the church. James became Bishop of Portland, Maine; Sherwood was a highly respected priest-theologian and for five years was rector of Boston Cathedral; Patrick, a Jesuit, became rector of Georgetown University (1873–82) and is sometimes referred to as its "second founder." The

74. Joe L. Feagen, "Black Catholics in the United States: An Exploratory Analysis," *The Black Church in America*, eds. Hart M. Nelsen, Raytha L. Yokely, and Anne K. Nelson (New York: Basic Books, 1971), p. 248.

Healy brothers were not "race men" and their singular distinction for the purposes of this study lies in the fact that they were the first men of color to be ordained priests and to function within the American church. Not one of these men was ordained by an American bishop. Their ordinations set no trend in the American church, nor did their ministries greatly affect the situation of black Catholics.[75]

In the years immediately following the Civil War a number of blacks defected from the ranks of the Catholic church, particularly in Louisiana. This phenomenon paralleled the defection of black Protestants from predominantly white churches. The American hierarchy made no effort to counter these losses. It was not until 1871 that the Mill Hill Fathers of England began an apostolate to the freedmen. The first missionaries from Mill Hill disembarked in Baltimore and established their work in that city. Subsequently several other societies began ministries among blacks, but it was not until the Third Plenary Council in 1884 that the national church launched the Commission for Catholic Missions among the Colored People and the Indians. The appointed purpose of the commission was to propagate the faith. The effectiveness of these varied Catholic initiatives are difficult to assess, since there is limited documentation of their efforts and since no statistics were compiled prior to 1928. In that year (1929) 200,000 blacks were listed on Catholic membership roles. Seventy-five percent of these persons resided in the southern or border states. By 1975 there were 916,854 black Catholics. Consistent with the continuing migration of blacks from the South, the largest gains were in eastern and midwestern urban centers.

The black Catholic population nearly doubled between 1940 and 1975, rising from 2.3 percent of the total black population to 4.0 percent.[76] The reasons for this dramatic increase must be sought in the appeal of Catholicism to a growing middle class among blacks coupled with dissatisfaction with traditional black Protestant churches. The increased numbers of blacks seeking to avoid segregated public schools and the assumed superiority of parochial education contributed to this dramatic growth as well. In addition, the displacement of immigrant groups by blacks in the urban centers changed the ethnic character of Catholic parishes and impacted parochial school populations as it did that of public school systems. The inevitable result was that many school children and their parents became Catholics. Another significant factor contributing to the growth of Catholicism among blacks was the

75. See Albert S. Foley, *God's Men of Color* (New York: Farrar, Straus, and Co., 1955) for a discussion of early black ordinations in the Catholic church.

76. George Shuster and Robert M. Kearns, *Statistical Profile of Black Catholics* (Washington, D.C.: Josephite Pastoral Center, 1976), p. 34.

practice of the church not to segregate nor to exclude worshipers on the basis of color. Moreover, the Catholic churches did not abandon the inner city as their Protestant counterparts frequently have done, and they reaped a harvest of new converts as a result.

At present the voices of black Catholics are being heard with increasing urgency throughout the American church. Rising black consciousness and self-awareness are expressed both at the parish level and through the National Office of Black Catholics.[77] Efforts are being made to increase the representation of blacks in the decision-making centers of church structures and to "indigenize" worship so that the cultural heritage of ethnic groups can be affirmed. Increasingly, black Catholics and black Protestants find themselves addressing the same agenda in their respective church groups and in the world outside of the churches. There is a developing ecumenism among these black Christians which has its origins in nontheological and nonecclesiastical considerations. This growing unity arises out of a concern to improve the quality of life for persons whom the churches serve. As black Catholics and Protestants abandon the historic suspicions and antagonisms which they appropriated from their white mentors, the Christian community among this minority group is being radically altered.

Pentecostalism, which is a term covering a broad range of groups, became a vigorous competitor for the allegiance of blacks early in the twentieth century. The movement is called "pentecostalism" because of its emphasis upon the gifts of the spirit, particularly that of glossolalia, or "speaking in tongues." W. J. Seymour, a holiness preacher, is credited with having triggered the revival that instituted the movement in the United States. The so-called Azusa Street Revival, which took place in Los Angeles in 1906, launched what was originally an integrated movement; by 1914 it had split into black and white branches.[78] This rapidly growing movement was soon organized into church bodies. Today there are approximately 200 separate pentecostal groups; the largest one among blacks is the Church of God in Christ, with headquarters in Memphis, Tennessee. Accurate statistics are very difficult to obtain since few records are kept, and polity is rather loose. However, in 1970 there were estimated to be 425,000 members in the Church of God in Christ. The reported growth of the Church of God in Christ—

77. See Fr. Lawrence Lucas, *Black Priest, White Church* (New York: Random House, 1970), for a discussion of rising black awareness in the church by an articulate spokesman and black activist.

78. John T. Nichols, *The Pentacostals* (Plainfield, N.J.: Logos International, 1966), contains a compact account of this development. See also Walter J. Hollenweger, "Black Pentacostal Concept," *Concept,* special issue no. 30 (June 1970).

from 53,558 members and 1,444 congregations in 1926 to an estimated membership of 413,000 and 4,000 congregations in 1963—is an index of its broadening appeal. The church estimated its worldwide membership in 1970 to be 3,000,000.[79] Pentecostal churches among blacks are primarily an urban phenomenon, though their existence in rural areas of the South is not uncommon. Pentecostalism is frequently the doctrinal affiliation of so-called "storefront" churches, though many of these smaller churches may be a pentecostal style worship service without holding to the primary doctrine of classical pentecostalism, that is, speaking in tongues and spiritual rebirth. The denominational affiliation of these churches, at least nominally, may be Baptist or any of a number of less well-known church bodies. The significance of the rise of pentecostalism among blacks for this study is that these churches do not explicitly trace their roots to any of the major denominational sources of black religion. Many of their converts, however, were originally members of Baptist and Methodist churches who were apparently drawn to them by their strict moral teachings and discipline and by the intimacy of their worship and congregational life style.

The twentieth century also witnessed the emergence of aggressive alternatives to institutionalized Christianity. Among the first of these alternatives emerged under the leadership of Marcus Garvey and his United Negro Improvement Association, which was primarily nationalistic and economic in character but which functioned as a veritable religion for many of its adherents. Its religious arm was the African Orthodox church, founded in 1920 with its membership consisting of a substantial number of Garveyites. This African Orthodox church was not officially related to the U.N.I.A. and never matched its mass membership. The number of blacks who abandoned orthodox Christianity for Garvey's black nationalism cannot be determined, but the opposition of established clergymen to it suggests that it was a significant figure. A number of explanations are offered for this clerical opposition, among which was the insistence that God is black.[80] Whatever the reasons, Garvey's movement as a movement was too shortlived and too soon deprived of his charismatic leadership to allow any prediction of the extent to which his popularity might have eroded support for traditional religious institutions.

A much more potent competitor for the religious allegiance of urban blacks is the Nation of Islam, the so-called "Black Muslims," which was

79. Nichols, p. 104.
80. E. David Cronon, *Black Moses: The Story of Marcus Garvey and the Universal Improvement Association* (Madison: University of Wisconsin Press, 1969), p. 182.

organized in Detroit in 1930. While Garvey's followers reinterpreted the Christian faith to harmonize it with their economic and nationalistic aims, the Muslims were initially aggressive in their denunciation of Christianity as a part of the slave-making strategy of white men to deceive and subjugate blacks. The Muslims have a carefully worked out social and economic theory working in conjunction with their theology, and have been particularly successful in winning urban blacks to their banner. Their membership is of "undetermined thousands."[81]

The Honorable Elijah Muhammad, who for forty-one years was the spiritual leader of the Nation of Islam, had begun to soften his criticism of Christianity and its black adherents prior to his death in 1975. This fostered a tentative rapprochement between black Christians and Muslims in the larger urban centers. The climate for this rapprochement was created on the Christian side by the fact that most blacks had begun to accept as axiomatic some of the teaching of Elijah Muhammad with respect to black self-awareness and by the pervasive appeal of black liberation as a rallying point. The "Black Muslims" did not place their greatest emphasis upon theology when they burst into prominence in the 1960s. They emphasized, rather, their social, economic, and ethnic tenets. C. Eric Lincoln, an authority on the history of the Nation of Islam, has said that it has "an ideology riding upon a theological vehicle."[82]

With the accession of the Honorable Wallace Muhammad to the leadership of the Nation of Islam, perceptible changes have been taking place in its attitude towards non-Muslim blacks. Supreme Minister Wallace Muhammad has argued, for example, that the Nation of Islam is that "Body-Christ (Jesus) in your midst that the world has been awaiting for almost 2,000 years."[83] In this view the Nation of Islam is the fulfillment of the Kingdom of God as understood in Christian theology. Muhammad writes further that

> it is time for the Black Man and the Black Woman of America to stand up and take on their Divine appointment as the Resurrected Christ, the World Saviour. You cannot escape the Divine Dictate of Almighty God, the Originator of all creation.[84]

Under the leadership of Wallace Muhammad some of the racial exclu-

---

81. C. Eric Lincoln, *The Black Muslims in America* (Boston: Beacon Press, 1961) provides a comprehensive account of the rise of the Nation of Islam. See also E. U. Essien-Udom, *Black Nationalism: A Search for an Identity in America* (New York: Dell Publishing Co., 1964).

82. Essien-Udom.

83. Interview with C. Eric Lincoln, 29 June 1972.

84. Wallace D. Muhammad, *Muhammad Speaks,* 9 May 1975.

sivism of the Nation of Islam has been repudiated and there is a spirit of openness not characteristic of the group during the tenure of his father. The full import of the new leadership is not yet clearly apparent, but it would appear to signal a clear turn towards the development and explication of Muslim theology as interpreted by the Nation of Islam.

Judaism has the fewest numbers of black adherents of any of the major religious traditions in the United States. The reason is not hard to deduce, since Judaism is essentially an ethnic and cultural religion, invested in the popular mind with social, economic, and especially political interests. Nevertheless, a small number of American blacks are "Jews." The origin of these "black Jews" are quite diverse:

> Black Jewish congregations are made up of Caribbean Island Negroes who are descendants of miscegenous marriages between Sephardic Jews and blacks, descendants of slaves of Jewish-owned southern plantations, leftovers from the Back-to-Africa Movement in the 1920s and recent recruits. The conversions began with the Great Migration in 1915 and hit their peak in the thirties and forties. They are almost solely a northern urban phenomena.[85]

New York City, Detroit, Los Angeles, and Philadelphia have significant numbers of black Jews. If their origins are diverse, so are the practices of the individual congregations which range from rigorous orthodoxy in all phases of public, family, and personal life, to impressionistic versions of Jewish ritual only. The most widely known group, the Commandment Keepers with headquarters in Harlem, is but one among relatively small all-black congregations. A limited number of converts to Judaism are members of integrated congregations. In the larger urban centers some children of black Jews receive their elementary education in Hebrew day schools. Black Jews have made modest beginnings in the development of institutions which parallel those of the larger Jewish religious community, such as the Israelite Board of Rabbis in Brooklyn, organized by blacks in 1971.

Signs that the numbers of black Jews will increase dramatically are not apparent, largely because black Jews tend to be relatively inconspicuous in the population, are not identified with popular race causes, and because their teachings run so directly counter to the rising tide of black self-affirmation.

While this essay has concentrated upon the major religious groupings among blacks, a number of smaller bodies which do not conveniently fit into any of the conventional classifications should also be

85. Lenora E. Berson, *The Negro and the Jews* (New York: Random House, 1971), p. 210.

mentioned. The great diversity of cults and sects, some of which have memberships in the thousands, are too numerous and too amorphous to be dealt with in depth here. Some of these groups have been in existence for more than half a century and are well established. Others are of more recent origin and have quite tenuous existences. The majority of these groups are Protestant in tone, derivation, spirit, and lineage, though a growing number claim African origins and purport to be unadulterated importations of black African worship, ritual, and belief. Still others have only peripheral relations to historic Protestantism or Catholicism.

One particular characteristic of sect and cult groups is that they invariably are led by charismatic leaders. Father Divine, Daddy Grace, and Prophet Jones are notable examples of such leadership. These men had great numbers of followers and left behind well-established institutions with sizable constituencies. The most prominent sect leader of the television era is the Reverend Frederick J. Eikerenkoetter—better known as "Reverend Ike"—whose United Church Science of Living Institute, Inc., was founded in 1966. Reverend Ike teaches that the Bible is a "psychology book" which helps persons to believe in the fact that God lives within them, after which all things are possible. "The love of money is not the root of all evil," Reverend Ike asserts, "but the lack of money is."[86] The United Church Science of Living Institute has its headquarters in New York but Reverend Ike carries on a nationwide ministry via television and public appearances. Statistics of its membership size are not available but if conspicuous wealth may be taken as an index, the number of contributors must be substantial.

The twentieth century witnessed the continuation of the development of social, political, and economic institutions and movements which took over many of the tasks which the church had had to assume because alternatives did not exist. The National Association for the Advancement of Colored People and the Urban League began to dominate the struggle for economic and civil justice early in the century. Moreover, the towering figure of Booker T. Washington and his pervasive influence, as well as the organizations which he fathered, dwarfed the efforts of groups led by less powerful men. Garvey was next on the scene and was perhaps the last national leader prior to the arrival of Martin Luther King who could claim a mass following. Thus, as the race developed more institutions with diversified functions and purposes, the importance of the role which the church had exercised in black affairs declined. The status of the clergy also was eroded during

86. Frederick J. Eikerenkoetter, *Action Magazine* 8:5 (July 1974).

these years. Organized religion took its place as chief among many ideologies, cults, sects, and movements competing for the allegiance of urban blacks, and seeking to minister, insofar as it could, to the ills to which they were subject. Its distinctiveness lay in the fact that (1) it had been among the earliest of the institutions laboring for the freedom and humanity of blacks; (2) it had the longest history in the black community; and (3) it continued to be the most stable institution that blacks controlled.

The civil rights struggles of the 1950s and 1960s have eclipsed all other events involving blacks in this century. Between the years 1955 and 1966 the preeminent personage in that struggle was Martin Luther King. King, a Baptist preacher possessed of deep Christian commitment, galvanized great numbers of persons of all races around his philosophy of social change through nonviolent means. He succeeded in mobilizing churchmen and persons outside the churches in quest of his vision of social justice. He pioneered the founding of the Southern Christian Leadership Conference and the Student Non-Violent Coordinating Committee. His campaigns were characterized by mass meetings reminiscent of revival times and, in the early years, he led a successful assault upon some of the more conspicuous forms of racial discrimination and segregation. King's movement was nondenominational but it was Christian in its premises and religious in its character.[87]

On the march to Selma in 1966 the cry for "Black Power" was raised, marking a turning away of the civil rights movement from its conspicuous religious and Christian character. The men contesting the preeminence of Martin Luther King were more secular, more pragmatic, and less idealistic than the preacher from Montgomery.[88]

The responses of the black churchmen to the new secularized initiatives of the new aspirants to leadership were at first ambiguous. Martin King himself applauded the objectives of the "Black Power" slogan but deplored its lack of a substantive program and its violent connotations. But whatever else could be said, it was clear that blacks, particularly the young, were impatient with the passive, patient, long-suffering strategies which King articulated and implemented. Clear, too, was the fact that the institutionalized character of racism in the United States would not finally yield to demonstrations in the street nor to strategies

87. Martin Luther King, *Stride Toward Freedom* (New York: Ballantine Books, 1958). Cf. David L. Lewis, *King: A Critical Biography* (New York: Praeger, 1970) .
88. King, *Where Do We Go From Here: Chaos or Community?* (New York: Bantam Books, 1967), pp. 27–37. Stokely Carmichael was one of the leaders of the Black Power movement. He delineates his views in a book which he coauthored with Charles Hamilton, *Black Power: The Politics of Liberation in America* (New York: Vintage Books, 1967).

of civil disobedience. Moreover, when Dr. King courageously declared his opposition to the Vietnam War, he lost whatever leverage remained to him in high places and his critics were quick to tell him, "I told you so!—The man is not going to change." In the intervening years the nationally organized and coordinated struggle for civil rights has virtually evaporated. However, at the local level a large share of the leadership in the struggle is still exercised by clergymen.

One of the consequences of the popularization of the Black Power slogan was the organization of the National Committee of Black Churchmen which came to national attention with their "Declaration on Black Power in July of 1966." This loose organization of clergymen, drawn from many denominations, held conventions annually and began several projects designed to fight racism in the nation, within ecclesiastical structures, and to make common cause with Pan-African concerns.[89] Two of its most active substructures are its African Commission, which seeks to recruit and send to Africa black Americans with skills which are needed in the emerging black nations of Africa. Its Theological Commission has been developing the parameters of a black theology and has spun off the Society for the Study of Black Religion, whose membership consists of persons engaged primarily in academic communities and in theological education.[90]

Another phenomenon among black Christians which was a direct result of the civil rights movement and of the urban riots of the mid-1960s was the emergence of black caucuses within virtually every white denomination with blacks in their overall membership. Eleven of these caucuses came into existence with the avowed purpose of fighting racism within the churches. They have been funded by their own churches and have been accorded official status by them. In addition, black Christians have raised their voices within the various ecumenical bodies in which they hold membership and have challenged the "benign neglect: and tacit paternalism of these bodies."[91]

As has been apparent throughout this essay, the efforts of blacks to improve their lot has more often than not been rooted in solid Christian motivation, but has found expression beyond the institutional church. This has continued to be the pattern, as it has been in the white reli-

89. The entire issue of *Renewal*, 10, no. 7 (October-November 1970) is devoted to the National Committee of Black Churchmen. It includes several of the initial documents which the NCBC issued. The NCBC has since been renamed the National Conference of Black Churchmen.

90. The Society for the Study of Black Religion was organized in 1971 at the Meeting of the American Academy of Religion in Atlanta.

91. Leon Watts, "Caucuses and Caucasians," *Renewal* 10, no. 7:4–6 (October-November 1970).

gious community as well. The Southern Christian Leadership Conference, the Montgomery Improvement Association, the Student Non-Violent Coordinating Committee were conspicuously and by design Christian in their conception and strategies. In part, these extra-ecclesiastical bodies were founded as a means of transcending denominational allegiances, and as organizations in which religious qualifications for membership were removed and yet which assured the Christian posture for the organization. The Southern Christian Leadership Conference, as its concerns became more and more focused on issues of economic justice, created "Operation Breadbasket" with the aggressive and charismatic Jesse Jackson as its national coordinator. In 1972 Jackson resigned this post and organized PUSH (People United to Save Humanity). The Southern Christian Leadership Conference has continued its Operation Breadbasket, but the resignation of Jackson deprived it of his creative leadership and amputated one of its strongest units—the Chicago Operation Breadbasket.[92] In Philadelphia the Reverend Leon Sullivan founded the Opportunities Industrial Centers whose operations have become international in scope. The O.I.C. has remained in the hands of clergymen and it has currently expanded to many cities and is an effective instrument in the training of persons for positions in industry.[93] These organizations are national in the scope of their operations and, except for the moribund SNCC organization, are still effective initiatives toward social change. As has been suggested, there are others, less well known, which operate on local levels.

The emergence of the Black Power slogan as a rallying point for persons and groups concerned to work for the liberation of black people also signaled the beginning of the development of black theology. Black theology is clearly an effort on the part of blacks to investigate the relationship between the black quest for power and the Gospel. The black religious community has not produced many theologians in the formal sense of that term. Though blacks have clearly had operative theologies, they have been informal and largely produced by clergymen in the course of their ministries; rarely have they been systematized. At the present time several theologians, teaching in seminaries and in universities, are writing in this field. Several parish clergymen are similarly engaged. Professor James Cone at Union Theological Seminary is perhaps the best known theologian writing within the categories of formal

92. *Wall Street Journal,* 16 March 1972; *New York Times,* 21 December 1971; *Amsterdam News,* 11 December 1971.
93. Leon H. Sullivan, *Build Brother, Build* (Philadelphia: Macrae, 1969).

theology.[94] The Reverend Albert Cleage of the Church of the Black Madonna in Philadelphia has been the leading practicing clergyman who has sought to harmonize the Gospel and the black liberation struggle. Cleage's writings tend to be more pragmatic and more related to strategies for change than Cone's.[95] We are, in fact, on the perimeters of what will doubtless be a burgeoning movement in the days ahead.

Organized black Christian religion has always had its detractors. Many slaves and freedmen refused to "hear" the Gospel because, as gerrymandered by white Christians, it appeared to rob them of their humanity and to sacralize an unjust status quo. Skepticism directed toward the church today has several aspects. Some of its critics reiterate the criticisms of their forebears. Others disparage the leadership of the church, viewing it as being primarily self-serving and exploitative of its membership. Still others reject Christianity because of the identification with the racist U.S. majority. They view the church as collusive in a system which oppresses its nonwhite minorities and which is one of the beneficiaries of that oppression. They point to the segregated structures of the Christian establishment and cannot reconcile the Christian faith with these manifestations of prejudiced racial attitudes.

In the context of the drive for black liberation, black churches are arraigned for failing to contribute to that drive proportionate to their numerical strength and financial resources. In a time when all institutions are being evaluated in functional terms relative to the "struggle," these are serious charges indeed. In a narrow, present-day sense these criticisms have a certain validity, but viewed through the spectrum of history they have limited merit. To properly appraise the contribution of black organized religion one needs to be aware that it, too, has shared in the powerlessness of all blacks. It has suffered from a leadership which, though dedicated, has been poorly prepared to cope with problems of institutionalized racism and with the complex demands which an ever-growing urban constituency has laid upon it. In the majority, black churches are poor, small, fragmented, in debt, and excluded from the sources of power which could effect change. Even so, the contribution that black Christians are making to the struggle through their churches is substantial. They have organized and loaned their facilities

94. See James Cone, *Black Theology and Black Power* (New York: Seabury Press, 1969), his *Liberation: A Black Theology of Liberation* (New York: J. B. Lippincott Company, 1970), and his *God of the Oppressed* (New York: Seabury, 1975).
95. Albert B. Cleague, Jr., *Black Messiah* (New York: Sheed and Ward, 1968) and *Black Christian Nationalism: New Directions for the Black Church* (New York: William Morrow and Co., 1972). For a survey of various views on black theology see James A. Gardiner and J. Deotis Roberts, eds., *Quest for a Black Theology* (Philadelphia: Pilgrim Press, 1971).

to community activities; for example, Headstart schools, day care centers, senior citizen programs, credit unions, employment offices, parochial schools, after-school tutorial programs, to centers devoted to combating drug abuse, and many other programs designed to make the communities more humane. Virtually every major city has church-sponsored housing projects. Moreover, one observes a new awareness among clergy of the need to equip themselves with secular skills appropriate to the demands of urban existence.

The major challenge to black Christian churches is of a more fundamental sort and concerns a conviction, shared by many, particularly among the young, that Christianity is inherently incapable of initiating and sustaining radical social change. These churches believe that the faith is fatally flawed by the constraints inherent in its ethical teachings. They are convinced that it mandates acquiescence in the face of injustice and that it promises rectification of wrong only in some distant future. Christianity is, in this view, a singularly inappropriate faith in a period where radical change is both desirable and being strenuously sought. Viewed from one perspective, black theology is an attempt to correct this "wrong" appraisal of the Christian faith. It is clear that these negative evaluations of Christianity are predicated upon estimates of the effectiveness of its churches and the people who claim to be its adherents. The burden of proof rests primarily upon the churches.

If the black churches are to remain viable in the black community in the years immediately ahead they will require leadership that is better trained theologically and better equipped with the secular knowledge and skills requisite for dealing with the chronic problems that continue to persist in the areas they serve—poverty, substandard housing, limited employment opportunities, injustice at the hands of law enforcement agencies and the courts, inadequate education, and the crippling lack of infrastructure. Moreover, they will have to overcome, as individuals, as congregations, and as denominations, the petty differences and inappropriate emphases which prevent them from studying, planning, and acting together to carry out the mandate of the Gospel which includes feeding the poor, clothing the naked, visiting those in prison, and preaching freedom to the captives. Unified strategies involving both the spiritual, human, and financial assets of all groups are requisite to any effective ministry. Personal ambitions and animosities must be subordinated to the common good. Common cause must be made with persons and groups seeking to effect constructive change without sacrificing Christian integrity and faithfulness.

What any institution in the black community that has a long tradition and history has to take into account is the new consciousness of the young, which demands that institutions validate their existence by contributing to the resolution of perennial problems. The recitation of past service, remembered glory, even of present contributions will not be enough to win the allegiance of persons who now see the opportunity to rectify historic injustices and are bent upon doing just that. Clearly the battle has been joined; the issues being contested are self-evident; only the outcome is in doubt. The humane spirit and life of the black community has, historically, been nurtured in its churches. Under the dehumanizing impact of rapid urbanization, institutionalized racism, and the parallel technological, political, and social revolution, the quality of life in the black areas has deteriorated. That new sources of community can be derived from reinvigorated nationalism is not self-evident. Whatever else may eventuate, organized religion in the black community will feel the impact, and while it is not moribund by any stretch of the imagination, it may find itself in a struggle for existence.

BIBLIOGRAPHY

Allen, Richard. *The Life Experience and Gospel Labors of the Rt. Rev. Richard Allen.* New York: Abingdon Press, 1970.

Berson, Lenora. *The Negroes and the Jews.* New York: Random House, 1971.

Bradley, David H., Sr. *A History of the A.M.E. Zion Church, 1796–1872.* Nashville, Tenn.: Parthenon Press, 1956.

Bragg, George F. *History of the Afro-American Group of the Episcopal Church.* Baltimore: Church Advocate Press, 1922.

Cleague, Albert E., Jr. *Black Messiah.* New York: Sheed and Ward, 1968.

––––––. *Black Christian Nationalism: New Directions for the Black Church.* New York: William Morrow and Co., 1972.

Cone, James H. *Black Theology and Black Power.* New York: Seabury Press, 1969.

––––––. *Liberation: A Black Theology of Liberation.* New York: J. B. Lippincott Co., 1970.

Davis, John P., ed. *The American Negro Reference Book.* Englewood Cliffs, N.J.: Prentice Hall, Inc., 1966.

DuBois, William E. B., ed. *The Negro Church.* Atlanta University Report no. 8, 1903. Atlanta University Publications, II. New York: Arno Press and the *New York Times,* 1969.

Fauset, Arthur H. *Black Gods of the Metropolis.* New York: Octagon Books, 1970.

Foley, Albert S. *God's Men of Color: The Colored Priests of the United States 1854–1954.* New York: Farrar, Straus and Co., 1955.

Frazier, E. Franklin. *The Negro Church in America.* New York: Schocken Books, 1963.

Freeman, Edward D. *The Epoch of Negro Baptists and Foreign Missions Boards.* Kansas City, Kans.: Central Seminary Press, 1953.

Gardiner, James A., and Roberts, Deotis, eds. *Quest for a Black Theology*. Philadelphia: Pilgrim Press, 1971.

Gillard, John T. *The Catholic Church and the American Negro*. Baltimore: St. Joseph's Society Press, 1929.

———. *Colored Catholics in the United States*. Baltimore: Josephite Press, 1941.

Hood, James W. *One Hundred Years of the African Methodist Episcopal Zion Church*. New York: A.M.E. Zion Book Concern, 1895.

Jordan, Winthrop D. *White over Black: American Attitudes Toward the Negro, 1750–1812*. Chapel Hill: University of North Carolina Press, 1968.

Jordon, Lewis G. *Negro Baptist History U.S.A. 1750–1930*. Nashville, Tenn.: Sunday School Publishing Board, National Baptist Convention, 1931.

King, Martin L., Jr. *Stride Toward Freedom*. New York: Ballantine Books, 1958.

———. *Where Do We Go from Here: Chaos or Community?* New York: Bantam Books, 1967.

Lincoln, C. Eric. *The Black Muslims in America*. Boston: Beacon Press, 1961.

Lucas, Lawrence. *Black Priest/White Church: Catholics and Racism*. New York: Random House, 1970.

Mabee, Carlton. *Black Freedom: The Non-Violent Abolitionists from 1830 Through the Civil War*. New York: Macmillan Co., 1970.

Mays, Benjamin E., and Nicholson, John W. *The Negro's Church*. New York: Institute of Social and Religious Research, 1933.

Mays, Benjamin E. *The Negro's God*. New York: Chapman and Grimes, Inc., 1938.

Murray, Andrew E. *Presbyterians and the Negro—A History*. Philadelphia: Presbyterian Historical Society, 1966.

Myrdal, Gunnar. *The Negro Social Structure*. Vol. 2 of *An American Dilemma*. New York: McGraw Hill Book Co., 1964.

Nelen, Hart M.; Yokley, Raytha L.; and Nelsen, Anne K. *The Black Church in America*. New York: Basic Books, 1971.

Nichol, John T. *The Pentacostals*. Plainfield, N.J.: Logos International, 1966.

Payne, Daniel A. *A History of the African Methodist Episcopal Church 1816–1856*. Nashville, Tenn.: A.M.E. Sunday School Union, 1891.

Phillips, Charles H. *History of the Colored Methodist Episcopal Church in America*. Jackson, Tenn.: Publishing House of the C.M.E. Church, 1925.

Quarles, Benjamin. *Black Abolitionists*. New York: Oxford University Press, 1969.

Reimers, David M. *White Protestantism and the Negro*. New York: Oxford University Press, 1965.

Shuster, George, and Kearns, Robert M. *Statistical Profile of Black Catholics*. Washington, D.C.: Josephite Pastoral Center, 1976.

Singleton, George A. *The Romance of African Methodism*. New York: Exposition Press, 1952.

Smith, Charles S. *A History of the African Methodist Episcopal Church, 1856–1922*. Philadelphia: Book Concern of the A.M.E. Church, 1922.

Tanner, Benjamin T. *An Apology for African Methodism*. Baltimore: 1867.

Washington, Joseph R., Jr. *Black Religion and Christianity in the United States*. Boston: Beacon Press, 1964.

———. *The Politics of God*. Boston: Beacon Press, 1967.

Woodson, Carter G. *The Negro Church*. Washington, D.C.: Associated Publishers, 1921.

Elmer W. Henderson

The Federal Government and the Fight for Basic Human Rights

FROM FREEDOM TO CITIZENSHIP TO INDIFFERENCE

Any review of recent federal efforts in the area of basic human rights must give attention to the earlier steps taken during the post-Civil War period (1865–75). Despite the tragic results for American blacks of the failure of government to fully meet its responsibilities during that era, the important precedent was established that the federal government did recognize an important duty to maintain equality among its citizens and to further the cause of human rights.

For the purpose of this paper, the adoption of the Thirteenth, Fourteenth, and Fifteenth Amendments to the Constitution, the Civil Rights Acts enacted thereunder, and the work of the Freedmen's Bureau will be discussed. These significant developments were among the first in the history of the United States in which the federal government took affirmative legislative and administrative steps to assist one of its constituent minority groups; this action constituted a reversal of the social doctrine of laissez faire which had guided the country since 1789.

With the military defeat of the South, some members of Congress feared that the emancipation of the slaves would be nullified, that the tragic war, with its terrible sacrifices, would be rendered futile unless the federal government did what was clearly necessary to protect the new status of the freedmen and provide help in their transition to hoped-for equality. These so-called Republican radicals thought that it was totally unrealistic to expect former slaves to prosper in a hostile

Elmer W. Henderson is counsel to the Committee on Government Operations, U.S. House of Representatives, Washington, D.C.

environment and they generally disagreed with President Lincoln, who seemed to feel that events should be allowed to take their own course— a sentiment even more forcefully held by his successor, Andrew Johnson of Tennessee.[1]

Historians of that period have variously ascribed to these radical Republicans such base motives as vindictiveness toward the South, the desire to insure the economic supremacy of the North in general, and the political supremacy of the Republican party in particular. But whatever the truth of these charges, the hopeful but helpless blacks and their descendants welcomed such efforts and the tantalizing vision of full citizenship which they evoked.

A federal administrative agency to provide food, clothing, and other elemental needs for the freed slaves was created before the end of the war to cope with the chaotic problems of thousands on the move. At the end of the war the radicals caused Congress to give to the Bureau of Refugees, Freedmen, and Abandoned Lands greater authority to meet these needs—but little in funds or resources. Nevertheless, the Freedmen's Bureau, under the leadership of General O. O. Howard, the founder of Howard University, carried on its work for more than five years. With the support of the War Department, of which it became a part, it rendered a major service in providing relief for the poor, in overseeing labor contracts between black workers and their employers, in making available to all blacks some lands in the South that had been abandoned or forfeited, in helping them to exercise the right to vote, and—more permanently—in setting up schools to enable some of the freedmen and their children to obtain an education.

The principal historian of this federal agency was George R. Bentley. He summarized its problems and its achievements in these words:

> To some extent the Freedmen's Bureau had succeeded in getting for its charges other things than the change in white people's mores the Negroes primarily needed. It had provided desperately needed relief to destitute freedmen; then it had helped them begin to earn their livings in a free-labor system. It had protected the Negroes at least temporarily from reenslavement in the form of peonage; it had been the most important agency in establishing schools and colleges for young colored people; and it had frequently enforced Negroes' civil rights.[2]

Congress, prodded by the Republican radicals, sought to insure equality for the freedmen by writing three human rights amendments.

1. John Hope Franklin, *Reconstruction After the Civil War* (Chicago: University of Chicago Press, 1961), pp. 25–31.
2. George R. Bentley, *History of the Freedmen's Bureau* (New York: Octagon Books, 1970), p. 214.

These amendments, added to the historic bill of rights, produced for all Americans a charter of civil liberties theretofore unparalleled in the history of nations. One thing should be clearly recognized: No matter how controversial the amendments appeared to be, nor how zealous the radicals were accused of being, they represented a consensus of the Congress, because constitutional amendments required a vote of two-thirds of both the House and the Senate.

The Thirteenth Amendment, ratified by the states on 6 December 1865, stated that "Neither slavery nor involuntary servitude, except as a punishment for crime whereof the party shall have been duly convicted, shall exist within the United States, or any place subject to their jurisdiction."[3] Thus, was cast into the basic law of the land what had only been decreed by executive fiat. The Emancipation Proclamation was made permanent and universal, covering the country in its entirety.

The Fourteenth Amendment was ratified on 9 July 1868. It declared that

All persons born or naturalized in the United States, and subject to the jurisdiction thereof, are citizens of the United States and of the State wherein they reside. No State shall make or enforce any law which shall abridge the privileges or immunities of citizens of the United States; nor shall any State deprive any person of life, liberty, or property, without due process of law; nor deny to any person within its jurisdiction the equal protection of the laws.[4]

The Congress thereby intended that the freed slaves, along with all persons born within the country or who emigrated here and became naturalized, had the full status and dignity of citizenship in both the United States as a whole and the state in which they resided. The amendment prohibited the states from abridging the privileges and immunities of citizenship (even today not plainly defined), required state power to be exercised with due process of law and, most significantly for modern Supreme Court interpretations, required the states to provide for all persons within their jurisdictions "equal protection of the laws."

Other provisions of the amendment related to the apportionment of the House of Representatives and the grounds for reduction in the number of seats held by a state in the event the right to vote is denied by a state. It also placed certain qualifications on elected and appointed

3. *The Constitution of the United States: Analysis and Interpretation* (Washington, D.C.: U.S. Government Printing Office, House Document 90–124, 1967), p. 13.
4. Ibid., p. 14.

officials of the United States and made secure the legitimate public debt of the United States.

The Fifteenth Amendment, ratified on 3 February 1870, was intended to safeguard the right of the freedmen to vote by declaring "The right of citizens of the United States to vote shall not be denied or abridged by the United States or by any State on account of race, color, or previous condition of servitude."[5]

Regretfully, it took nearly 100 years for the Supreme Court to place upon these amendments the meaning which the Congress and most of the ratifying states certainly intended.[6] But the importance of the amendments must not be gainsayed, for many observers have expressed doubt that the three could gain passage by two-thirds of the House and Senate and ratification by three-fourths of the states in the climate of today.

The Congress next implemented the amendments by the adoption of the Civil Rights Acts and other significant legislation. The most far-reaching of these was the Civil Rights Act of 1875, subtitled "An Act to Protect All Citizens in their Civil and Legal Rights."[7] Professor Konvitz summarized its provisions as follows:

> The preamble stated that Congress deemed it essential to just government that "we recognize the equality of all men before the law, and hold that it is the duty of government in all its dealings with the people to mete out equal and exact justice to all, of whatever nativity, race, color, or persuasion, religious or political," and that it is "the appropriate object of legislation to enact great fundamental principles into law." The new act provided that "all persons within the jurisdiction of the United States shall be entitled to the full and equal enjoyment of the accommodations, advantages, facilities, and privileges of inns, public conveyances on land or water, theaters, and other places of public amusement; subject only to the conditions and limitations established by law, and applicable alike to citizens of every race and color, regardless of any previous condition of servitude." The person aggrieved by a violation could recover $500, and the offender was also to be guilty of a misdemeanor. Federal courts were given exclusive jurisdiction.[8]

If these constitutional amendments and civil rights laws had been faithfully carried out and enforced by the federal government and the states, the course of race relations in this country during the last century would doubtless have been far different and, unquestionably, the social

5. Ibid., p. 15.
6. *Brown v. Board of Education of Topeka*, United States Reports, vol. 349 (1954), p. 294.
7. U.S., *Statutes at Large*, vol. 18 (1975), p. 335.
8. Milton R. Konvitz, *The Constitution and Civil Rights* (New York: Columbia University Press, 1962), p. 6.

and economic condition of the black minority would have been greatly improved. The spirited efforts of the radicals soon flagged however, and the attention of the populace was turned to other matters. The Supreme Court held the principal provisions of the civil rights acts to be unconstitutional,[9] and even the Fourteenth Amendment was twisted from its historic purpose as a charter of human rights into a tool of the great corporate giants formed during the latter decades of the nineteenth century.

The great progress which this federal legislation seemed to promise turned to ashes with the collapse of the reconstruction governments in the states during the 1870s, and for nearly sixty years neither the Congress nor the executive made any serious effort to involve the federal government in the protection of human rights.

THE AWAKENING FEDERAL RESPONSIBILITY

Franklin D. Roosevelt's New Deal administration represented a dramatic shift from the doctrine of laissez faire in the U.S. government. The deepening depression and its attendant unemployment and hardship for millions of Americans stirred Roosevelt to mobilize the power of government to relieve economic distress and to regulate the economic system. The New Deal programs were not directed at the black minority but at all of the poor, of which that minority was, unfortunately, a prominent constituent.

Thus, in the period preceding World War II—and in anticipation of it—Roosevelt issued Executive Order 8802 in June of 1941.[10] His decision was reluctant and was clearly made to defuse A. Philip Randolph's threatened march on Washington. But it was done, nevertheless, and it represented the use of executive power in the federal government to curb rampant discrimination in employment in the defense industries and government service. The Executive Order stated:

> I do hereby reaffirm the policy of the United States that there shall be no discrimination in the employment of workers in defense industries or government because of race, creed, color, or national origin, and I do hereby declare that it is the duty of employers and of labor organizations, in furtherance of said policy and of this order, to provide for the full and equitable participation of all workers in defense industries, without discrimination because of race, creed, color, or national origin;
> And it is hereby ordered as follows:
> (1) All departments and agencies of the Government of the United States

9. *Civil Rights Cases,* United States Reports, vol. 109 (1893), p. 3.
10. Fair Employment Practices Committee, *Final Report* (Washington, D.C.: U.S. Government Printing Office, 1947), p. 98.

concerned with vocational and training programs for defense production shall take special measures appropriate to assure that such programs are administered without discrimination because of race, creed, color, or national origin;

(2) All contracting agencies of the Government of the United States shall include in all defense contracts hereafter negotiated by them a provision obligating the contractor not to discriminate against any worker because of race, creed, color, or national origin. . . .

The order created a Committee on Fair Employment Practice to receive and investigate complaints of discrimination in violation of its provisions and to take appropriate steps to redress grievances which it found to be valid.

The Committee on Fair Employment Practice served through the duration of the war. It held a number of public hearings and settled nearly 5,000 cases of discrimination by peaceful negotiation, including forty strikes caused by racial differences.[11] There were many unresolved cases as well, but the committee, in spite of tremendous opposition and harassment and with no enforcement powers of its own, did a truly remarkable job in achieving the integration of Negroes, Jews, and other minorities into defense-related industries in skills and occupations from which they had been barred.

In accepting the resignation of the members of the committee, President Truman said: "The degree of effectiveness which the Fair Employment Practice Committee was able to attain has shown once and for all that it is possible to equalize job opportunity by governmental action, and thus eventually to eliminate the influence of prejudice in the field of employment."[12]

After the war, a strong effort was made to have Congress enact legislation banning discrimination in employment in interstate commerce, but Congress failed to do so.

On 5 December 1946, Harry S. Truman created the President's Committee on Civil Rights "to inquire into and to determine whether and in what respect current law-enforcement measures and the authority and means possessed by Federal, State and local governments may be strengthened and improved to safeguard the civil rights of the people."[13] A year later the committee, after making a careful study of the subject, issued one of the first official reports of its kind entitled "To Secure

11. Ibid., p. viii. See also Malcolm Ross, *All Manner of Men* (New York: Reynal and Hitchcock, 1948).
12. Harry S. Truman, Letter of Acceptance. Fair Employment Practice Committee, *Final Report* (Washington, D.C.: U.S. Government Printing Office, 1947), p. vii.
13. Executive Order no. 9809, *Code of Federal Regulations*, Title III, 1943–48 Compilation, p. 590.

these Rights."[14] It proposed a reorganization and expansion of the Civil Rights Section of the Department of Justice and the establishment of a permanent Commission on Civil Rights. It also recommended to Congress the passage of a federal fair employment practices law and new legislation to correct discrimination in voting and in the administration of justice.[15] This report, issued thirty years ago, may well have been the turning point in official governmental determination to deal with the problem of equality among citizens and the elimination of discrimination.

President Truman sent Congress a special message urging that the recommendations of the commission be enacted into law and made Congress' failure to act an issue in the presidential election of 1948. Undoubtedly, the impact of this report had been significant.

Two further steps were taken by President Truman. The disgraceful manner in which Negro soldiers were relegated to segregated units in World War II had pricked the conscience of many Americans in the immediate postwar period. On 26 July 1948, the president, exercising the powers vested in him as the president and as commander-in-chief of the armed services, promulgated Executive Order 9981 declaring the equality of treatment for all persons in the armed services without regard to race, color, religion, or national origin. To help carry out the order, he created in the military establishment the President's Committee on Equality of Treatment and Opportunity in the Armed Services, headed by a highly regarded judge of the U.S. Court of Appeals.[16] He further directed all executive departments and agencies of the federal government to cooperate with the committee in its work. Thus began the task of desegregating the U.S. Army, Navy, Air Force, and Marine Corps that some years later proved to be an outstanding achievement in governmental action in the field of human rights. Of course it was not done instantly, nor even today has it been perfected, but it demonstrated that social patterns built up by nearly 200 years of institutional practice could be changed.

Another of President Truman's executive orders attacked the problem of employment discrimination in an area under his control—the federal government itself.[17] He directed that "all personnel actions taken by federal appointing officers shall be based solely on merit and fitness; and such officers are authorized and directed to take appropriate

14. The President's Committee on Civil Rights, *To Secure These Rights* (Washington, D.C., U.S. Government Printing Office, 1947).
15. Ibid., p. 139.
16. Executive Order no. 9981, *Federal Register,* vol. 13 (1948) p. 4313.
17. Executive Order no. 9980, *Federal Register,* vol. 13 (1948) p. 4311.

steps to insure that in all such actions there shall be no discrimination because of race, color, religion or national origin." He made the head of each department and agency personally responsible for an effective program to insure that fair employment policies were fully observed within his department. He also established a Fair Employment Board within the U.S. Civil Service Commission to review departmental decisions and to advise the departments on problems and policies relating to fair employment.

A moderate effort was also made by President Truman to influence the employment practices of private industry, which had reverted to its pre-World War II discrimination against minority workers. After the Korean War began, he issued an executive order reaffirming the policy that government contracts contain a provision obligating the contractor not to discriminate against any employee or applicant for employment because of race, creed, color, or national origin.[18] He also established a Committee on Government Contract Compliance to help carry out the policy. Considering the tremendous scope of government purchases, the policy, if successfully implemented, would have had a profound effect on private industry and enabled many minority workers to be employed in accordance with their highest skills. The committee was given no enforcement powers, however, and little was accomplished.

The 1950s were dominated, for the most part, by actions in the courts and particularly by the landmark Supreme Court decision outlawing racial segregation in public education. Possibly the outstanding event involving federal executive action was President Eisenhower's response to the defiance of the courts by the Governor of Arkansas in the Little Rock school cases. In this instance, the Arkansas General Assembly enacted a number of laws to block desegregation of a Little Rock high school, and when school opened in September of 1957, Governor Faubus ordered the Arkansas National Guard to prevent Negro children from entering the school as had been ordered by a federal court. During the disorder which followed, President Eisenhower directed federal troops to remove any obstructions to compliance with the court's order.[19] The use of the troops established, for the first time since the reconstruction period, that the power of the federal government would be used to prevent state action, contrary to law, that sought to maintain racial segregation.

18. Executive Order no. 10308, issued 3 December 1951, *Federal Register,* vol. 16 (1951) p. 12303.
19. Executive Order no. 1–930, issued 24 September 1957, "Providing Assistance for the Removal of an Obstruction of Justice within the State of Arkansas," *Code of Federal Regulations,* Title III, 1954–58 Compilation, p. 389.

Another noteworthy event occurred during this decade when, in 1957, Congress enacted the first statute dealing with civil rights in eighty years. Congress had repealed a number of statutes but had not enacted new ones. The principal device for thwarting congressional action was by the filibuster in the Senate. Historically, senators from the South had abused the Senate's privilege of unlimited debate by talking to death any measure remotely beneficial to American blacks. Many times efforts to apply cloture (shut off debate) had been made, but none had ever succeeded. The climate of opinion, due in great measure to the National Association for the Advancement of Colored People (NAACP), had improved and conditions became ripe for change. It was Lyndon B. Johnson of Texas, then Majority Leader of the Senate, who distinguished himself by leading the fight against the filibuster to eventual success—and who was catapulted into national prominence and candidacy for the presidency thereby.

The Civil Rights Act of 1957 had as its chief purpose "to provide means of further securing and protecting the civil rights of persons within the jurisdiction of the United States among other purposes."[20] It authorized the federal government to bring civil suits in its own name to obtain injunctive relief where any person is denied or threatened in his or her right to vote (this legal remedy was formerly available only to private persons). The act also elevated the Civil Rights Section of the Department of Justice to the status of a division to be headed by an assistant attorney general. The act created the U.S. Commission on Civil Rights and empowered it to investigate allegations of denial of the right to vote; to study and collect information concerning legal developments constituting a denial of equal protection of the laws under the Constitution; and to appraise the laws and policies of the federal government with respect to equal protection.

This breakthrough in civil rights legislation, although modest in its effect, paved the way for more significant statutes to follow and is, therefore, an important historical precedent for federal actions. The Civil Rights Commission is still in existence, continuing to stimulate governmental progress in this area.

THE RANGE OF FEDERAL POWER

The 1960s constituted a period when, at long last, the federal government agreed to commit itself by statute and policy to equality among citizens. Of course *statute* and *policy* are not always followed by *action*, but action can scarcely be expected without a prior accord on policy.

20. U.S., *Statutes at Large*, vol. 71, p. 634.

The federal government's commitment to human rights was not founded on ideological or abstract grounds, but was a response to the pent-up demands of American blacks and other minority groups, led by the NAACP and the Leadership Conference on Human Rights. These demands were based on the very practical and high priority needs that those groups felt must be met to give them a chance for equality with other Americans: the right to vote; the right to equal employment; the right to decent housing; the right to enjoy all public accommodations; and the right to serve (and die, if necessary) equitably and honorably in the armed forces, among others. The drive to establish these policies, combined with a series of major Supreme Court affirmations of equality under the Constitution, made the decade of the 1960s the most important for human rights in U.S. history.

The first enactment was the Civil Rights Act of 1960.[21] Its major aim was to strengthen the federal guarantee of the right to vote contained in the 1957 act. Recognizing that full participation by blacks in the political process would be their most effective entree into full citizenship, southern registrars had developed a tactic involving their refusal to register blacks, followed by their resignation to avoid prosecution. The new law declared that discriminatory acts of registrars "shall be deemed that of the State and the State may be joined as a party defendant." Thus, if a registrar resigned, a proceeding could be instituted against the state. The act also required that voting records be preserved for twenty-two months following any general, special, or primary election. It permitted the attorney general of the United States to gain access to them for inspection, reproduction, and copying before filing suit in order to determine if proceedings were warranted. The act also included a provision for the appointment of judicial voting referees so that if a district court found a pattern or practice of voting deprivation, it could appoint such voting referees to receive applications from prospective voters who alleged that they had been denied an equal opportunity to register or otherwise qualify to vote. If the referee agreed with the prospective voter, he or she would report such findings to the court, which could then issue a decree ordering that the qualified voter be permitted to vote. Refusal to honor the decree would be punishable as contempt of court.

The 1960 act also provided penalties for those who obstructed orders of the court and made such obstructionists subject to civil suit. Further, in response to the severe violence, bombing, and terror practiced against blacks in the South at that time, the law made flight across state lines to avoid prosecution for such crimes a federal offense.

21. U.S., *Statutes at Large*, vol. 74, p. 86.

The Civil Rights Act of 1964,[22] enacted over the bitter and determined opposition of the anti-civil rights bloc in the House and the Senate, was a major turning point in congressional efforts to establish firm, unequivocal policy in the field of human rights. It was broad and comprehensive in scope and came to grips with many of the problems which had plagued minorities for years. The conscience of the country had been shocked by a wave of terror in the South which was capped by the bombing of a church in Birmingham, Alabama, in the spring of 1964 in which four young girls had been killed. The NAACP and many other groups were aroused and insistent. Here again the leadership of Lyndon B. Johnson, by then president of the United States, was crucial.

In Title I of the act Congress further attacked discrimination in voting and the devices used to thwart voters by declaring that no person under penalty of law could apply any standards of qualification to one individual different from those applied to others; could deny the right to vote because of nonmaterial errors or omissions in filling out application forms; or could employ any literacy test unless it was given in writing and unless the individual, upon his or her request, was furnished a copy of the test and answers within a specific period of time. It also created an important rebuttable presumption that persons who had completed the sixth grade possessed the necessary intelligence and comprehension to vote. In addition, the procedures for obtaining court action in voting cases were strengthened.

Title II provided equal access to virtually all places of public accommodation, ending the practice which, for so many years, had been a source of humiliation and inconvenience to minorities. The act declared that:

All persons shall be entitled to the full and equal enjoyment of the goods, services, facilities, privileges, advantages, and accommodations of any place of public accommodation, as defined in this section, without discrimination or segregation on the ground of race, color, religion, or national origin.

It then indicated the breadth of the coverage in the following manner:

Each of the following establishments which serves the public is a place of public accommodation within the meaning of this title if its operations affect commerce, or if discrimination or segregation by it is supported by State action:
(1) any inn, hotel, motel, or other establishment which provides lodging to transient guests, other than an establishment located within a building which contains not more than five rooms for rent or hire and which is

22. U.S., *Statutes at Large,* vol. 78, p. 241.

actually occupied by the proprietor of such establishment as his residence;

(2) any restaurant, cafeteria, lunchroom, lunch counter, soda fountain, or other facility principally engaged in selling food for consumption on the premises, including, but not limited to, any such facility located on the premises of any retail establishment; or any gasoline station;

(3) any motion picture house, theater, concert hall, sports arena, stadium or other place of exhibition or entertainment; and

(4) any establishment (A)(i) which is physically located within the premises of any establishment otherwise covered by this subsection, or (ii) within the premises of which is physically located any such covered establishment, and (B) which holds itself out as serving patrons of such covered establishment.

The act defined "commerce" in a fashion designed to make it quite difficult for any such place to escape coverage.

The law made it clear that "all persons shall be entitled to be free, at any establishment or place, from discrimination or segregation of any kind on the ground of race, color, religion, or national origin, if such discrimination or segregation is or purports to be required by any law, statute, ordinance, regulation, rule, or order of a State or any agency or political subdivision thereof."

It prohibited interference with the enjoyment of the rights conferred and set up procedures by which remedies could be obtained in the courts.

The act authorized the Community Relations Service to make investigations of complaints under this title.

Title III of the Civil Rights Act of 1964 clarified the role of the federal government in enforcement of the constitutional bar against any state that deprived or threatened a person with the loss of his or her right to the equal protection of the laws on account of race, creed, or color, by authorizing the attorney general to file suits on behalf of persons so deprived or threatened. The prohibited state action included any denial of equal utilization of any public facility owned, operated, or managed by or on behalf of any state or subdivision thereof, except a public school or college.

Title IV directed the United States commissioner of education to provide technical assistance to school districts preparing to desegregate and to make grants to school boards to help them deal with the problems incident to desegregation. This title also authorized the attorney general of the United States to sue to achieve desegregation whenever a parent or group of parents complained that their minor children were being deprived by a school board of the equal protection of the laws, or whenever an individual or his or her parent complained that he or she had been denied admission to a public college.

Title V renewed and broadened the scope of the studies and investigations to be conducted by the U.S. Civil Rights Commission.

Title VI charted entirely new ground in federal-state relations by creating a new right to participate in, receive the benefits of, and be free from discrimination under any state program or activity receiving federal financial assistance. Thus, it required that any program or activity involving federal funds, no matter the administrator, must be carried out without discrimination and with equal participation by all. All federal departments and agencies extending grants, loans, or contracts were required to issue rules and regulations consistent with the objectives of this statute. Federal financial assistance could be terminated if discrimination was detected. In view of the ever increasing role of federal assistance, many observers believed that this was one of the most powerful of all weapons in enforcing nondiscrimination policies.

Title VII, for the first time, provided congressional legislation (rather than only executive action) which made it unlawful for employers or labor organizations engaged in interstate commerce to practice job discrimination. This historic affirmation of a policy established by President Roosevelt for war-related industries was broadened and codified into law. Its essential provision reads as follows:

(a) It shall be an unlawful employment practice for an employer—
  (1) to fail or refuse to hire or to discharge any individual, or otherwise to discriminate against any individual with respect to his compensation, terms, conditions, or privileges of employment, because of such individual's race, color, religion, sex, or national origin; or
  (2) to limit, segregate, or classify his employees in any way which would deprive or tend to deprive any individual of employment opportunities or otherwise adversely affect his status as an employee, because of such individual's race, color, religion, sex, or national origin.
(b) It shall be an unlawful employment practice for an employment agency to fail or refuse to refer for employment, or otherwise to discriminate against, any individual because of his race, color, religion, sex, or national origin, or to classify or refer for employment any individual on the basis of his race, color, religion, sex, or national origin.
(c) It shall be an unlawful employment practice for a labor organization—
  (1) to exclude or to expel from its membership, or otherwise to discriminate against, any individual because of his race, color, religion, sex, or national origin;
  (2) to limit, segregate, or classify its membership, or to classify or fail or refuse to refer for employment any individual, in any way which would deprive or tend to deprive any individual of employment op-

portunities, or would limit such employment opportunities or otherwise adversely affect his status as an employee or as an applicant for employment, because of such individual's race, color, religion, sex, or national origin; or

(3) to cause or attempt to cause an employer to discriminate against an individual in violation of this section.

Employers with less than twenty-five workers were exempt and labor organizations with less than twenty-five members are to be exempt after the third year the act was in force.

The act set up an Equal Employment Opportunity Commission somewhat similar to President Roosevelt's Fair Employment Practice Committee to investigate complaints of discrimination and to prevent unlawful employment practices, but the Congress refused to give the commission enforcement powers. If the commission's efforts at conciliation failed, the only remedy for a worker discriminated against was to file a suit against the employer in court or attempt to convince the attorney general to do so. Not until 1972 did Congress allow the commission itself to file charges against recalcitrant employers in the courts. After such filing, the court could enjoin an employer from continuing to practice discrimination and could direct the employer to provide such relief to the worker suffering discrimination as it found appropriate, including back pay. Civil rights leaders continue to find these enforcement provisions inadequate and are hoping to convince a future Congress to give the commission power to issue cease and desist orders.

Title VIII directed the secretary of commerce to compile registration and voting statistics. Title IX provided authority for the attorney general to intervene in cases where relief was being sought from the denial of equal protection of the laws, and Title X established the Community Relations Service to assist communities in resolving disputes or difficulties based on discriminatory practices.

In spite of the legislation enacted by the Congress in 1957, 1960, and 1964, the South was still adamant in its refusal to permit Negro citizens to fully exercise their franchise. The devices used ranged from the literacy test to intimidation and even violence. The country had become so concerned about this denial that President Johnson appeared before a specially called joint session of Congress on 15 March 1965 to plead for the enactment of more effective legislation. He told the assembled Senators and Representatives:

Many of the issues of civil rights are very complex and most difficult. But about this there can and should be no argument. Every American citizen must have an equal right to vote. There is no reason which can excuse the denial of that right. There is no duty which weighs more heavily on us than the duty we have to insure that right.

Yet the harsh fact is that in many places in this country men and women are kept from voting simply because they are Negroes.

Every device of which human ingenuity is capable has been used to deny this right. The Negro citizen may go to register only to be told that the day is wrong, or the hour is late, or the official in charge is absent.

And if he persists, and if he manages to present himself to the registrar, he may be disqualified because he did not spell out his middle name or because he abbreviated a word on the application.

And if he manages to fill out an application he is given a test. The registrar is the sole judge of whether he passes this test. He may be asked to recite the entire Constitution, or explain the most complex provisions of State law and even a college degree cannot be used to prove that he can read and write.

For the fact is that the only way to pass these barriers is to show a white skin.

Experience has clearly shown that the existing process of law cannot overcome systematic and ingenious discrimination. No law that we now have on the books—and I have helped to put three of them there—can insure the right to vote when local officials are determined to deny it.

In such a case our duty must be clear to all of us. The Constitution says that no person shall be kept from voting because of his race or his color. We have all sworn an oath before God to support and to defend that Constitution.

We must now act in obedience to that oath.[23]

Congress subsequently enacted the Voting Rights Act of 1965,[24] designed to attack the problem on a more generalized basis than through case by case litigation. The act as passed authorized the courts to suspend the use of any test or device which it found had been used to deny or abridge the right of citizens to vote in violation of the Fifteenth Amendment. The courts were empowered to authorize the appointment of federal examiners by the U.S. Civil Service Commission and the federal examiners could register and maintain lists of persons eligible to vote in federal, state, or local elections. It particularly applied the action to six states in which the number of registered voters was less than 50 percent of those eligible (because of age) among the residents of those states, as determined by the Bureau of the Census. It also authorized federal observers to "enter and attend at any place for holding an election . . . for the purpose of observing whether persons who are entitled to vote are being permitted to vote." It barred the levy of any poll tax as a precondition to voting and ordered stronger penalties

23. U.S., Congress, House of Representatives, *Congressional Record*, 89th Cong., 1st sess., 1965, pt. 4:5058.
24. U.S., *Statutes at Large*, vol. 79, p. 437.

against those who attempted to intimidate or coerce those seeking to vote.

This legislation has proved to be quite successful in achieving its objectives. The U.S. Commission on Civil Rights said in 1970:

> The Voting Rights Act of 1965 has also resulted in dramatic, statistically measurable progress. Before its passage, registration of black citizens of voting age in the six southern states affected by the law was less than 31 percent. By the spring of 1969, approximately 57 per cent of eligible blacks in these States were registered. . . . To be sure, the Voting Rights Act has not resulted in full use of the franchise. Means other than disqualification such as exploitation of continuing economic dependence of rural Negroes in the South, still constitute deterrents to the exercise of the right to vote. Nonetheless, impressive progress has been made as a result of the Voting Rights Act.[25]

One of the major handicaps under which blacks have labored is that of inadequate housing—due in part to a long-standing and deliberate policy by real estate brokers and managers of property to refuse to sell or rent to blacks outside of certain circumscribed areas. The consequences of such discrimination have been seen in the nationwide growth and exploitation of inner-city ghettos surrounded by suburbs from which blacks have virtually been excluded. Much of the current furor over busing and the slow pace of school integration stems from the hard fact of housing segregation. For decades this problem was either acquiesced in or ignored by government at all levels; by 1968, however, Congress decided to take action. It did so by creating, in the Civil Rights Act of 1968, a new right not previously recognized by statute, declaring it to be unlawful

> (a) To refuse to sell or rent after the making of a bona fide offer, or to refuse to negotiate for the sale or rental of, or otherwise make unavailable or deny, a dwelling to any person because of race, color, religion, or national origin.
> (b) To discriminate against any person in the terms, conditions, or privileges of sale or rental of a dwelling, or in the provision of services or facilities in connection therewith, because of race, color, religion, or national origin.
> (c) To make, print, or publish, or cause to be made, printed, or published any notice, statement, or advertisement, with respect to the sale or rental of a dwelling that indicates any preference, limitation, or discrimination based on race, color, religion, or national origin, or an intention to make any such preference, limitation, or discrimination.

25. U.S. Commission on Civil Rights, *Federal Civil Rights Enforcement Effort—A Report* (Washington, D.C.: U.S. Government Printing Office, 1970), p. 31.

(d) To represent to any person because of race, color, religion, or national origin that any dwelling is not available for inspection, sale, or rental when such dwelling is in fact so available.

(e) For profit, to induce or attempt to induce any person to sell or rent any dwelling by representations regarding the entry or prospective entry into the neighborhood of a person or persons of a particular race, color, religion, or national origin.[26]

The law prohibited any bank or other financing organization from denying a real estate loan or other financial assistance to any person because of race, creed, color, or national origin. It placed the administration of the law under the Department of Housing and Urban Development. When the secretary of the department is unable to obtain voluntary compliance, the person aggrieved may commence civil action in any U.S. District Court, which may enjoin such discrimination or order such affirmative action as the court deems appropriate. The law also states that:

Whenever the Attorney General has reasonable cause to believe that any person or group of persons is engaged in a pattern or practice of resistance to the full enjoyment of any of the rights granted by this title, or that any group of persons has been denied any of the rights granted by this title and such denial raises an issue of general public importance, he may bring a civil action in any appropriate United States district court by filing with it a complaint setting forth the facts and requesting such preventive relief, including an application for a permanent or temporary injunction, restraining order, or other order against the person or persons responsible for such pattern or practice or denial or rights, as he deems necessary to insure the full enjoyment of the rights granted by this title.

The essential provisions of the literacy test prohibitions of the Voting Rights Act of 1965 were only put into effect for a period of five years. At the time of enactment, Congress thought this to be sufficient time for the states to eliminate any restrictions on voting in violation of the Fifteenth Amendment, and that Negro citizens would by then have sufficient voting power in the affected states so that federal protection would no longer be needed. However, in 1970, although considerable progress had been made, Congress did not feel it could return to the states the complete discretion in selecting qualified voters. The House Judiciary Committee in its report on the 1970 bill said ". . . the committee concludes that it is essential to continue for an additional five years all the foregoing provisions of the Act in full force and effect in order to safeguard the gains in Negro voter registration thus far

26. U.S., *Statutes at Large*, vol. 82, p. 73.

achieved, and to prevent future infringements of voting rights based on race or color."[27]

The 1970 act also contained several important new features. Congress abolished the durational residency requirement as a prerequisite for voting for president and vice president and undertook to establish nationwide, uniform standards relative to absentee registration and absentee voting. It also reduced the age requirement from twenty-one to eighteen in federal, state, and local elections.

Another congressional action to further human rights came with the passage of the Equal Employment Opportunity Act of 1972, in which Title VII of the Civil Rights Act of 1964 was, to a considerable degree, rewritten.[28] Civil rights organizations had pointed out the difficulties in obtaining compliance with that law for a number of years and had urged the Congress to give to the Equal Employment Opportunity Commission the right to issue cease and desist orders—a power conferred upon a number of other federal agencies. The EEOC was devoid of any enforcement authority and could only try to eliminate discrimination by conferences and conciliation. It had only limited effectiveness.

In its report on the 1972 act, the Committee on Education and Labor of the House of Representatives stated:

Despite the progress which has been made since passage of the Civil Rights Act of 1964, discrimination against minorities and women continues. The persistence of discrimination and its detrimental effects require a reaffirmation of our national policy of equal opportunity in employment. It is essential that seven years after the passage of the Civil Rights Act of 1964, effective enforcement procedures be provided the Equal Employment Opportunity Commission to strengthen its efforts to reduce discrimination in employment.[29]

Congress continued its refusal to give the EEOC cease and desist powers, but in the 1972 act it did give the commission the authority to file suits in the federal courts against employers and labor unions which were charged with discrimination. The courts then, if they saw fit, could provide relief.

Other changes made by the new law included a transfer to the EEOC, after two years, of the attorney general's authority to take court action in those cases in which a person or group of persons are engaged in a pattern or practice of discrimination as distinguished from a single in-

27. U.S., *Statutes at Large*, vol. 84, p. 314, cited as the "Voting Rights Act Amendments of 1970."
28. U.S., *Statutes at Large*, vol. 86, p. 103.
29. U.S., Congress, House of Representatives, Committee on Education and Labor, *House Report no. 92–238,* June 2, 1971.

stance of discrimination against a particular individual. It broadened the coverage of the act to include employees of educational institutions and of state and local government. It reduced the size of business firms affected from twenty-five to fifteen workers, thus increasing the number of firms covered, among other changes.

The 1972 act improved the effectiveness of the commission, even though until today it has not received the enforcement authority required to carry out its difficult task.

A BACKWARD STEP

Although the 1960s were banner years for congressional action in the field of human rights, the 1970s began rather ominously. Several strong congressional moves were made to restrict the courts in their efforts to carry out the Supreme Court's ruling that public education must be equally available to all children. The ruling had resulted in court-ordered transportation of students out of the neighborhoods where they resided to effect such equalization. Busing became very unpopular with many parents and Congress responded by attaching riders to various bills to prohibit busing when ordered for the purpose of achieving racial balance in the schools.

In the Education Amendments of 1972, enacted as Public Law 92–318 on June 23 of that year, Congress included a provision which declared that no busing order issued by a United States District Court could be carried out until all appeals had been exhausted or until the time for such appeals had expired. This provision has remained in effect. The law also virtually barred the use of federal funds for busing to achieve desegration.

This restriction, however, was modest compared to the legislation proposed to Congress on 20 March 1972 by President Nixon. In his Special Message on School Busing, the president urged the Congress to place a moratorium on the courts preventing them from issuing any new orders requiring local educational agencies to transport students and to declare that local educational agencies would not be required to implement desegregation plans in order to be eligible to receive federal funds.[30]

Inasmuch as busing had always been treated by the courts as a method of last resort in implementing desegregation and was used only when other methods had proved ineffective, the president's plan was clearly a reversal of course for the federal government in its previous

30. U.S., Congress, House of Representatives, *Message from the President of the United States,* 20 March 1972, House Document 92–195.

compliance with the constitutionally based policy of school desegregation. Although the bill embodying the Nixon plan was passed by the
House, it fortunately failed of passage in the Senate. Civil rights advocates fervently hoped that this move by President Nixon would not
signal other, more regressive actions on the part of the executive and
the Congress.

IMPLEMENTING POLICY

The foregoing has shown the changes in human rights policy in the
federal government from laissez faire to one of positive expression. The
language of the law now clearly states that all citizens are equal and
are to be treated equally by all branches of the government—federal,
state, and local. Citizens are also to be treated equally in most areas
of employment, housing, and public accommodations, even though
these may be controlled by private individuals or corporations. Thus,
the basic needs and rights of minorities as well as the majority are elo-
quently guaranteed in the Constitution, the statutes, the judicial opinions, and in national policy.

The next question is: Has policy been translated into effective results? In some areas the answer must be "yes." The military has virtually
eliminated segregation of troops by race. The polls have been opened,
and unrestricted voting is the norm in most parts of the South and
elsewhere in the country. Places of public accommodation are open and
accessible to a degree not thought conceivable a few years ago. Instru-
ments of government on all levels are now providing services to citizens
in a manner many did not dare to expect until recently. But many problems still remain—particularly those of access to quality education;
access to jobs, both in government and private business, in accordance
with skill or potential; access to decent housing not restricted to the
ghetto; and access to the real centers of power and decision making in
government and the economy.

In its comprehensive survey of the federal government's implementation of civil rights policy, the U.S. Commission on Civil Rights pointed
out the persistence of discrimination in various of these areas.[31] The
commission found that in federal employment where the degree of federal control is absolute, black and Spanish-surnamed Americans are still
grossly underrepresented in the higher salary brackets. It also found
that despite nondiscrimination requirements in the merit system applicable to federally aided state programs, minority group employment

31. U.S. Commission on Civil Rights, *Federal Civil Rights Enforcement Effort*
(Washington, D.C.: U.S. Government Printing Office, 1971).

often remains low. For example, the Mississippi Welfare Department had only 3 blacks on its staff of more than 1,500 in a state where the ratio of blacks and whites is nearly even.

Even though equal employment opportunity requirements are imposed on government contractors, evidence gathered by the commission indicates that employment discrimination in the private sector is still prevalent throughout the United States. Many examples of private firms throughout the country were given. The McDonnell Douglas Aircraft plant—the nation's fourth largest defense contractor—employed more than 33,000 persons in its plant outside of St. Louis, of whom only 2,500, or less than 8 percent, were Negro. Yet blacks represent at least 14 percent of the population of the St. Louis metropolitan area. Less than 1 percent of the company's officials, managers, and professionals were Negroes. No black person was a general foreman or a salesworker in the plant.[32]

The commission pointed out that the denial of equal opportunity in *housing* remains a severe problem. As late as 1967 a national Federal Housing Administration survey of minority group occupancy in subdivisions built within the previous five years found that of the more than 400,000 units surveyed, only 3.3 percent were reported as having been sold to black families. In many areas even less encouraging results were shown. Another federal program which, like FHA, operated with a supposedly nondiscrimination policy, was Urban Renewal. It had the effect, however, of intensifying the concentration of blacks in ghettoes, as revealed in St. Louis.[33]

The commission also discovered that discrimination continued in the operation of programs under the Department of Agriculture and in state employment offices supported by the U.S. Department of Labor. Among other forms of unequal treatment, the latter included discrimination in the referral of applicants to employers. This important study, which exposed facts that are common knowledge to members of minority groups themselves, indicates that only a beginning has been made in the task of eliminating the hard facts of discrimination.

The commission pointed out that despite the fact that the federal arsenal of civil rights protection is impressive, in many areas the government has not yet developed the mechanisms and procedures necessary to secure this right in fact as well as in legal theory. It listed a number of fundamental weaknesses and inadequacies in civil rights

32. Ibid., p. 13.
33. Ibid., p. 14.

compliance and enforcement common to most federal agencies. They were:

—Inadequate staff and other resources to conduct civil rights enforcement activities with maximum effectiveness.
—Lack of authority and subordinate status of agency civil rights officials.
—Failure to define civil rights goals with sufficient specificity or breadth.
—Failure to coordinate civil rights and substantive programs.
—Undue emphasis on a passive role, such as reliance on receipt of complaints, in carrying out civil rights compliance and enforcement responsibilities.
—Undue emphasis on voluntary compliance and failure to make sufficient use of available sanctions to enforce civil rights laws.
—Failure to provide adequate coordination and direction to agencies having common civil rights responsibilities.
—Failure to collect and utilize racial and ethnic data in planning and evaluating progress toward goals.[34]

The commission noted that many of these weaknesses reflect more deep-seated problems, "problems of hostile bureaucracies that view civil rights as a threat to their prerogatives and programs." It concluded that "in the final analysis, achievement of civil rights goals depends on the quality of leadership exercised by the President in moving the Nation toward racial justice. The Commission is convinced that his example of courageous moral leadership can inspire the necessary will and determination, not only of the Federal officials who serve under his direction, but of the American people as well."[35]

BIBLIOGRAPHY

Bennett, Lerone, Jr. *Black Power, USA*. Chicago: Johnson Publishing Co., 1967.
Bentley, George R. *A History of the Freedmen's Bureau*. New York: Octagon Books, 1970.
Berman, Daniel M. *A Bill Becomes A Law—Congress Enacts Civil Rights Legislation*. 2nd ed. New York: Macmillan Co., 1966.
Berger, Monroe. *Equality by Statute*. New York: Columbia University Press, 1952.
Carr, Robert K. *Federal Protection of Civil Rights*. Ithaca, N.Y.: Cornell University Press, 1947.
Committee on Fair Employment Practice. *Final Report*. Washington, D.C.: U.S. Government Printing Office, 1947.
DuBois, W. E. B. *Black Reconstruction*. New York: Harcourt Brace and Co., 1935.

34. Ibid., p. 362.
35. Ibid., p. 364. See also U.S. Commission on Civil Rights, *Federal Civil Rights Enforcement Effort—A Reassessment* (Washington, D.C.: U.S. Government Printing Office, 1973).

Equal Employment Opportunity Commission. *Sixth Annual Report*. Washington, D.C.: U.S. Government Printing Office, 1972.

Franklin, John Hope. *From Slavery to Freedom: A History of American Negroes*. 1st ed. New York: Alfred A. Knopf, 1947.

———. *Reconstruction After the Civil War*. Chicago: University of Chicago Press, 1961.

Greenberg, Jack. *Race Relations and American Law*. New York: Columbia University Press, 1959.

Konvitz, Milton R. *The Constitution and Civil Rights*. New York: Columbia University Press, 1962.

Logan, Rayford W. *The Negro in American Life and Thought: The Nadir, 1877–1901*. New York: Dial Press, 1954.

Mangum, Charles S. *The Legal Status of the Negro*. Chapel Hill: University of North Carolina Press, 1940.

President's Committee on Civil Rights. *Freedom to Serve*. Washington, D.C.: U.S. Government Printing Office, 1950.

———. *To Secure These Rights*. Washington, D.C.: U.S. Government Printing Office, 1947.

Ross, Malcolm. *All Manner of Men*. New York: Reynal and Hitchcock, 1948.

U.S. Commission on Civil Rights. *Federal Civil Rights—Enforcement Effort—A Report*. Washington, D.C.: U.S. Government Printing Office, 1971.

White, Walter. *How Far the Promised Land?* New York: Viking Press, 1955.

Woodward, C. Van. *The Strange Career of Jim Crow*. New York: Oxford University Press, 1955.

Mack H. Jones

**Black Politics:
From Civil Rights
to Benign Neglect**

The late Kwame Nkrumah, the first president of Ghana, is generally given credit for the phrase "Seek ye first the political kingdom and all other things shall be added unto you." Much of the history of black people in the United States suggests that Nkrumah's dictum has undergirded their struggle for equal status. Beginning with the efforts of free blacks during the slavery era and continuing to the present, black people have placed inordinate faith in politics as *the* vehicle for liberation. To be sure, there have been those who assigned primacy to other means such as education, or economics, or religion as the optimum structure through which liberation might be achieved, but politics has invariably been accepted, consensually, as the most auspicious arena for promoting desired social changes. Consequently, much of the black struggle has been directed toward achieving full participation in the U.S. political process, with the implied assumption that such participation would bring about equal status.

The level of black participation, which has never approached anything approximating full participation, has been characterized by peaks and troughs as blacks have achieved new levels of participation only to be followed by greater white resistance and concomitant decline in participation. The contemporary epoch should be understood simply as one segment in this undulating progression. This chapter will focus primarily upon political developments, both electoral and nonelectoral, of the 1960s and early 1970s. Specifically it will deal with the various

---

The author chairs the Department of Political Science, Atlanta University.

black political groupings, their philosophies, tactics, goals, and political gains achieved, and with white resistance to their efforts.

Before dealing with the contemporary epoch, present developments should be placed in proper perspective by briefly citing salient historical developments in the black struggle for political equality and by establishing a frame of reference for analyzing and interpreting black political activity in the United States.

The history of black political activity may be divided into five fairly distinct periods: (1) pre-Civil War, 1619–1865; (2) post-Civil War and Reconstruction, 1865–76; (3) post-Reconstruction and reimposition of white supremacy, 1876–1944; (4) struggle for equal status under the Constitution, 1944–54; and (5) struggle for full socioeconomic and political participation, the contemporary epoch, 1954 to the present.

During the first period, 1619–1865, most blacks were slaves and had no political rights. At one time or another every colony recognized slavery and sharply defined the legal status of slaves and free blacks.[1] The latter, who numbered 59,557 in 1790; 313,466 in 1830; and 475,209 in 1860, although technically free, were only slightly better off than slaves.[2] Consequently, black political activity during this period was concerned mainly with securing legal rights, particularly the franchise, for freedmen, whose conditions were desperate. Some states limited their mobility and required that all freedmen carry passes, while others placed severe proscriptions on occupations in which they might engage.

The position of the federal government was hardly more benevolent than that of the states. According to one prominent historian,

Reflecting the popular concept of the United States as a white man's country, early Congressional legislation excluded Negroes from certain federal rights and privileges and sanctioned a number of territorial and state restrictions. In 1790 Congress limited naturalization to white aliens; in 1792, it organized militia and restricted enrollment to able bodied white male citizens; in 1810, it excluded Negroes from carrying the United States mail. . . . On the basis of such legislation, it would appear that Congress had resolved to treat Negroes neither as citizens nor aliens.[3]

Blacks achieved no major national victories during this period. The most significant development was the Dred Scott decision of 1857, which declared that blacks were not included under the Constitution and,

1. This discussion draws heavily on Leon Litwack, *North of Slavery* (Chicago: University of Chicago Press, 1961) chapters 1–3.
2. Figures computed from table 1 in Hanes Walto, *Black Politics, A Theoretical* and *Structural Analysis* (New York: J. B. Lippincott Co., 1972), p. 57. Walton's data are taken from Bureau of the Census figures on Negro population, 1790–1915.
3. Litwack, p. 31.

consequently, could not lay claim to any of the rights and privileges provided U.S. citizens.

The most striking political gains ever for black Americans occurred during the second period, 1865–77. The Thirteenth Amendment (1865) outlawed slavery, while the Fourteenth, passed three years later, repealed Dred Scott by bestowing citizenship upon blacks and guaranteeing to them equal protection of the laws. The Fifteenth Amendment (1870) expressly guaranteed the right to vote.

In addition to the three Constitutional amendments, Congress passed several statutes designed to protect the rights of blacks. The act of 1866 was and still remains the most far-reaching civil rights law ever passed by Congress. It was meant to insure for blacks the same rights "as [are] enjoyed by white citizens."[4] The so-called "force" acts of 1870 and 1871 sought to protect black access to the franchise by making it a crime for individuals or groups either privately or under the color of law to interfere with the right to vote. Significantly, the first act covered not only direct and immediate interference, but indirect economic pressure as well. The act made it a crime to interfere with voting by "means of bribery, threats, or threats of depriving such persons enfranchised by the 15th Amendment of employment or occupation, or of ejecting such persons from rented house, lands, or other property, or by threats of refusing to renew leases or contracts for labor, or by threats of violence to himself or family."[5] The second act sought to eliminate organized terrorist interference by groups such as the Ku Klux Klan by declaring that such interference "shall be deemed a rebellion against the government of the United States."[6] The final civil rights statute of this period, the act of 1875, guaranteed blacks access to public accommodations and the right to serve on petit and grand juries.

Collectively, the Civil War amendments and the several civil rights acts represented unprecedented political gains. By 1875 blacks had been legally or constitutionally accorded all rights and privileges enjoyed by white persons and the federal government was specifically empowered to protect the exercise of them.

The third period, although characterized by intense black protest, was one of reversals rather than victories. Many of the rights won during the preceding period were nullified through nonenforcement, while others were specifically reversed. Between 1876 and 1883 the Supreme

---

4. This language appears in the enactment clause of the act of 1866. See Richard Bardolph, *The Civil Rights Record, Black Americans and the Law, 1849–1970* (New York: Thomas Y. Crowell, 1970), p. 51.

5. Sections of the act quoted in Bardolph, p. 51.

6. Section 4, act of 1871, quoted in Bardolph, p. 53.

Court virtually eliminated all federal protection by ruling that the national government had no power to prevent discrimination and interference by private individuals and groups. According to Blaustein and Zangrando, "the Civil Rights Cases of 1883 confirmed the fact that the National government was officially abandoning the Negro to the caprice of state control. The next thirty years indicated the extent to which the Negro, though nominally freed from slavery, could be repressed and reduced to the status of second-class citizenship by the force of law and the force of custom sustained by state control."[7]

Blacks did not win a significant national victory during this period until 1944 when the Supreme Court, in *Smith* v. *Allwright,* outlawed the white primary.[8] Between 1944 and 1954 blacks won several significan victories in the Supreme Court including the seminal *Brown* decision outlawing state-sanctioned segregation as a denial of equal protection of the laws. It was the logic of the Brown decision which paved the way for the elimination of all forms of discrimination and segregation and laid the foundation for the contemporary struggle for full socio-economic and political participation.

With this brief historical sketch behind us, it remains for us to establish a frame of reference through which we may analyze black political activity. Such activity, like all other forms of social activity, can be understood only in terms of some conceptual scheme or frame of reference. Traditionally, the melting pot theory of American pluralism has been used most often as a conceptual scheme for interpreting the socio-political life of black people in the United States.[9] This approach assumes that U.S. society can be explained in terms of successive waves of ethnic groups who move in linear progression from politically impotent subjects to full citizen-participants over time. Under this frame of reference, the political history of other ethnics—Irish, Jews, Poles, Italians—is used as a referent or benchmark for interpreting black political life.[10]

The essential assumption of the ethnic pluralist model is that society moves predeterminedly toward a state of equilibrium characterized by countervailing forces which insure that no one group gets too much and that every group gets substantially something. The pluralist frame

7. Albert Blaustein and Robert Zangrando, eds., *Civil Rights and the American Negro* (New York: Washington Square Press, 1968), p. 283.

8. Smith v. Allwright, 321 U.S. 649 (1944).

9. For example of works based upon this approach see James Q. Wilson, *Negro Politics* (New York: Free Press, 1960); and Nathan Glazer and Daniel Moynihan, *Beyond the Melting Pot* (Cambridge, Mass.: MIT Press, 1967).

10. See Matthew Holden, "Black Politicians in the Time of the 'New' Urban Politics," *Review of Black Political Economy II* 56–72 (Fall 1971).

of reference assumes further that it is only a matter of time before blacks become an equal partner in a new equilibrium.

During the 1960s the pluralist frame of reference came under attack for being inappropriate for understanding the black political experience.[11] In an earlier work I argued that a frame of reference for black politics should not begin with superficial comparisons of blacks and other ethnic minorities in this country or elsewhere, because such an approach inevitably degenerates into normative reformist speculation around the question of what can be done to elevate blacks to the position (real or imagined) occupied by the group with which they are being compared. This, in turn, leads to the establishment of a linear model of ethnic or out-group politics which forces the black political experience to fit a contrived model that obscures, rather than clarifies, the crucial variables in the black political experience. In developing a frame of reference for black politics, one should rather begin by searching for those factors which are inherent in the black political experience, for these are the things which will facilitate our understanding of the role and position of blacks in the U.S. political system.[12]

Consistent with Blalock,[13] I went on to argue in the earlier work that the key to understanding black politics in America is the realization that those in superordinate positions invariably act in such a manner as to preserve their position of dominance and that, therefore, whites in the United States act toward blacks in such a manner as to maintain white hegemony. Thus, rather than conceptualizing black politics as a process through which black people, propelled by some unseen hand, move inexorably to a position of equal status, it is more appropriate to conceptualize it as a power struggle between two groups, one bent on maintaining its position of dominance and the other struggling for liberation. These groups may be thought of respectively as the dominant and submissive group.

Historically, dominant groups have used several basic political strategies to maintain their position of dominance. These include: (1) assimilation; (2) legal protection of minority rights; (3) pluralism; (4) population transfer; (5) continued subjugation; and (6) extermination. On the other hand, submissive or oppressed groups have attempted to use

11. For an incisive analysis of the inappropriateness of the ethnic pluralist model for understanding black political life, see Chandler Davidson, *BiRacial Politics* (Baton Rouge: Louisian State University Press, 1972), especially chapters 1–4.
12. For further elaboration see Mack H. Jones, "A Frame of Reference of Black Politics," in *Black Political Life in the U.S.: A Fist as the Pendulum,* Lenneal Henderson, Jr., ed. (San Francisco: Chandler, 1972), pp. 7–20.
13. Hubert Blalock, *Toward a Theory of Minority Group Relations* (New York: John Wiley & Sons, 1967), p. 191.

the first four strategies along with a fifth—reversal of status through revolutionary activity—to alleviate their oppressed condition. At any point in time there will be identifiable forces within the dominant community advocating the use of any one or any combination of the six strategies as the optimum method for maintaining control while, conversely, within the submissive community there will always be groups advocating the use of any one or any combination of the four counter strategies as the optimum means for alleviating their oppressed condition.

Generally speaking, factions within the respective communities seek, first of all, to solicit intracommunity support for their position and then to influence elements in formal political structures such that a faction's position becomes national, state, or local policy. For example, the National Association for the Advancement of Colored People (NAACP) seeks, first of all, to convince the black community that integrationism is the proper strategy for political advancement and then to have its position adopted as national policy.

Thus, black politics have four distinct dimensions: (1) a struggle within the white community regarding the optimum means for maintaining white control with minimum systematic stress and strain; (2) a struggle within the black community over the optimum strategy for liberation; (3) conflict and collaboration between and among black and white factions; and (4) struggle within formal governmental structures over authoritative policy decision. These four struggles occur simultaneously and interdependently. Black politics is their sum. It must be noted here, however, that these struggles cannot be neatly separated from all the other power struggles going on simultaneously in society, and that therefore developments within the realm of black politics are often influenced, disproportionately, by other conflicts. To emphasize the point being suggested, black politics of the Reconstruction era was influenced considerably by the economic conflict between competing northern and southern elites and, similarly, the pivotal *Brown* v. *Board* decision of 1954 was not uninfluenced by the "Cold War" situation existing at the time between the United States and the Soviet Union.[14] Moreover, the politics of rewards and status within the black community may take precedence, from time to time, over black-white issues. For example, one civil rights organization may take a particular posi-

14. Editorial reactions to the Brown decision demonstrate this point graphically. The *Pittsburg Courier,* one of the country's best known black weeklies, said "This clarion announcement will also stun and silence America's communist traducers behind the Iron Curtain." The NAACP heralded that decision as a "victory of America's leadership in the free world"—*Crisis* 61:358–59 (1954).

tion more because of the impact which that position may have on its relative position vis-a-vis a competing group than its probable impact on the black-white situation.

Part two of this paper will utilize the foregoing conceptual framework in discussing black political activity during the 1960s and 1970s.

CONTEMPORARY BLACK POLITICS

Historically, as Harold Cruse and others have pointed out, blacks in the United States have vacillated between integrationism and nationalism as the optimum political strategy for achieving equality, with the former being dominant for the most part. At the same time, until the post-World War II period, the white community followed a policy of continued subjugation of blacks moderated by legal protection. Although blacks first came to America as indentured servants, they were soon reduced to the status of slaves, and even though there were "free blacks" the official white policy was one of domination through continued subjugation. The Dred Scott decision alluded to earlier put the matter this way:

> The question before us is, whether the class of persons described in the plea in abatement compose a portion of this people, and constituent member of this sovereignty? We think they are not, and that they are not included, and were not intended to be included under the word "citizens" in the Constitution and can therefore claim none of its rights and privileges which that instrument provides for and secures to citizens of the United States.[15]

The opinion of the court went on to say that for more than a century before the Declaration of Independence opinion which prevailed in the "civilized and enlightened" portions of the world regarded blacks as being of an "inferior order altogether unfit to associate with the white race and "had no rights which the white man was bound to respect."[16] The Scott decision argued further that continued subjugation as national policy was necessary to protect not only white society but also black people from themselves.

Continued subjugation remained the dominant policy among white Americans throughout the pre-Civil War years, but not exclusively so. Strands of legal protection and population transfer were clearly evident. Support for policies other than one of continued subjugation was essentially a northern phenomenon supported primarily by church-based societies. However, it was not solely a sectional issue, inasmuch as the

15. Dred Scott v. Sanford, 19 Hon. 393 (1857).
16. Ibid.

advocates of continued subjugation had considerable support in both the North and South. The abolitionist movement, comprised primarily of northern whites and free blacks, led the way in lobbying for the end of slavery and for the protection of free blacks in nonslave territory. John Hope Franklin has documented the negative response accorded the abolitionist by northern elements, including the federal government.[17]

Population transfer as a strategy for dealing with the black political presence received support from diverse quarters, including prominent whites such as Thomas Jefferson and President James Monroe, as well as southern plantation owners and northern emancipation societies.[18] These forces, led by the American Colonization Society, advocated emigration of free blacks to Africa. Most blacks opposed such schemes because they felt that emigration of free blacks would reinforce slavery; however, some blacks endorsed population transfer as the appropriate strategy.[19]

The victory of the North in the Civil War ushered in an era in which the strands of legal protection and continued subjugation through terror became the primary currents for maintaining white dominance, while legal protection and assimilation (integration) became the primary tactic of blacks struggling for liberation.[20] Legal protectionists prevailed during the 1860s and 1870s and succeeded in having a number of statutes adopted which guaranteed basic political and social rights to the black populace. As discussed earlier, the Civil War amendments established legal protection against involuntary servitude, bestowed citizenship upon blacks, affirmed the right to vote, and guaranteed due process and equal protection of the laws. The U.S. Congress reinforced these amendments by statutes which guaranteed access to public accommodations and freedom from terror and intimidation in the exercise of these rights.[21]

17. John Hope Franklin, *From Slavery to Freedom* (New York: Alfred Knopf, 1948), chapters 14–15.
18. President Monroe was instrumental in promoting the migration of free blacks to settle in what was to become Liberia. Its capital, Monrovia, still bears his name.
19. Scores of prominent blacks advocated population transfer at one time or another. Some favored migrating within the U.S. to establish black dominated areas while others argued for migration to Africa. See August Meier, *Negro Thought in America 1880–1915* (Ann Arbor: University of Michigan Press, 1966), chapter 4.
20. Due to the taboo on mixed marriages no major white faction can be said to have advocated complete assimilation as a solution to the race problem; integrationism may be a more descriptive term.
21. The Civil Rights Act of 1866 conferred upon blacks complete civil rights and empowered federal officials to project freedmen from infringements by any and all persons. The act of 1870 affirmed the right to vote and provides means for enforcement, while the act of 1875 provided for access to public accommodations without regard to race.

After the Compromise of 1877, in which the forces of legal protection tacitly capitulated to those subscribing to continued subjugation through terror bordering on extermination, protection of black rights waned. During the early decades of the twentieth century, lynching and burning at the stake was commonplace not only in the South but as far north as Indiana, Illinois, and even Wyoming, Maryland, Oklahoma, Missouri, Kansas, Ohio, and West Virginia.[22] Burnings and hangings were public spectacles attended by whites, including women and children, and covered by newspapers in a manner not unlike contemporary coverage of sporting events.[23]

By 1901, black participation in U.S. political life which had been made possible by the ascendance of legal protectionists following the Civil War had virtually disappeared and not until the early 1930s did legal protectionists begin to rise once more and politics become a significant vehicle in the struggle for black advancement. Migration of blacks from the South to the urban centers of the North made blacks a political force of consequence. In 1929 black voters in Chicago were able to send Oscar DePriest to Congress, and elsewhere black voters were instrumental in helping to defeat several senators whose posture toward blacks was something less than benevolent. As a result of growing black electoral strength, the northern wing of the Democratic party, under the leadership of Franklin D. Roosevelt, began to court black voters by advocating legal protection of black rights. Bills were introduced in Congress, albeit unsuccessfully, to outlaw lynching and other flagrant abuses. While such measures were not pushed through by Roosevelt, he reinforced the renaissance of black political activity by involving black advisors on a systematiç basis in various New Deal programs and by generally recognizing and respecting black political leaders.

The pace of black political regeneration which began in the 1930s under auspices of legal protectionists quickened during the next decade. In 1944 in *Smith* v. *Allwright* the U.S. Supreme Court declared white primaries unconstitutional and thereby gave blacks in the South legal access to the franchise for the first time since Reconstruction. Prior to the Smith decision, political parties could determine eligibility criteria for participating in party primary elections. Since victory in party primary elections was tantamount in victory in the general election, by prohibiting black participation in party primaries, southern whites effectively precluded black political participation. Ten years later the

22. See Ralph Ginzburg, *100 Years of Lynching* (New York: Lancer, 1962), pp. 253–70.
23. Ibid, p. 46. The author reproduces a news clipping which describes the chagrin of newspaper reporters when those who had scheduled a lynching granted a reprieve to the victim in order to allow him to have a farewell interview with his family.

Court in *Brown* v. *Board* overturned the separate but equal doctrine enunciated during the years of retreat following the Compromise of 1877.

The Brown decision marked the beginning of the first phase of the contemporary epoch. For the purpose of analysis, the contemporary epoch may be divided into two phases; the first was the civil rights era, characterized by dominance of integrationism in both white and black communities as the optimum strategy for liberation, and the attendant protest movement for black inclusion in all phases of U.S. life. This period extended from 1954 until approximately 1965. The next phase, commonly referred to as the "Black Power" period,[24] began in 1966 when Willie Ricks, an ally of Stokely Carmichael, is said to have shouted those words on the Meredith march through Mississippi.[25] This phase, which extended through the 1960s, has been characterized by the rise of those advocating pluralism, nationalism, and revolution as a means for dealing with black oppression and by a concomitant diminution in the strength of the integrationist strand (although polls continue to show that integrationism remains the dominant theme among the black public[26]). The distinguishing factor of the contemporary epoch is that increasing numbers of blacks, particularly intellectuals, no longer believe that integrationism is tantamount to progress and hence to liberation. Criteria for progress are more directly related to the power to make binding decisions in one's own interest.

During the first phase of the current epoch, the struggle was borne mainly by national organizations such as NAACP, Congress on Racial Equality (CORE), Student Non-Violent Coordinating Committee (SNCC), the National Urban League, Southern Christian Leadership Conference (SCLC), and by countless local groupings either affiliated with, or patterned after, one of these national bodies. None of these groups had a clearly stated ideology. Essentially, they were content to work within the confines of a loose set of assumptions best described as the "civil rights perspective." The key assumption in this perspective, though never clearly stated as such, is the notion that integrationism is the only programmatically sound option open to blacks in the United States and that nationalist or separatist notions are inherently escapist.

24. To the extent that the term "Black Power" is taken literally its use is misleading since blacks did not exercise any more power during this period than previously. However, the tempo and tone of black political activity did change around 1965 when greater emphasis was placed on the need for blacks to wrest political power from white authorities.

25. James Foreman, *Sammy Younge, Jr.* (New York: Grove, 1968), p. 11.

26. For the most thorough analysis of black opinions, see William Brink and Louis Harris, *Black and White* (New York: Simon and Schuster, 1966).

Deference to this assumption precluded the raising of other fundamental political questions and led to unquestioning acceptance of the assumption that the problems facing blacks in America could be alleviated simply by the passage of statutes proscribing discrimination. The essential tenet of civil rights groups during this period was that blacks should pursue practical or responsible alternatives. For the most part, this meant that blacks sought progress through alliances with certain white factions which, according to their rhetoric, were also committed, more or less, to black progress through integration. Unfortunately for black groups, white allies almost always had disproportionate command over resources and political influence and therefore exercised undue influence over the initiatives of their black allies.

During the 1960s these groups, along with allied white factions, were successful in getting a number of statutes passed and court decisions rendered which recommitted the country to legal protection of civil and political rights of black citizens and equal access, at least legally so, to jobs, education, and housing. However, as the 1960s came to a close and as the nation moved into the fateful 1970s, these statutes and court decisions, seemingly far-sweeping, were clearly seen as falling far short of bringing about equal protection of the laws.[27] This assertion becomes clear when we look at their substance, patterns of enforcement, and their impact upon the socioeconomic and political conditions under which black people live.

The important civil rights statutes of the present epoch include the acts of 1957, 1960, 1964, 1965, and 1968. The act of 1957 sought to remove arbitrary interference to voting in primaries and general elections for federal offices by empowering the U.S. attorney general to obtain court orders to halt threatened interference in the exercise of the franchise. The act of 1957 also created the U.S. Commission on Civil Rights and gave it general investigatory and reporting responsibilities. But Congress deliberately declined to give the commission authority to initiate action to end discrimination. Nor did the act provide for executive enforcement but rather relied upon cumbersome judicial relief. Consequently, the major impediments to black voting remained. Indeed, in many areas white opposition intensified. Blatant acts of terror and intimidation occurred in the South to such an extent that Congress passed a second civil rights act in 1960 which made it a crime to obstruct federal court orders, to transport explosives in interstate com-

---

27. This point was stressed with vigor by the United States Commission on Civil Rights. See *Federal Rights Enforcement Effort* (Washington, D.C.: U.S. Government Printing Office, 1971), pp. xv-xvii.

merce for purposes of damaging buildings, and to flee to avoid prosecution for burning and bombing. The act of 1960 also attempted to protect further the right to vote by requiring local officials to keep records of federal elections and by providing that federal courts, when they found patterns of discrimination, might appoint federal referees who could issue voting certificates to persons who had been discriminated against by local authorities.

The acts of 1957 and 1960 were limited in terms of both their scope and their enforcement procedures, and consequently blacks continued to receive unequal treatment by both governments and private individuals and groups. In the face of white intransigence black-oriented groups, particularly SNCC, CORE, NAACP, and SCLC, utilized direct action protest to create societal tensions and pressure the federal government into taking a more forthright position against racial discrimination. The direct strategy involved civil rights groups singling out governments or private groups practicing racial discrimination and mounting protest campaigns against them. The protests were designed and conducted in a fashion which prevented the target government or business from carrying on its day-to-day functions and this, in turn, created a crisis-laden situation which threatened the social peace of the larger community. Thus, failure to make concessions consistent with demands of black protest groups threatened social consequences more detrimental to important vested interests than consequences which would flow from conceding to black demands. As custodian of national social peace, the federal government, particularly the executive branch, was compelled to take the initiative to defuse the situation and, inasmuch as the Democratic party which controlled the White House from 1960 to 1968 depended heavily upon black votes, its own self-interest dictated that some deference be given to black demands. Such direct action protests led directly to the two most important civil rights statutes to date: the acts of 1964 and 1965.

The act of 1964 was the most comprehensive statute since Reconstruction; it covered not only voting rights, but the right to education, jobs, and public accommodations as well. The first section sought to deal with the continuing troublesome question of voting by forbidding local registrars to deny the franchise because of minor errors in application forms, by requiring that all literacy tests used to establish eligibility for voting be administered in writing, and by making a sixth-grade education a presumption of literacy.

Perhaps the most significant features of the act of 1964 were those dealing with economic protections, since these were the first such protections guaranteed by federal statutes since the Reconstruction period. The act barred discrimination in federal programs or activity and outlawed federal assistance in any activity or project where there was evidence of discrimination. The act also sought to give blacks full access to the job market by bringing all major employers, hiring halls, and labor unions under fair employment regulations. Racial discrimination by firms employing twenty-five workers or more was expressly forbidden. This provision, along with the prohibition against any federal involvement in, or assistance to, any program or activity tainted by discrimination, brought most of the job market under fair employment discrimina- The pervasive coverage of the act of 1964, however, was weakened by the fact that enforcement procedures leaned heavily on voluntary compliance and injunctive relief.

The Voting Rights Act of 1965 sought to guarantee the franchise to blacks in the South once and for all by summarily suspending for five years literacy and good character tests as prerequisites for voter registration in those states and counties where patterns of discrimination existed. Specifically, the act covered states and counties which used such devices and in which less than 50 percent of the voting-age residents were registered or less than 50 percent voted in the 1964 presidential election. This formula brought seven states under the act—Alabama, Georgia, Louisiana, Mississippi, South Carolina, Virginia, and Alaska. Forty counties in North Carolina, three in Arizona, and one each in Hawaii and Idaho were also covered.[28] Additionally, the U.S. attorney general was authorized to send federal examiners to recalcitrant counties to list persons qualified to vote and to assign federal observers to monitor elections in designated counties. Section 5 of the act sought to prohibit governments, both state and local, from manipulating electoral laws to disfranchise blacks by requiring that all proposed changes in such laws and regulations be submitted to the U.S. attorney general for review. The attorney general was given power to veto changes which, in his view, were designed to discriminate against black voters.

The act of 1968 attempted to eliminate racial discrimination in housing by forbidding such discrimination in the sale of housing except transactions involving single-family dwellings and in which no real estate brokers were involved. This act covered approximately 80 percent of all housing.[29] During the same year, the U.S. Supreme Court upheld a more pervasive open occupancy position in the case of *Jones*

28. U.S. Commission on Civil Rights, *Political Participation* (Washington, D.C.: U.S. Government Printing Office, 1968), p.11.
29. *Federal Rights Enforcement Effort*, p. 141.

v. *Mayer* when it upheld an 1866 statute which "bars all discrimination, private as well as public, in the sale or rental of property."[30]

Thus, collectively, the several civil rights statutes and court decisions of the 1960s eliminated de jure discrimination in voting, employment, and in access to housing and public accommodations. These proscriptions against discrimination were buttressed by the passage of several pieces of social welfare legislation designed to temper the socioeconomic conditions of the poor. These programs, which became known as the "War on Poverty," were important to blacks because they provided needed social services for the poor and middle-income jobs for black professionals.

The Economic Opportunity Act of 1964, the flagship act of the War on Poverty,[31] established the Office of Economic Opportunity (OEO) and gave it responsibility for planning and coordinating antipoverty programs. This act also established a multifaceted approach to alleviating poverty through a series of experimental and conventional programs. Job training aimed at improving the employability of the poor was provided, with separate training programs for youths and adults. Neighborhood health centers were established to provide medical and dental care for thousands who could not afford private care. OEO also provided legal assistance to the poor. Special programs, including loans, were established for dealing with rural poverty and with migrant and seasonal laborers, and educational programs for both preschool age children and for college-bound high school youth were also established.

The basic philosophical assumption underlying OEO programs was the belief that the most effective way to eliminate poverty was through active participation of the poor in planning and administering the programs. Accordingly, Community Action Agencies were established to insure such participation. On its face this represented a fundamental change in the country's philosophy regarding the poor. Although the War on Poverty never came close to vanquishing its stated adversary—indeed it was never given resources nor power commensurate to the task—its provisions complemented the several civil rights statutes of the 1960s and, taken together, they provided potential structures within which some of the political and socioeconomic conditions of black citizens could be addressed. However, de facto qualitative changes in the lives and life chances of blacks in the United States during the 1960s

30. Ibid, p. 142.
31. The following discussion draws heavily on Sar A. Levitan, *The Great Society's Poor Law: A New Approach to Poverty* (Baltimore: Johns Hopkins Press, 1966), especially chapter 1.

were in no way commensurate with the promise of these statutes, court decisions, and executive orders.

Black families and individuals continue to be much worse off than their white counterparts on all accepted indicators of socioeconomic well being. In employment in 1974, as table 1 indicates, average unemployment for black workers was 9.9 percent compared to 5.0 for whites. Black unemployment was constantly high throughout the period, usually about twice as high as that of whites.

Even these figures probably create a more optimistic picture than is warranted, because unemployment rates are considerably higher among black teen-agers and residents of low-income areas in central cities than the rates shown in table 1. Among black teen-agers, persons 16 to 19 years old, 32.9 were unemployed in 1974 as compared to 14.0 among whites. In a special study of low-income neighborhoods in 60 urban areas, the Census Bureau reported in 1970 that 284,000, or 11.1 percent, of the black labor force was unemployed, with another 932,100, or 26 percent, out of jobs but not counted as unemployed because, while they desired to work, they were not actively seeking it. Whatever the reasons, 37 percent of blacks in the selected low-income areas had no jobs.[32]

Black family income continued to lag, with a median figure of $6,400, or 60 percent of that of white families ($10,670), in 1971. Twenty-nine percent of black families were below federally defined poverty level, as compared to 8 percent of all white families. Black workers continued to be overrepresented in lower-paying menial jobs and underrepresented in those paying higher wages. While blacks constituted 10 percent of the employed population in 1971, only 5 percent of professional workers, 3 percent of managers and administrators, and 6 percent of craftsmen were black.[33] Conversely, 17 percent of service workers, 20 percent of laborers, and 50 percent of private household workers were black.[34]

The above figures demonstrate clearly that the objectives of the several civil rights statutes, executive orders, and court decisions designed to insure blacks equal access to the economy have not been realized. To be sure, to expect parity overnight would be unreasonable, but no upward trend is yet discernible. Some might argue that inferior educational preparation explains the persistent gap between black and white income and employment figures now that de jure job discrimination has been eliminated. However, a more convincing explanation is to be

32. Figures in the preceding paragraphs were taken from U.S. Department of Commerce, *The Social and Economic Status of the Black Population in the United States, 1971* (Washington, D.C.: U.S. Government Printing Office, 1972), pp. 1–7.
33. Ibid., p. 3.
34. Ibid.

Table 1.
Unemployment Rates:
1968 to 1974
(Annual Averages)

Year	Black and other races	White	Ratio: Black and other races to white
1960	10.2	4.9	2.1
1961	12.4	6.0	2.1
1962	10.9	4.9	2.2
1963	10.8	5.0	2.2
1964	9.6	4.6	2.1
1965	8.1	4.1	2.0
1966	7.3	3.3	2.2
1967	7.4	3.4	2.2
1968	6.7	3.2	2.1
1969	6.4	3.1	2.1
1970	8.2	4.5	1.8
1971	9.9	5.4	1.8
1972	10.0	5.0	2.0
1973	8.9	4.3	2.1
1974	9.9	5.0	2.0

Source: Adapted from U.S. Bureau of the Census, Current Population Reports, Series P-23, *The Social and Economic Status of the Black
Population in the United States,* for 1971, 1972, and 1974.

found in the thesis advanced by economist Don Harris, who argues that
the U.S. economy operates in a fashion prescribing high unemployment
and underemployment with racism providing a convenient tool for
rationing these debilities, disproportionate amounts being visited upon
black workers. The logic of this proposition becomes inescapable when
one realizes that it is not the presence of unskilled workers which
creates menial, low-paying jobs or the reserve army from which such
job holders come, but rather that both menial jobs and the reserve
army are systemic conditions which the economy produces and reproduces.

The civil rights laws dealing with political rights, as discussed above,
were addressed primarily to nondemocratic processes in the states of the
old Confederacy. During the 1960s, they led to significant increases in
black political participation as measured by voting and holding elected
office, but not to significant increases in real black political power. The
number of elected officials in the southern states rose from 72 in 1965 to
873 in 1973 and to 1,944 in 1976 (see table 2). For the nation as a whole,
3,069 blacks held office in 1975.[35] These figures are impressive, but

35. U.S. Department of Commerce, *The Social and Economic Status of the Black
Population in the United States, 1974* (Washington, D.C.: U.S. Government Printing
Office, 1975), p. 151.

Table 2.   Black Elected Officeholders in the South, January, 1976

State	Total	Congressmen (U.S.)	Senators (State)	Representatives (State)	Commissioners, Supervisors & Councilmen (County)	Election Commissioners (County)	Others (County)	Mayors (City)	Vice Mayors (City)	Councilmen, Aldermen & Commissioners (City)	Others (City)	Judges (Law Enf.)	Magistrates (Law Enf.)	Constables (Law Enf.)	Marshals, Sheriffs & Chiefs of Police (Law Enf.)	Justices of the Peace (Law Enf.)	Others (Law Enf.)	Superintendents (Educ.)	State (Educ.)	School Bd. County	School Bd. City	School Bd. District	Other School Officials
ALABAMA	193		2	13	12		12	10	2	63	3	1		48	4					21	2		
ARKANSAS	212		1	3	30		1	9	2	78	14				1						9	62	2
FLORIDA	79			3	3			6	3	51	1	7				6				4	1		
GEORGIA	221	1	2	20	12		2	3	4	110	1	4				6	1	1		34	21		1
LOUISIANA	278		1	9	65	13	10	10	3	74	17	4		13	7	13	1			71	4		
MISSISSIPPI	237			4	16			7	4	63		1		28	1	19	1	4	3	26	1	21	1
NORTH CAROLINA	210		2	4	16		1	8		131		2								33	14		
SOUTH CAROLINA	153			13	24			7		60			16							19	1	12	
TENNESSEE	118	1	2	9	48					29		4	7	5						9	11		
TEXAS	155	1		9	1			5	5	62		2		2	2	2						60	
VIRGINIA	88		1	1	25		3	3	5	41			7		1		1		1				
Total Offices[1]	1,944	3	11	88	252	13	29	68	28	762	37	25	23	96	16	40	4	5	4	217	64	155	4

Source: Voter Education Project (VEP), 52 Fairlie St., N.W., Atlanta, Georgia 30303

[1]Five officials hold dual offices. In Georgia, a mayor is a city council member. In Mississippi, a county election commissioner also serves as an alderman. In Louisiana, an alderman also serves as a justice of the peace. Twenty-four of the black elected officials now holding office were appointed to fill the unexpired terms of vacated seats.

begin to pale when the level of black office holding is compared to black population strength. Blacks constitute only 0.5 percent of the nation's 522,000 elected officials, as opposed to 11 percent of the population (see table 3). In no state are blacks represented in proportion to their numbers, nor is black officeholding significant in any particular category. Further, in those areas where blacks constitute sizeable portions of the electorate (see table 4), they have not been able to convert their numbers into political power.

My 1975 study showed that even though blacks constituted 40 percent or more of the population in 205 of 1105 southern counties, a majority of the population in 102 counties, and a majority of registered voters in at least 21, black citizens served on the governing boards of only 80 counties. In 45 of the 80 there was only one black on the governing body. At present blacks control major governing bodies in only a few counties including Macon and Greene in Alabama; Hancock in Georgia, Jefferson in Mississippi, and Charles City in Virginia.[36]

In those counties where black control is numerically possible, whites have made determined efforts, both legal and extralegal, to diminish black participation. The 1970 study demonstrated that in such counties every effort is made to maintain a preponderance of white registrants:

> This becomes abundantly clear when voter registration figures are examined on a county by county basis. Generally speaking, white registration tends to vary in direct proportion to black voting strength. . . . In 52 Georgia counties whose population is 40 percent or more black, white registration is more than 100 percent in 40 of them; in Louisiana 7 of 22 similarly situated parishes have more than 100 percent white registration and another 11 parishes show white registration between 90 and 100 percent. Twenty-three of Mississippi's 43 counties which are 40 percent or more black have more than 100 percent white registration. . . . Even in Florida the pattern remains unaltered. White registration is 100 percent or more in three of the four counties 40 percent or more black.[37]

In addition to maintaining a preponderance of white registrants, other techniques used to maintain white control include, among others, switching to at-large elections, abolishing elective positions, extending terms of incumbent white officials, outright harassment, and intimidation.[38]

36. Mack H. Jones, "Black Officeholding and Political Development in the Rural South," Report to the Task Force on Southern Rural Development, Atlanta, Georgia, 1975.
37. Federal Courts ruled that census data are not accurate enough to say that 100 percent plus registration necessarily represents fraud. See *Gray* v. *Main*, Civil no. 2430–N.M.D. Ala. 29 March, 1968, and discussion in *Political Participation*.
38. *Political Participation*, especially part 3, pp. 19–114.

Table 3.
Elected Officials
of State and Local
Governments
by Race, 1975

Level of Government	Total Elected Officials	Total Black Elected Officials	Percent Black
Total U.S.[1]	521,758	3,485	0.67
State	13,038	281	0.4
Local	508,720	3,204	0.63
County	74,199	305	0.41
Municipal (city)	143,927	1,573	1.09
School district	107,663	939	0.87
Other local government[2]	182,931	307	0.17

1 These figures do not include the 535 members of the U.S. Congress: the 435 Representatives and 100 Senators. At present there are 18 black Representatives and 1 black U.S. Senator.
2This includes elected officials in townships and special districts. The 1975 figures were taken from the *Roster of Black Elected Officials*, 1975, Joint Center for Political Studies, Washington, D.C. Figures on total number of elected officials in state and local governments were taken from *Abridging the Right to Vote*, National Urban League, New York, 1972.

Detailed information regarding black political participation outside the South is unavailable. However, a recent analysis by the Citizenship Education Department of the National Urban League suggests that the situation is quite similar:

> Outright refusal to register blacks and the use of fear are not the style of the North. Discrimination, intentional or not, takes a more subtle turn. The result, however, is much the same. Blacks are denied the right of full participation in the political system.[39]

Even though the actual number of black officeholders is small, the question of their impact on policy outcomes still must be discussed. Possible impact can be divided into two abstractions: (1) reordering the priorities of various governing bodies on which they serve and persuading them to seek novel solutions to outstanding problems which are particularly salient in black communities, and (2) garnering for the black community a more equitable distribution of existing services and benefits provided by government within present priorities. My earlier study on black officeholders revealed that their success in reordering priorities has been negligible at best. Most of the initiatives of black officeholders have been designed to increase the black community's share of existing services and benefits. And while noticeable changes were effected in the quality of public services—streets, lights, drainage,

39. National Urban League, Citizenship Education Department, *Abridging the Right to Vote* (New York, 1972), p. 9.

Table 4. Black Officeholders in the South. Selected Statistics on Black
Population Registration and Representation in Southern Counties, Summer 1970

Number of Counties

State	40 to 49% black	50% black	with voting age black majority	with majority black registrants	with blacks on governing bds.	governing bds. with black majority
ALABAMA	8	12	10	4	2	2
FLORIDA	2	2	2	0	2[1]	0
GEORGIA	20	32	19	4	3	1
LOUISIANA	13	9	5	2	7	0
MISSISSIPPI	15	28	21	9	4	0
NORTH CAROLINA	19	8	4	0	1	0
SOUTH CAROLINA	8	15	9	0	2	0
TENNESSEE	0	2	2	. .[2]	5	0
TEXAS	2	3	0	0	0	0
VIRGINIA	11	15	7	2	2	0
Total	98	126	79	21	28	3

Source: Mack H. Jones, "Black Officeholders in the South," *Politics 71* (March 1971), p. 53.
Figures appearing in columns 2 and 3 were computed from data in *City County Data Book 1967.*
Figures in columns 4 and 5 were supplied by Voter Education Project and those in columns 6 and 7
were computed from information gathered through field research for this study.
[1]Dade County which has a metropolitan commission and the consolidated government of Jackson-
ville-Duval County.
[2]No official figures available.

and so forth—the study concluded that wide disparities between the
quality of services in black and white communities still remained. No
comparable study has been made of the impact of black officeholders in
the non-South, but studies of Gary, Indiana, Cleveland, Ohio, and Newark, New Jersey—cities in which blacks succeeded in electing mayors—
suggest that the impact was much the same.[40]

How may we account for the apparent paradox growing out of the
foregoing analysis—a plethora of statutes and regulations purporting to
insure for blacks equal access to the political and economic system but,
at the same time, in spite of much activity, no significant appreciation
in the conditions under which blacks live? We can begin by turning to
Murray Edelman's thesis on the symbolic uses of politics.[41] Edelman
argues that political analysis must proceed on two levels by examining
how, on the one hand, political acts get some groups tangible things

40. See William E. Nelson, *Black Politics in Gary: Problems and Prospects* (Washington, D.C.: Joint Center for Political Studies, 1972). For information on Cleveland
see Philip Meranto and William E. Nelson, Jr., *Electing Black Mayors: Political Action
in the Black Community* (Columbus: Ohio State University Press, 1977).
41. Murray Edelman, *Symbolic Uses of Politics* (Chicago: University of Illinois
Press, 1970), p. 12 passim.

they want from government while, on the other hand, political acts may be used to placate or arouse mass publics. Implicit in Edelman's theory is the notion that political acts may give symbolic assurance to a given public that its concerns have been dealt with, while the actual administration or implementation of such acts may leave the problem situation more or less unchanged. Passage and implementation of the several civil rights laws and regulations in the 1960s would seem to have been consistent with this notion. For example, the Voting Rights Act of 1965, as previously mentioned, was drafted to apply to states and subdivisions in which less than 50 percent of the eligible black population was registered. The act was enforced with modest vigor during its first two years. Between 1965 and 1967 the national government was responsible for adding 150,767 black registrants and raising the percentage of registered voting age blacks above 50 percent in each of the southern states. However, federal efforts appeared to stop at that point. By the end of 1971 the number of black registrants enrolled by federal examiners had increased only to 159,915.[42] Moreover, of 185 counties covered by the law, federal examiners were sent to only 58 during the first two years. Since that time only 10 counties have been added to the list.[43]

The same story prevails in regard to the enforcement of other civil rights statutes. The U.S. Commission on Civil Rights concluded in 1971 that

> the principal impediment has been the failure of departments and agencies having civil rights responsibilities to make maximum use of the procedures and mechanism available to them. As a result, there is danger that the great effort made by public and private groups to obtain civil rights laws we now have will be nullified through ineffective enforcement. The focus of civil rights must shift from the halls of Congress to the corridors of the Federal bureaucracies that administer these laws.[44]

In sum, due to lack of enforcement, the civil rights statutes of the 1960s served to give symbolic reassurance to those making broad unspecified demands for equal treatment. Tangible policy payoffs which would eliminate structural impediments to equal treatment were negligible. Perhaps the realization of this fact by many blacks was the reason they began to explore other forms of political activity, both within, and external to, formal electoral politics.

42. U.S. Civil Service Commission, *Cumulative Totals on Voting Rights Examining, December, 1971* (Washington, D.C.: U.S. Government Printing Office, 1972).
43. Information supplied in personal letter of 3 January 1973 from Mr. Charles J. Dullea, Director, Voting Rights Task Force, U.S. Civil Service Commission.
44. *Federal Civil Rights Enforcement Efforts*, p. 362.

Within the electoral arena, the most significant departure from conventional black politics was the convening of the Gary National Black Political Convention in the spring of 1972. The convention grew out of a series of meetings of black leaders of national standing who were disenchanted with the role played by blacks within the existing two-party system. Some were especially concerned with the dependency relationship between the Democratic party and black voters and wanted to change that by creating an independent black force. Others, particularly those of nationalist persuasion, were more interested in creating an independent black political force as a precursor to developing a sense of nationhood among blacks in America. Whatever their diverse reasons, approximately 3,500 delegates and several thousand observers assembled and adopted an agenda for action which departed fundamentally from the usual prescriptions of U.S. political culture. The convention also approved the establishment of a permanent National Black Assembly designed to become the primary coordinating body for black political activity in the United States.

The *National Black Agenda* adopted by the convention was based upon the assumption that "the American System does not work for the masses of our black people, and it cannot be made to work without radical fundamental change."[45] The *Agenda* went on to argue that "white liberalism" was incapable of solving black problems; it denounced both the Republican and Democratic parties, arguing that

> both . . . have betrayed us whenever their interest conflicted with ours (which was most of the time) and whenever our forces were unorganized and dependent, quiescent and compliant. Nor should this be surprising, for by now we must know that the American political system, like all other white institutions in America, was designed to operate for the benefit of the white race: It was never meant to do anything else.[46]

Specifically, the *Agenda* called for proportionate (15 percent) black representation in the House, Senate, and federal employment at all levels; a permanent voting rights act with registration based solely on age and residency; local community control over the police, the courts, and prisons; and the calling of a national constitutional convention. On economic matters, the *Agenda* called for, among other things, a national minimum wage of $2.50 per hour for all workers, and a guaranteed minimum annual income of $6,000 for all families of four, free

45. *National Black Political Agenda*, p. 2. For a discussion of the genesis on implications of Gary. See Immamu Baraka, "Toward the Creation of Political Institutions for All African Peoples," *Black World* 21:54–78 (October 1972).
46. Ibid.

public transportation, ceiling price for rents for all families of four or
more earning less than $20,000, and the creation of a "well-funded"
black agency within the U.S. Department of Agriculture to work toward
solving problems of black rural development.

In addition to specific agenda items, the convention, in its waning
hours, adopted two general resolutions which became the subject of
much debate and which caused considerable strain among black political figures. One of the resolutions, Point 12, expressed agreement with
the position of the Organization for African Unity (OAU) on the Arab-
Israeli question. The OAU, which is the principal regional organization
of African heads of state, had condemned Israel for its "expansionist
policy and forceful occupation of sovereign territory of another state."[47]
The other controversial resolution expressed opposition to busing
school children to achieve racial balance in the public schools.

These proposals, both specific agenda items and general resolutions,
clearly represented radical departures from past black political strategy,
and the fact that they were endorsed by an assembly comprising black
elected officials, including U.S. congressmen and mayors of major cities,
representatives from prestigious national civil rights organizations, both
integrationist and nationalist, as well as individuals of diverse ideological positions, made it all the more persuasive. However, the radical
posture taken by the Gary declaration was quickly dissipated when
various factions within the black community began to dissociate themselves from various specifics of the *Agenda*. Integrationist forces led by
the NAACP issued a disclaimer on the basis of the draft preamble
which was released before the convention fully opened. The NAACP's
statement charged that the "preamble is rooted in the concept of separate nationhood for black America. . . . It proclaims a doctrine of black
racial superiority in that it holds that only persons of African descent
are capable of spearheading movements toward desirable change in the
society."[48] Others were quick to repudiate the resolution condemning
Israeli occupation of Arab territory. Indeed, two of the three coconve-
nors of the Convention, Congressman Diggs of Michigan and Richard
Hatcher, mayor of Gary, Indiana, issued statements to that effect, leaving only Imamu Baraka supporting the *Agenda* completely.

The Congressional Black Caucus, which is a consulting body of all
blacks in the U.S. House of Representatives, further blunted the edge
of the Gary declaration when it adopted its own *Black Bill of Rights*
as an agenda for the 1970s and as a bargaining ploy for the 1972 presi-

47. Point 12 of the *Agenda*.
48. Quoted in Edwin Jaffe, "Coming Together in Gary," *Nation* (3 April 1972).

dential election. While the specifics of the caucus' *Bill of Rights* were similar to the Gary *Agenda,* its very promulgation served to undercut the unified thrust envisioned by Gary and to reinstitute the traditional patron-client relationship between black voters and the Democratic party, with black elites serving as brokers. During the presidential election campaign of 1972, the National Black Political Council, the executive arm of the National Black Assembly, had no noticeable impact. After 1972 the promise of Gary continued to degenerate such that by 1976 the National Black Assembly seemed destined for oblivion. The assembly's 1974 and 1976 biennial conventions were only sparsely attended. Internal wrangling led to the deposing of Baraka as president following his announced conversion to Marxism. And the organization reached its nadir in 1976 when both Julian Bond, Georgia state senator, and Ronald Dellums, congressman from California, refused to accept the assembly's nomination for president of the United States for the 1976 presidential election.

Black political activity during the 1960s was not limited to the formal variety. A number of groups predicated upon the assumption that electoral politics could not solve the social, economic, and political problems of blacks came to the fore. Some of these were in the historical tradition of self-help organizations which eschewed politics in favor of education and economic activity; others, perceiving the black condition as a systematic result of international monopoly capitalism, advocated change through revolutionary activity; and, finally, those groups which saw black problems in the United States as being inextricably connected with the fate of African people throughout the world. A plethora of groups subscribing to one or the other of these notions received national attention during the period under discussion but they, too, had little discernible salutary impact on the political status of blacks in the United States. A look at an example of each type may dramatize this point.

Probably the best known of the self-help organizations prominent during the 1960s was the Nation of Islam, known to the uninitiated as the "Black Muslims." The Nation of Islam is a religious sect based upon its version of the Holy Koran. Under the leadership of its founder, the Honorable Elijah Muhammad, its doctrine asserted that whites were devils and advised blacks to remain separate from whites. Members of the sect were instructed to eschew politics and concentrate on self-help economic schemes. Mixing its version of the Koran with generous portions of the Protestant ethic, the Nation of Islam established a chain of small businesses in several major cities and, during the latter years of the decade, the nation purchased two farms in the deep South to supply its retail outlets in urban areas. Precise figures on its economic worth during the reign of Elijah Muhammad were unavailable, but it was agreed that the Nation was a multimillion dollar enterprise.[49]

However, when Wallace Muhammad took over the organization in 1975 following the death of his father, Elijah Muhammad, the new leader reported that the Nation of Islam was not as solvent as many thought it to be, with current debts of almost a million dollars and a long term deficit of approximately $4.6 million.[50]

Wallace Muhammad instituted several far-reaching changes in the organization. These included opening membership to whites, encouraging its followers to become involved in politics, and deciding to sell all the Nation's business holdings except its newspaper and fish import business. The implications of these changes are not yet apparent, but by divesting itself of its businesses the Nation of Islam has certainly diminished its appeal to many blacks.

Although during most of the period covered by this analysis the Nation of Islam was officially nonpolitical, insofar as its members did not participate in formal politics, it was nevertheless an important political force during the 1960s. From its ranks came one of the most charismatic figures of the decade, Malcolm X. As a minister of the nation, Malcolm X had access to impersonal channels of communication and used them to great advantage. He interpreted the complex web of public and private contrivances which combined to maintain the unequal status of blacks in a manner readily understood by laymen.

Largely because of the lucidity of Malcolm's analysis and his consummate skill in articulating it, the Nation of Islam, during the early 1960s, was considered by the U.S. government to be a dangerous or subversive organization. When Malcolm was suspended because of questions internal to the Nation of Islam, he formed the Organization of Afro-American Unity (OAAU) which, while continuing the spiritual mission of the Nation, would also be expressly political. The OAAU was designed to serve as an umbrella under which blacks of diverse ideological persuasion could work toward black unity and liberation.[51] Unfortunately, Malcolm X was felled by assassins' bullets before the

---

49. A good indication of the Nation of Islam's economic success can be gleaned from stories in its weekly paper *Muhammed Speaks.* See also W. Haywood Burns, "The Black Muslims in America: A Reinterpretation," reprinted in *Black Liberation Politics* ed., Edward Greer (Boston: Allyn and Bacon, 1971), pp. 72–85.

50. See accounts in *New York Times,* 26 February and 8 August 1976.

51. See George Breitmen, ed., *Malcolm X, By Any Means Necessary* (New York: Pathfinder, 1970), pp. 133–56.

OAAU became functional. At the time of his death most assumed that Malcolm's death resulted from intragroup strife among members of his sect. However, in his autobiography (in preparation when he was killed), Malcolm X expressed his fears that other unnamed sources, but presumably intelligence agencies, were plotting his death. Subsequent revelations of extensive and intensive harassment of black leaders and organizations by federal agencies during the 1960s gave new credence to Malcolm's speculation.

The Black Panther Party, a self-styled Marxist-Leninist group, also received considerable attention during the decade. The Panthers emphasized self-defense, as opposed to nonviolence, for individuals and argued for the insulation of black neighborhoods from white interference, particularly interference by police authorities, whom they identified as an occupation army. To dramatize their position, the Panthers adopted paramilitary trappings including uniforms, organizational structure, and weapons. The federal government quickly declared the party to be a danger to internal security, and subsequent raids by municipal police forces with the apparent support if not guidance of federal authorities quickly decimated the party.[52] Party headquarters were raided in several cities and party members jailed, even though many were subsequently acquitted after lengthy trials.[53] Party leaders were killed by police in a number of cities. Police invariably reported that the deaths occurred in police-panther shoot-outs while the panthers claimed that the assaults were unprovoked. In a case involving the death of Chicago Panther leader Fred Hampton, the *New York Times* editorialized that it was more of a "police shoot-in" than a shoot-out.[54] Police tactics, along with internal dissension, severely crippled the party.[55] By 1971 its paramilitary emphasis was dropped and the party began to rely on more conventional tactics. One of its famous members, Bobby Seale, ran unsuccessfully for mayor of Oakland, California, in 1973.

Finally, the Pan-African thrust, which has had a long history in black politics going back to the days of Martin Delany, W. E. B. DuBois, and Marcus Garvey, resurfaced during the decade, and took on two

52. In February of 1970 the mayor of Seattle, Washington, reported that a federal law enforcement agency had asked for his participation in a raid on Panther headquarters in his city. See the *New York Times,* 9 February 1970, p. 30. See also "F.B.I. Seeks Panther Data," *New York Times,* 14 December 1969; and Roy Wilkins and Ramsey Clark, *Search and Destroy* (New York: MARC, 1973).
53. This was true of cases in both New York and New Orleans.
54. See editorial in *New York Times,* 18 May 1970.
55. For discussion of internal differences in the party see Earl Anthony, *Picking Up the Gun* (New York: Dial, 1970).

fairly distinct dimensions. One, as personified by the Congress of African People (CAP) led by Imamu Baraka, called for a united front of all black groups for the purpose of capturing political power within the existing political system while working simultaneously for ultimate self-determination of all African people. At its first annual meeting held in Atlanta, Georgia, in 1969, the congress accepted a tentative program designed to achieve political power by starting at the local level and working upward.[56] In subsequent years the congress became involved in local politics in Newark, New Jersey, the home base of its leader, Immamu Baraka.

The Congress of African People was instrumental in the election of Kenneth Gipson as the first black mayor of Newark in 1970. The marriage between electoral politics and Pan-Africanism proved, however, to be short lived. By 1974 Mayor Gipson and CAP were at odds with each other. In the 1974 elections in Newark, CAP-backed candidates were soundly defeated. CAP has yet to become an important political force.

The second strand of Pan-Africanism was represented by the New Republic of Africa (NRA) which revived the old idea of establishing an independent black state in the "Black Belt" of the South. In 1972 NRA sent a cadre to Mississippi to purchase a site to serve as headquarters for their self-declared nation. This, like several other black political experiments of the decade, ended in violence when Mississippi state patrolmen, who allegedly were attempting to serve a warrant on the residence housing NRA members in Jackson, exchanged gunfire with the occupants. In the shoot-out, one police officer was killed and NRA members who were in the house along with others not present were charged with, and later convicted of, murder by Mississippi courts. Their convictions were upheld by federal district courts. Final appeals to the Supreme Court are now pending.

The foregoing brief discussion of groups which pursued nonelectoral political activity as a means toward black liberation is not meant to be exhaustive, but rather suggestive of the pattern of initiatives tried and results achieved. They demonstrate that politics of the nonelectoral variety were no more productive than electoral politics during the 1960s. Neither was able to overcome white opposition. Significant prima facie gains were registered in the electoral arena, but failure to enforce them reduced their importance. Those engaging in aggressive nonelectoral politics were crushed by the power of the state.

56. Report of Committee on Political Liberation, Congress of African People, mimeographed (1969).

EPILOGUE

The political gains, limited though they were, recorded by blacks during the 1960s depended largely upon supportive action by the national government. Since the period of the New Deal, the national government has taken a more progressive position on matters involving black citizens than has the white rank and file. For example, it is doubtful that the civil rights acts of 1964 and 1965, or the decisions of the Supreme Court on open housing or school integration, would survive public referenda. This should not be interpreted as a paen for the federal government, since the data previously produced indicates that it, too, lacks a fundamental commitment to the black struggle for equal status. The argument advanced here is that while the American political system has never been especially kind to black people, the factions which have controlled the executive branch of the nation's government, for political reasons dictated by the winner-take-all structure of the electoral college system and the strategic location of blacks in the urban centers of the populous industrialized states, have spewn forth a stream of rhetoric, albeit timorously, which decried racism and advocated a better deal for blacks. As scholars have long observed, any theme which is repeated often enough affects its audience. In our case, the rhetoric of the dominant national factions, along with myriad other contributory factors, led the white masses to tolerate a political system which was a bit more sensitive to the plight of blacks than the prevailing attitudes of white rank and file would justify. During the 1960s the dialectic of black political agitation with the concomitant passage of remedial civil rights legislation and resultant white opposition to such symbolic assurance set in motion an ambiguous counterforce which threatens, on the one hand, to reduce the attitude of the national government toward the black power movement to indifference, if not outright hostility, while on the other hand it promises to facilitate unprecedented black political participation at the federal level.

The ambiguous nature of this counterforce may be illuminated by analyzing and synthesizing several diverse yet related salient political developments of the period, such as those exemplified in the political fortunes of Alabama's George Wallace in national politics; the federally sponsored efforts to destroy the Black Power movement; the posture of the Nixon and Ford administrations on civil rights; and the election of Jimmy Carter, former governor of Georgia, as president of the United States.

When Governor Wallace ran as the American party candidate for the presidency in 1968, he had a national reputation as a hard line segregationist. Nevertheless, he was able to secure a position on the ballots of all of the states, primarily through either citizen's petition or by his showing in primary elections. He received 13.5 percent of the vote on election day. This meant that in spite of the usual disinclination on the part of voters to "waste" their votes on a third party, one of every seven voted for Wallace. Perhaps of more importance, Wallace was able to convince a former chairman of the Joint Chiefs of Staff of the U.S. Armed Forces, a prestigious position in the American political system, to run as his candidate for vice president.

During the 1972 presidential campaign, Governor Wallace was considered a major candidate for the nomination of the Democratic party and given all the deference and respect of serious presidential aspirants. An avowed segregationist had not known such national acceptability in more than twenty years. This campaign was cut short when he was paralyzed by the bullet of a would-be assassin. However, Wallace kept his political machine alive and again competed for the Democratic party's presidential nomination in 1976. After a relatively poor showing in several state primaries Wallace withdrew from the race, but not before his conservative position on many major social issues became a respectable part of the American political culture. This point was accentuated by Wallace when he, along with other respected elder statesmen of the party such as Hubert Humphrey, was invited to address the 1976 Democratic National Convention.

The Nixon administration, elected in 1968 and returned to office in 1972, in deference to sentiment made manifest in the popular support of Governor Wallace and his views, began to weaken the federal government's support for black interests. During its first term, for example, the administration supported efforts to weaken the Voting Rights Act when it came up for renewal in 1970. This was seen by many observers as part of the administration's plan to build a new national majority by appealing to parochial sentiment in middle and southern America.[57]

Following the reelection of President Nixon in 1972, he announced a policy of returning to what he called the work ethic, or self-reliance, as opposed to welfare. Accordingly, his 1973 budget called for drastic reductions in "Great Society" and other social welfare programs. The Office of Economic Opportunity was to be dismantled and the Community Action Program, the structure designed to facilitate participation

---

57. For two interesting discussions of this point see Leon Panetta and Peter Gall, *The Nixon Team and the Civil Rights Retreat* (New York: J. P. Lippincott, 1971) and Reg Murphy and Hal Gulliver, *The Southern Strategy* (New York: Charles Scribner's Sons, 1971).

by the poor, was to be eliminated outright. Additional cutbacks were announced in social welfare programs administered by other departments. These cutbacks would reduce the already limited but sorely needed services to blacks and the poor and also eliminate significant numbers of middle-income jobs for black professionals.

Reactions by black leadership to the changing posture of the national government under Nixon was uniformly apprehensive. Roy Wilkins, executive director of NAACP and a moderate, charged that blacks were under a state of siege launched by "the executive branch of the Federal Government."[58] A group of black southern mayors called for a meeting with the president to discuss the impact of the president's budget cuts.[59] In an unprecedented move, the Congressional Black Caucus prepared a rejoinder to the president's 1973 State of the Union message which was presented to the U.S. House of Representatives. The fifteen black congressmen in their statement, which was billed as the "true state of the Union," cited wide differences between blacks and whites in terms of income, employment, housing, and so forth, and charged that self-reliance was a viture demanded only from minorities, the poor, and the disadvantaged.[60]

The Nixon administration's plan to forge a new political majority in the U.S. by appealing to parochial interests of the South, the West, and the Midwest was short-circuited when revelations of the president's Watergate-related transgressions forced him to resign. The policies of his appointed successor Gerald Ford, however, were more benevolent toward blacks.

Two final issues need to be addressed before this narrative is closed. One deals with the revelation of concerted action by the federal government, particularly the FBI, to disrupt the black movement of the 1960s and 1970s, and the other relates to the dynamics of the 1976 presidential election process.

Information made public by the FBI in 1974 pursuant to a suit under the Freedom of Information Act and data uncovered by a Senate select committee demonstrate conclusively that the FBI worked systematically to neutralize the efforts of various black groups and individuals through surveillance and disruption. Such tactics were used against diverse black groups including the Southern Christian Leadership Conference, Nation of Islam, Black Panther Party, Student Non-Violent Coordinating Committee, NAACP, and campus based black student unions.[61]

58. "Wilkins Terms Blacks in State of Seige," *New York Times*, 9 January 1973.
59. "Black Mayors Ask for Nixon Parley," *New York Times*, 11 February 1973.
60. Quoted in "Black Caucus Scores Budget Cuts," *New York Times*, 1 February 1973.

Senate documents demonstrate that the FBI invoked a wide range of legal, extralegal, and patently illegal tactics to stifle and destroy black political groupings. These tactics included character assassination of leaders, discrediting black groups in the eyes of potential supporters by providing unfavorable (often false) information, instigating conflicts between and among black groups, encouraging local police to harass black groups, and even burglarizing the offices of such groups. While it may be impossible to assess precisely the impact of FBI harassment on the black movement, clearly it was in no way salutary.

The currents of the 1960s and mid-1970s discussed in this paper seem to have dovetailed in the 1976 campaign for the presidential nomination of the Democratic party. The liberal wing of the party, the faction considered most sympathetic to black aspirations, did not fare well in the 1976 nominating process. But neither did the Wallace faction. Instead another southerner, a relatively unknown former Georgia governor, won the nomination by running an ecumenical campaign which appealed to, among others, white Wallace supporters and black voters in both the North and South.

Carter's ascendance was facilitated greatly by the efforts of prominent black politicians from his home state who traveled throughout the country to convince blacks and liberals that a white southerner was an acceptable presidential candidate. On his part, Carter did not present any specific plan or programs designed to ameliorate the black condition. Instead he promised that blacks would be fully integrated into the decision-making structures of his administration.

Although many commentators gave black voters primary credit for Carter's victory, a close analysis yields a more ambiguous picture. Carter received 85 percent of the black vote, but so did Hubert Humphrey in his unsuccessful campaign in 1968. George McGovern received 87 percent of the black vote in his losing 1972 campaign. Thus it was not Carter's share of the black vote that distinguished his victorious campaign from that of the two unsuccessful Democratic nominees who ran in 1968 and 1972, but rather it was Carter's success in attracting conservative white votes. This result meant that Carter's victory heightened the ambiguities growing out of the sixties because he assumed office

61. For a summary of the FBI's account of its indiscretions see "Statement of Clarence Kelley, Director Federal Bureau of Investigation, November 18, 1974," mimeographed (Washington, D.C.: U.S. Department of Justice) and "FBI Cointelpro Activities," (attached to Kelley's statement). Also Cathy Perkus, ed., Cointelpro, the FBI's Secret War on Political Freedom (New York: Monad, 1975). See also U.S., Congress, Senate, Select Committee to Study Governmental Operations with Respect to Intelligence Activities. Supplementary Detailed Staff Reports on Intelligence Activities and the Rights of Americans, book 3, 94th Cong., 2d sess. 1976, pp. 3–223.

beholden to both the black and conservative white vote at a time when special affirmative action programs in both public and private sectors designed to facilitate black access to the fruits of the U.S. political and economic system are under attack as being discriminatory against whites.

A full assessment of the meaning of the political gains made by blacks during the 1960s and early 1970s, then, must await the denouement in this latest chapter in the labyrinth of U.S. racial politics.

Robert Arthur Smithey

The New Militancy and Its Impact on the Afro-American Middle Class

Three presumptions are immediately reflected in the title of this chapter: (1) that militancy is not a new phenomenon in the Afro-American community, hence the term, "new militancy"; (2) that socioeconomic, cultural strata are present in the overall black American community, just as in other ethnic communities that make up this republic; and (3) that the new militancy has had some demonstrable effect on those classed as middle class in the Afro-American community. Nothing in these presumptions makes them mutually exclusive: both militant black intellectuals and militant black nonintellectuals exist, as do both militant black members of the middle class and militant black paupers, and so on. These observations must be made here, because for too long too many persons, even among those whose training and experience should have taught them better, blacks as well as whites, have insisted that all black Americans fall into one of two categories: those who submit to and/or subscribe to the status quo and those who oppose it.

History denies to us the name of the first Afro-American militant, but somewhere, long years before Nat Turner's famous insurrection in 1831, at some point in time between the landing of the first black slaves in America in 1619 and Lincoln's Emancipation Proclamation in 1863, somewhere in "those improbable fields down South,"[1] a voice of protest was raised against the "system" and this republic's legally sanctioned inhumanity to the minds and bodies of blacks. The form of this first militant act, like the name of its source, is forever denied to us. So is the

1. James Baldwin, *Go Tell It on the Mountain* (New York: Dell, 1965), p. 17.

Dr. Smithey is professor of English, Norfolk State College, Norfolk, Virginia.

initial reaction of the establishment and its consequences. Such data would be helpful here, were it available, for among other things it would put to rest at once and forever the too-widely held, mistaken notion that dissent and protest in the black American community is a new phenomenon sprung full-grown from the heads of blacks born in the 1940s; that prior to the advent of the Student Non-Violent Coordinating Committee (SNCC) and its progeny, the appearance of Malcolm X and Stokely Carmichael and their disciples, *all* black Americans, "Uncle Toms" by nature, sat complacently by while the great white father exploited and emasculated at will and with impunity the offspring and descendants of the survivors of 1619 and beyond.

A question might well be raised concerning the presence of this cloud over the origin and evolution of militancy in the Afro-American community in particular and the American community in general, groups which comprise the most enlightened nation in the annals of civilization. The answer is quite simple. Until very recently the significant deeds of Afro-Americans in the development of this Republic were ignored, deprecated, or forgotten, and the names and faces of the men and women behind those deeds were invisible. These phenomena, Afro-American invisibility and its malignant offspring, general historical disregard of Afro-American contributions and achievements, have both served to outrage and enrage many contemporary black Americans and, consequently, have effected and nurtured the new militancy among their numbers. And whereas the earliest and older militants among blacks in this country had as their primary concern delivery from the bonds of slavery and a realization of the letter of the "slave amendments" to the federal Constitution, the new militants have expanded their goals to include, in addition to equal justice under the law and due process, an insistence upon an honest inclusion of their forebears and brothers' participation in those accounts of our nation's past, posited as American history. Some of the new militants go so far as to argue for a separate history, a "black history," because of the glaring omissions in received history.[2]

So that the new militancy may be examined in proper historical perspective, a look must be given at the forerunners of this movement. The last decade of the nineteenth century and the first decade of this century were critical periods in black American history. Jim Crowism, denial of the ballot, ghetto living, unequal treatment under the law were all commonplace for a majority of black Americans. In protest

2. Vincent Harding, *Beyond Chaos: Black History and the Search for the New Land,* Black Paper no. 2 (Atlanta: Institute of the Black World, 1970) *passim.*

against such treatment, courageous liberal whites and militant blacks began to organize to complain about the increasing number of monstrous acts by whites against blacks. Two important protest organizations were the Committee of Twelve for the Advancement of the Interests of the Negro Race and the Niagara Movement. The former group was black and aimed largely at challenging Booker T. Washington's appeasement program. Washington believed that the best road for blacks to follow to achieve full equality was through economic-industrial education. DuBois and his cohorts believed that economic-industrial education was but one facet of the quest for equality; that higher education, political and civil rights were equally important.

Anti-Washington sentiments prevailed in the Committee of Twelve and DuBois resigned from its membership. The immediate consequence of his resignation was the establishment of a more militant organization, the Niagara Movement, so named because of its initial meeting place. This organization's main objective was active opposition to the reactionary methods of Washington and the generation of a more militant policy of struggle against "Jim Crowers" and lynchers. The principles agreed on by the Niagara Movement were:

1. Freedom of speech and criticism
2. An unsettled and unsubsidized press
3. Manhood suffrage
4. The abolition of all caste distinctions based simply on race and color
5. The recognition of the highest and best training as the monopoly of no class or race
6. The recognition of the principle of human brotherhood as a practical present creed
7. A belief in the dignity of labor
8. United effort to realize these ideals under wise and courageous leadership.[3]

The organization's department of civil rights devoted itself to four major objectives:

1. The enactment of an effective civil rights bill in each of the northern states
2. The organization in each of the northern states of a sympathetic group to be composed mainly of persons not members of the movement
3. The improvement of traveling accommodations on local carriers in the south

3. Warren D. St. James, *The National Association for the Advancement of Colored People: A Case Study in Pressure Groups* (Hicksville, N.Y.: Exposition Press, 1958), p. 37. See also Mary White Ovington, *The Walls Came Tumbling Down* (New York: Schocken, 1970), chap. 4.

4. The attainment of service of colored men on grand and petit juries in southern states.[4]

While DuBois and Washington, with their divergent views, were struggling for ascendancy in the black American community, recurring manifestations of white hostility were taking place throughout the nation in the form of lynchings and race riots.[5] On 14 August, 1908, race riots broke out in Springfield, Illinois. These riots had been preceded by similar riots in New York; Atlanta; Springfield, Ohio; Greensburg, Indiana; and Brownsville, Texas.[6] The liberal white press was outraged;[7] their anger led to the convocation, several months later, of a group of liberal whites at the instigation of Mary White Ovington to devise methods to combat the increasing spread of terror and racism in the black community.[8] From this meeting and subsequent meetings of the group assembled, there emerged a committee of forty called the Negro National Committee. In May of 1910 this group was incorporated under the laws of the state of New York into the National Association for the Advancement of Colored People.[9] The organization's platform of "absolute political and social equality" shocked many people, and the association was denounced as radical, revolutionary, and subversive.[10] The same epithets applied to the NAACP in its early days were to be repeated fifty years later with reference to the Student Non-Violent Coordinating Committee (SNCC), the Congress of Racial Equality (CORE), the Southern Christian Leadership Conference (SCLC), the Black Panthers, and all black groups challenging the continuation of the anti-black status quo of the American system. The NAACP, however, unlike some of the more vocal latter-day militant groups, has centered its efforts for equality in litigation. Its success is inspiring and need not be repeated here.[11] Life for *all* blacks in America has been positively affected because of the successes of the NAACP in its legal efforts to make democracy in America a reality for *all* Americans!

4. St. James, pp. 37–38.
5. James W. Johnson, *Along This Way* (New York: Viking, 1933), p. 312. For an account of the Negroes' plight following the Civil War, see Benjamin Quarles, *The Negro in the Civil War* (Boston: Little, Brown, 1953).
6. St. James, pp. 35–36; Charles Flint Kellogg, *NAACP: A History of the National Association for the Advancement of Colored People* (Baltimore: Johns Hopkins University Press, 1967), pp. 23–24.
7. Mary White Ovington, *How the NAACP Began* (NAACP, 1914).
8. Ibid.
9. For a history of the NAACP, see Kellogg.
10. See Kellogg; also Robert Jack, *The History of the NAACP* (Boston: Meador, 1943).
11. The NAACP has been successful in twenty-four out of twenty-six cases before the U.S. Supreme Court in its efforts to make the U.S. Constitution a reality for all Americans. For a detailed account of these cases, see Kellogg; also St. James.

The NAACP has centered its efforts for equality in litigation, and litigation for blacks in America is a long and tedious process if any semblance of equal justice is to be obtained. Some disaffection evolved among certain blacks because of what often seemed an interminable span of time in the NAACP's efforts. Thus, two major thrusts have evolved in the black American's struggle to achieve equality: (1) A "give the courts a try" thesis, tantamount to leaving all matters relating to the pursuit of equal justice under the law to due process in the courts; and (2) the "we have waited long enough" thesis, seeking equality now, within or without the law. History would seem to have vindicated the "give the courts a try" thesis, in view of the opportunities available now to all Americans as compared with those available to blacks in 1910, the year of the NAACP's founding.

The spirit of the time plays an important role in the operations of any pressure group, and it was a recognition of this factor, undoubtedly, which helped to determine the course the NAACP would follow in pursuit of its goals. A nation that had held its black population in slavery for nearly 250 years, whose highest court had once held that a black was only three-fifths of a man, was not likely to unequivocally subscribe to the notion that black Americans were created equal to the Founding Fathers or their offspring and descendants, at least not without a struggle. But the NAACP was relentless in its pursuit of equal justice under the law for America's black citizens, and in May of 1954, in the case of *Brown* v. *Board of Education of Topeka, Kansas,* it achieved a victory before the U.S. Supreme Court that seemed to virtually mark an end to all our woes. For the high court held unanimously, in effect, that the "separate but equal" doctrine condoned for more than fifty years by the nation's highest tribunal was unconstitutional. The promised land seemed at hand, the dream long hoped for imminent.

Years began to slip by, however, and little of the dream was realized. "With all deliberate speed" seemed to many, blacks as well as liberal whites, legal sanction for prolonging the status quo. Blacks in public schools at the beginning of the 1960s (six years after the historic decision outlawing segregation) were actually just as segregated as they had been at the beginning of the 1950s, four years before the historic 1954 decision. This apparent foot dragging in making the outlawing of segregation a reality gave rise to the new militancy of the 1960s, the "we have waited long enough" thesis. And it is with the militancy of this period, the most widely publicized of all the black protest movements in this country, that this chapter will be primarily concerned as it examines the new militancy and its impact on the Afro-American middle class. The reader is emphatically asked to remember, however, that just as militancy in the black American community is not new, neither is protest among black American youth, especially black American college students.[12]

What was peculiar about the early years of the new militancy was its point of emphasis. As Saunders Redding put it:

What black students of the year 1960 wanted was simply an end to segregation and discrimination. Although integration was undoubtedly their ultimate goal, they did not say so. All their talk was of "desegregation," and all they asked was that the process begin on a basic level that everyone could understand and all ordinary folk could relate to. As if to emphasize this, the students began their campaign at a lunch counter in a five and ten cent store in Greensboro, North Carolina.[13]

This action precipitated similar sit-in demonstrations throughout the nation, especially in the South, wherever racial discrimination was practiced. The immediate result was the establishment of black student unions throughout the nation to coordinate and plan subsequent demonstrations. The resultant organization was called the Student Non-Violent Coordinating Committee, or SNCC, and it was headed by two young Negroes—James Forman, executive secretary, and John Lewis, chairman. In 1961 SNCC expanded its campaign to include the elimination of discrimination in voting. By this time many concerned white students had joined their ranks.

SNCC's early impact on the American sociopolitical scene is too familiar to repeat here.[14] The great attraction it had for the American public and its initial successes quickly engendered interest in the group's activities and methods of direct action. And so, established protest groups ("protest" in the sense of "extreme devotion to a cause," in

12. Those interested in pursuing this subject further will find August Meier et al; *Black Protest Thought in the Twentieth Century* (Indianapolis: Bobbs-Merrill, 1971) especially helpful, as well as essays by Herbert Aptheker, "The Negro College Student in the 1920s—Years of Preparation and Protest: An Introduction," *Science and Society,* 33:150–67 (1969; and Edward K. Graham, "The Hampton Institute Strike of 1927: A Case Study in Student Protest," *American Scholar* 668–82 (Autumn 1969); and Margaret Mead, "Postscript: The 1969 Demonstrations," *American Scholar* 682–83 (Autumn 1969); Ernest Kaiser, "Recent Literature on Black Liberation Struggles and the Ghetto Crisis," *American Scholar* 168–96 (Autumn 1969). For related discussions, see also Wayne Cooper, "Claude McKay and the New Negro of the 1920s," *Phylon* 25:297–306 (1964); Gilbert Osofsky, "Symbols of the Jazz Age; The New Negro and Harlem Discovered," *American Quarterly* 18:229–38 (1965); and Hugh M. Gloster, *Negro Voices in American Fiction* (Chapel Hill: University of North Carolina Press, 1948), chap. 3.

13. Saunders Redding, "The Black Youth Movement," *American Scholar* 584 (Autumn 1969).

14. Essays reciting the history of SNCC by members and observers are to be found in Meier; also see William Brink and Louis Harris, *The Negro Revolution in America* (New York: Simon and Schuster, 1963).

this case the cause of black liberation from second-class citizenship) such as the NAACP and CORE adopted direct involvement. Heretofore, the NAACP's tactics had been legalistic in nature; that is, changes had been sought in opposition to practices operating against the Negro through court action, seeking an interpretation of the U.S. Constitution which would in deed and in fact offer equal justice under the law for black Americans. CORE, on the other hand, was originally formed in Chicago in 1942 by a group headed by James L. Farmer, a former director of the NAACP, and had, as its cardinal principle, "to translate law and morality into practice."[15]

SNCC's sit-ins, by the time of the great March on Washington in August of 1963, had forged an amalgam of the leading black action groups in the nation—NAACP, CORE, and the Urban League. The long-awaited, much-desired unity of the black American community seemed at hand. Furthermore, the large white liberal support mustered for the great march seemed to herald, finally, a realization of this Republic's great motto: "E Pluribus Unum."

But this great expectation was short-lived. The first wind of change was noted in the ranks of SNCC. The exact cause of the change will perhaps never be known, but change was imminent. In 1965, James Forman was ousted as the head of the SNCC and succeeded by Stokely Carmichael, whose first public announcement was that henceforth SNCC would be all black, and while contributions from whites would still be acceptable, they would not be permitted to join the organization or to work in its program. SNCC's avowed determination to "keep it black" and its announced policy of black self-determination, coupled with Stokely Carmichael's now famous "Black Power"[16] speech, marked the beginning of what may aptly be called the new militancy in the black American experience. (The term "Black Power," incidentally, did not originate with Stokely Carmichael. It was originated by the late Adam Clayton Powell, who first mentioned it at a Chicago rally in May, 1965, and elaborated upon it in his Howard University commencement speech of 29 May 1966.)

The essence of Carmichael's Black Power concept is as follows: The

15. Brink and Harris, p. 43.
16. For a full explanation of Stokely Carmichael's concept of "Black Power," see Charles V. Hamilton and Stokely Carmichael, *Black Power; The Politics of Liberation in America* (New York: Random House, 1967); and Charles V. Hamilton, "An Advocate of Black Power Defines It," *New York Times Magazine*, 14 April 1968, pp. 22–23. For some opposing views on the subject, see Martin Luther King, Jr., "Showdown for Nonviolence," *Look*, 16 April 1968, pp. 23–25; Roy Wilkins, "Whither Black Power?" Excerpts from keynote address delivered at NAACP 57th Annual Convention, Los Angeles, 5 July 1966, published in Meier, pp. 596–621; and Bayard Rustin, "Separate Is Not Equal," news release of the A. Philip Randolph Institute, 13 February 1969.

concept of Black Power calls for black people in this country to unite, to recognize their heritage, to build a sense of community. It is a call for black people to define their goals to lead their own organizations and to support those organizations. It is a call to reject the racist institutions and values of this society.

The concept rests on a fundamental premise: Before a group can enter the open society, it must first close ranks. Only black people can convey the revolutionary idea—and it is a revolutionary idea—that black people are able to do things themselves. Only they can help create in the community an aroused and continuing black consciousness. In areas where black people have a majority, they will attempt to use power to exercise control. When black people lack a majority, Black Power means proper representation and sharing of control.

Black visibility is not the same as Black Power. The power must be that of a community, and emanate from it. The ultimate values and goals are an effective share in the total power of the society. The goal of Black Power is full participation in the decision-making processes affecting the lives of black people, and recognition of the virtues in themselves as black people.

Hard upon Carmichael's call for Black Power, factions within the black community were joined, almost immediately, to determine what future course black Americans would take to obtain equal justice under the law; whether, in fact, the "American Dream" is an ignis fatuus unworthy of the quest that black Americans have pursued for the hundred years plus since their emancipation;[17] to determine who speaks for the Negro and the specific group within the Afro-American community the Negro represents; whether separatism in this Republic, that is, separate black and white states, is in fact as viable as accommodation and/or integration;[18] whether it was feasible to continue on the well-trod, notably successful road the NAACP had been following since its founding at the turn of this century. What ultimately erupted as a consequence of SNCC's Black Power stand was what Dr. Vera M. Green calls "the confrontation of diversity within the Black Community."[19] The old order, the patience-oriented proponents of integration through the tactic of legal maneuvers, stood poised against the new order, the impatient, "disenchanted with the system" advocates of black determin-

17. See Harding, *Beyond Chaos.*
18. See Robert S. Browne, "A Case for Separation," in Robert S. Browne and Bayard Rustin, *Separation or Integration: Which Way for America?—A Dialogue* (New York, 1968), pp. 7-15.
19. See Vera M. Green, "The Confrontation of Diversity Within the Black Community," *Human Organization,* 29, no. 4 (Winter 1970).

ism who were bent on change at once, within the system, if possible, without, if necessary. America's black population seemed at Armageddon.

An insistence on black pride, pride in things black—color, history, culture—generally unnoted before in the American community arose and, simultaneously, supporters of the new order joined hands with its authors in rejecting the traditional ambiguous, racist epithet "Negro" for what was regarded as the more accurate appellation, "black," spelled, for emphasis, with a capital "B."[20] The term "Negro" became anathema. Black Americans who insisted on using it were labeled "Uncle Toms" by the new militants and to be so called by anyone, black or white, was regarded as a term of opprobrium, as offensive as the racist insult "nigger."

But a great deal more than name calling was involved in the polarization effected by this sociopolitical renaissance initiated by SNCC and its adherents to its new militancy. It challenged the entire black American community to a reassessment of the contemporary position and prospects for the future of black Americans in this Republic's scheme of things. For the insistence on black pride, charged by the new militants, would brook no further toleration of the "go slow now" admonitions of the past.[21]

Understandably, the strongest negative reaction to the proposed urgency of reassessment of black status in the American community came from the members of the black establishment, the traditionalist NAACP,[22] and the black intellectuals and middle class,[23] members of the black American community "adopted" by white American society, and/or those in the black community who had "made" it in white America, in spite of racial oppression, and cultural and racial emasculation.

As hinted above, one of the sharpest drawn battles resulting from the

20. For a pre-1960 declaration of pride in blackness, such as implied in the black pride manifesto of the new militants of the 1960s, see Langston Hughes, "The Negro Artist and Racial Mountains," *The Nation*, 23 June 1926, pp. 692–94. For a complimentary view to Hughes's essay, see John O. Killens, "Explanation of the Black Psyche," *New York Times Magazine*, 7 June 1964, pp. 37–38.

21. The expression is William Faulkner's. See "A Letter to the North," *Life*, 5 March 1956, pp. 51–52.

22. See especially excerpts from Roy Wilkins's keynote address delivered at the NAACP 57th Annual Convention, Los Angeles, 5 July 1966, printed in *Crisis* 353–54 (August-September 1966). Wilkins said of CORE, SNCC, and SCLC, "Here today and gone tomorrow. There is only one organization that can handle a long, sustained fight—the NAACP."

23. See James Farmer, "We Cannot Destroy Segregation with a Weapon of Segregation," *Equality*, 1:2 (November 1944). An interesting observation on the black youth movement and some of its inconsistencies and contradictions relevant to Black Power is to be found in Saunders Redding's essay, "The Black Youth Movement," cited above.

emergence of the new militancy in the black American community has been the confrontation between the new militants and the Afro-American middle class.[24] That such groups (imaginary or real) even exist in the black community offers a formidable challenge to the more verbal segments among the exponents of the new militancy, especially since their abusive harangues against the system frequently suggest that all black Americans are of a piece. Somewhat less caustic, but equally as uninformed, are those who, like the early Malcolm X, group all Afro-Americans in one of two classes, Negroes and blacks. Negroes, that is the middle class or "Uncle Toms," were portrayed as having been descended from pre-Civil War house servants, while blacks, that is, those interested in black pride—with all of its accompanying symbols— were descended from the field hands.[25] The overall suggestion of such classifications is that descendants from slave house servants inherited the brainwashing of their forebears on the Negro's "place," the latter-day, contemporary manifestation of which is accommodationism, "Tomism," a desire for integration, and so on. Conversely, descendants of field hands escaped this inherited taint of wanting to be with or like white folks, their historic oppressors.

One of the great ironies of the theories of the new militancy is that, despite their avowed contempt for "whitey" and all that whites stand for, often their own pronouncements are corroboration of the same racist theories they purport to disavow. For example, the often-expressed notion among some militant blacks that *all* Afro-Americans are alike is but an echo of popular theories held by rabid white racists that "all niggers are the same." But the reason for such attitudes is directly related to the new militancy; an ancient political maxim, quoted by Caesar and Machiavelli, suggests that one clear road to domination of a people is a division of that people. The maxim was "Divide et Impera" (Divide and Rule).

As the recently televised showing of Alex Haley's *Roots* clearly demonstrated, one of the primary means used by the slave masters to prevent any semblance of unity or organization among early black slaves was to keep them divided. This was often achieved in *Roots* and in historical accounts by establishing, through certain "privileges" rendered to some (such as living and eating in the kitchen of the "Big

---

24. Orde Coombs in his brilliant essay on the black middle class, "Soul in Suburbia," *Harper's* (January 1972), p. 24, gives an incisive commentary on the conflict between the new militancy and the Afro-American middle class.

25. See Green, p. 268. The views of the early Malcolm X on this subject can be found in Malcolm X, "Message to the Grass Roots," Record Jacket, Afro-American Broadcasting and Recording Company, Detroit, 1965.

House"; entertaining white guests, and so on) and denied to others, a quasi-caste and class system, the instilling of a false and unfounded notion among the blacks that there were, indeed, "differences" among them. A slave, in short, was not always a slave.

In a desperate effort to escape in some degree the rigors of slavery, unwitting blacks (and some knowledgeable ones) accepted the fantasy as reality. Generations of blacks descended from holders of these "Kafka-esque" fantasies have perpetuated these notions of difference in the black community. These notions, in turn, aided in no small measure by racist whites, liberals, and conservatives alike, have contributed to keeping blacks in their "place." Thus the call to unity among black proponents of the new militancy fell all too frequently on deaf ears. I remember vividly the indifferent, negative response I received to a call to black unity in my hometown to fight segregation and the sometimes exclusion from our city auditorium back in 1944, shortly after I had been elected chairman of the National Youth Conference of the NAACP. A commonly expressed opinion was "I don't blame whites for not wanting to associate with some blacks. Opening the city auditorium to all blacks will set back those of us who have arrived a hundred years." There were dissidents to such notions, but the majority won the day. Thus the new militancy's call among blacks to black self-respect, black unity, black assertiveness, black celebration, was a Sisyphean task. The antebellum germ of black division based on the fantasy of black "differences" proved and is proving a Herculean force, opposing the black middle class acceptance of the new militancy.

Granted that none of the "Jim Crow" legislation distinguishes between classes of Negroes; nonetheless, the absolutistic principle embraced by many whites and many blacks that *all* Afro-Americans are the same is not nor has ever, in Gunnar Myrdal's words, "been fully realized even in the South."[26] A social stratification in the slave community based on jobs and emergence of a class of free Negroes strengthened the trend toward distinctions. Even today, with or between the class structures of white and black society there is still a line, with whites above and blacks below.

One of the obvious direct consequences of black achievements (socio-economic and educational) being ignored or looked down upon by whites has been the emergence of an isolated black middle class, just as black businesses—banks, insurance, churches, and so on—emerged as a consequence of blacks being ignored or denied a meaningful role in the

26. Gunnar Myrdal, *An American Dilemma* (New York: Harper and Row, 1962), p. 689.

development of the American economy and the white American religious community. It is a matter of indisputable fact that blacks did indeed have a meaningful role in the development of the American economy (blacks built the roads, for instance), but little if any role was given to them in the decision-making process or in the positions where fortunes were being made. One of the tragic ironies of the American experience is that black Americans who ape the white community's patterns of achievement find themselves, at the pinnacle of their efforts, not in the promised land, socially accepted in the American middle class as middle class, nor even in limbo, waiting for room at the top, but in a veritable wasteland with no hope of unbiased recognition or acceptance. Such awareness among middle class blacks leads to fantasy, the embracing of revolutionary nonclass ideologies such as socialism, communism, despair, or black militancy. Black militants are acutely aware of the ambiguous state of would-be black middle-class aspirants and have capitalized on it, as we shall see later.

E. Franklin Frazier describes the black middle class as "constituted of those Negroes who derive their income principally from the services they render as white collar workers."[27] "White collar," according to Webster's *Collegiate Dictionary*, "designates or pertains to the class of salaried workers whose duties permit a well-groomed appearance." Surprisingly, the earliest white collar workers among black Americans were bankers.[28] This fact is indeed surprising, since the American black has been and still is almost completely insignificant as a banker.[29] The early ventures in this area were those of Negroes freed before the Civil War.[30] These men, few in number and, ultimately, unsuccessful, nevertheless were the lineal forebears of what comprise today the black bourgeoisie as well as black businesses in America. The most successful of these early ventures in banking was Freedmen's Savings Bank and Trust Company—backed by the Freedmen's Bureau—which opened on 4 April 1865 in New York City. By the time of its failure during the depression of 1874, less than ten years after opening, the bank had at one time deposits of $57,000,000 and branches in 36 cities.[31] I would hazard that today, one hundred years later, no black American bank has nearly so many branches or such deposits.

Other precursors of the present-day black American middle class,

27. E. Franklin Frazier, *Black Bourgeoisie* (Glencoe, Ill.: Free Press, 1957), p. 43.
28. Ibid., pp. 29–42.
29. Myrdal, pp. 314–18.
30. For a full discussion of Negroes freed before the Emancipation Proclamation, see Carter G. Woodson, *The Negro in Our History* (Washington, D.C.: Associated Publishers, 1941), pp. 243–78.
31. Frazier, pp. 34–38.

more successful than the bankers, were the pioneers in insurance.[32] Myrdal stated that the fact that Negroes made some headway in life insurance was due to their high mortality rates. One of the principal consequences of this discriminatory treatment against blacks by white insurance companies has been the development of such respected, black owned, black controlled companies as the Atlanta Life Insurance Company, North Carolina Mutual, and Supreme Liberty Life Insurance Company of Chicago.[33]

Like the modern black insurance companies, the history of black American undertakers, doctors, and lawyers, perhaps the most affluent segment of the black middle class, had its origin in black protest; protest against the discriminatory practices of white practitioners of the professions involved, a fact lost on or unknown to the majority of the black American community. Ira De A. Reid rightly observes, for example, that "the Negro has had a chance as an undertaker because of the character of his work; corpses usually are segregated even more meticulously than live people."[34] The related unhappy history of blacks attempting to bury their dead in unsegregated cemeteries is common knowledge.

Black doctors—physicians and surgeons as well as dentists—and black lawyers depend largely, if not totally, on the black community for their existence. As a matter of fact, services rendered by these professions are, in many places, nonexistent for black Americans if they are not available from black practitioners. That blacks are almost totally dependent on black undertakers, dentists, physicians and surgeons, and lawyers for needed services accounts for the usual affluence of members of these professions. The frequent exploitation of their patrons and clients by such professionals is also common knowledge.

Membership in county and state medical societies even in the northern and western states, where racial prejudice is not always as apparent or blatant as in the deep South and border states, is still uncommon among black doctors, however. Exclusion from membership in these societies is an important contributing cause to the restriction of areas where black physicians are able to obtain competence. Board member-

32. Ibid., pp. 316–18.
33. See Myrdal, p. 163, for an abbreviated history of the antecedents of modern Negro insurance. The National Benefit Life Insurance Company of Washington and the Standard Life Insurance Company of Atlanta, two of the earliest black insurance companies, were unable to survive largely because of unwise investments in projects far outside the sphere of ordinary life insurance investments.
34. Ira De A. Reid, "The Negro in the American Economic System," unpublished manuscript prepared for Gunnar Myrdal's *An American Dilemma*, vol. 1 (1940), pp. 102–3.

ship in the various medical specialties in medicine is infinitesimal among black doctors. Only a few hospitals in the United States, such as Harlem Hospital in New York City, have black and white doctors on the staff who work together under a system of absolute equality.

The black physician not only depends on black patients for a livelihood, but within that group the majority of his patients are those with low incomes. This phenomenon is largely due to a lack of faith in black physicians (black lawyers and dentists suffer in a similar fashion) on the part of the upper and middle class blacks, caused primarily by an awareness on the part of these two groups of the limited training and professional experience ordinarily available to black professionals. This reluctance to patronize black professionals by the black upper and middle class is not always scientifically founded, since there is little distinction between the basic training received by black or white physicians in America. But the equality ends with basic training: in the recent past, four-fifths of Negro physicians received their training in one of two medical schools, Meharry in Nashville, Tennessee, and Howard in Washington, D.C.[35]

Part of the syndrome of the upper and middle class black style of living is to seek out professional services not readily or easily available to the less fortunate, not so much for the services themselves but for the exclusiveness such selectivity affords. That such practices perpetuate the notion of white supremacy and insult the intelligence of many of their own select group never seems to occur to the black perpetrators of these myths.

Difficulties resulting from discrimination against blacks also hamper black lawyers in the practice of their profession and in their rendering of meaningful service to their clients, almost always black. The principal difficulty black lawyers encounter is the racist judge before whom they must plead their clients' cases. The incidence of legal insecurity of black lawyers in American courts, particularly in the South, like the professional insecurity of black doctors (inability to treat patients in racist-run hospitals), causes many blacks, both rich and poor, to seek the services of some "respectable" white lawyer in preference to representation by the best black members of the bar. Few major law firms anywhere in America have black associates, and the legal work of a large majority of black lawyers is restricted to domestic relations, criminal matters, and routine services to black real estate brokers, such as searching titles.

35. E. Franklin Frazier, *Negro Youth at the Crossways: Their Personality Development in the Middle States* (New York: Schocken, 1967), p. 290.

The most insidious consequence of discriminatory practices among what might be called the "needed professions," medicine, law, dentistry, and undertaking, is the engendering of a false sense of excellence among the practitioners of these professions, largely the result of an almost inevitable affluence as a consequence of a near-monopoly on the services rendered. Frazier, speaking of the characteristics of the Afro-American community in general, sees its chief limitation growing

> out of the fact that the Negro is kept behind the walls of segregation and is not permitted to compete in the larger community. This produces an artificial situation in which inferior standards of excellence and efficiency are set up. Since the Negro is not required to compete in the larger world and to assume its responsibilities and suffer its penalties, he does not have an opportunity to mature. Moreover, living within a small world with its peculiar valuations and distinctions, he may easily develop on the basis of some superficial distinction a conception of his role and status which may militate against the stability of his own little world.[36]

Equally as insidious as the fostering of inferior standards of excellence among members of the needed professions is the false sense of importance they assume because of their socioeconomic superiority in their communities. This false sense of superiority and importance causes, says Frazier, "members of the black bourgeoisie to live largely in a world of make-believe," a frustrating world in the absence of any relevance to society as a whole.[37]

One would think such rejection and frustration would lead to extreme militancy among such groups and deep-seated hostility and constant protests against the system; however, the facts of the Afro-American experience do not substantiate such a history or offer such portents for the future, as we shall see later.

The remaining three principal groups which make up the black middle class—white collar workers, entertainers, and teachers (the largest group comprising the black middle class)—suffer from the same type of discriminatory practices as blacks in the previously described groups. Even so, these groups also indulge in delusions of grandeur about their actual significance in the total American experience and often subscribe to inferior standards of excellence and efficiency.

Successful members of the entertainment group are among the most affluent of the upper black bourgeoisie, their salaries often running into hundreds of thousands of dollars a year. Notwithstanding, they have

36. Frazier, *Black Bourgeoisie*, p. 213.
37. Ibid., p. 237.

never played a significant role in American life. Most of the "big name" black professional entertainers have, in fact, sought to escape the strictures of blackness by marrying whites or nonblacks.

Recently findings and observations have been made which appear to dispute some of Frazier's conclusions about the black middle class. Apparently, some of these individuals may draw their values from a number of sources. Joseph Scott offers some dissenting views from Frazier's thesis that all middle class blacks operate in a world of delusion about who they are, or that most show a universal antipathy toward the black masses. Scott does not take issue with Frazier's position that middle class blacks "practice a particular ideational and behavioral style of life which involves status-seeking and conspicuous consumption."[38] But he takes issue with the fact that Frazier "imputes these orientations and behaviors to what appears to be nearly *all* those of middle socioeconomic status."[39] Scott believes that the middle class has at all times drawn upon its identification with the black American majority. Currently this identification has served to carry the liberation struggle beyond the demagogy of the early leaders of the current movement.

Scott's viewpoint is strengthened by William Sampson's (unpublished) findings. Sampson found that middle class blacks maintain a strong sense of black cultural identity and racial pride, contrary to earlier findings in other sociological studies.

Scott and Sampson represent the position that blacks can be both middle class and proud, in partial contradiction to Frazier. While Frazier's insight will thus have to be modified, we still must not conclude that the black middle class maintains an undivided cultural identification with the new militants. Actually there is an ambivalent mentality both within the middle class and within each of its members. Despite pride, one cannot identify too much activism in this group; if their ambivalence has grown in the last ten years, the new militants are responsible.

The phenomenon of survival is the source of much of the woe in the contemporary black American community. Those who have somehow "made it" in spite of the system are loath to give up what they feel they have achieved, whatever the cost to their psyche. "Half a loaf is better than none" is more than a cliché; it is a way of life for a significant portion of the Afro-American community, especially so for those who have escaped from some of the more objectionable manifestations of blatant racism into the seeming comfort of middle class status. These

38. *The Black Scholar,* p. 12.
39. Joseph Scott, *The Black Bourgeoisie and Black Power* (Sausalito, Calif., 1973).

persons look with deep fear and resentment on any efforts of dissident blacks to challenge the system. And their feigned contempt for the more obvious victims of the system—exploited, downtrodden, hopeless blacks —is matched only by their hatred of themselves and their African heritage, a heritage more often visible in their complexions and features than not.

This matter of self-hatred is, of course, not confined to middle class blacks, who often attempt escape from the frustration of invisibility and nothingness by aping their white counterparts. For example, they join black fraternities and sororities, black social clubs such as The Guardsmen; Sigma Pi Phi Boule; Links, Incorporated; Girl Friends; and so on, organizations unknown or unheard of in white society (and much of the black community as well), organizations which wield little political or economic power even in the black community. Self-hatred among lower class blacks is demonstrated daily in the heinous crimes its members commit against one another; the largest percentage of crimes committed by blacks occurs in poor black communities, and involves criminal acts often barbaric in nature. For, unlike their middle class blacks, these individuals lack the faculties and/or facilities to escape their invisibility and nothingness, and thus their frustrations and despair turn into violence which they vent upon one another. The old guard black middle class, the fair-skinned, fair-haired third- and fourth-generation college graduates and professionals who believe they have escaped their blackness or who feel they stand on the brink of exodus therefrom, are shaken mightily and angrily when the white controlled, often racist news media announce the crimes of their black brothers. The nouveau riche among the black middle class, indeed, are less perturbed by what these unhappy stories relate than are their established peers, since their roots are often only one generation removed, if that, from those described sociologically and economically as poor and underprivileged.[40] The delusion of wealth and power still obsesses many middle-class black Americans, and they still seek identification with the white America which continues to reject them. The call of the new militancy, celebrating blackness, apparently falls on deaf ears among much of the black middle class.

Orde Coombs, writing of the dilemma of the black middle class, seems to be writing a modern addendum to Frazier's indictment of black make-believe, written two decades ago. Coombs provides both an admonition and a warning to the complacent black middle class:

40. *Time*, 17 June 1974, pp. 19–28.

The material comfort of the Northeastern middle-class black is, in 1972, a direct result of the urban fires of the North and of the black Southerners who marched determinedly along their dustscapes and gave a semblance of change to this country. The thirty-to-forty-year-old black who holds down a good job in the North must know that his present success is a direct result of past tumult. All his talent, all his effort would not have otherwise given him a toehold in television, in consulting firms, in brokerage firms, in advertising, and in publishing. If he doubts this, he has only to look around and see how small his numbers are and how quickly the thrust to recruit blacks has abated. Many of these black men know that they owe their livelihoods to their poorer, more militant brethren. They know, too, that with all the marching, the rioting, and the dying, the relative condition of most black people has not greatly improved. In fact, only one black group has really benefited from the turbulence; and that is the middle class. Seizing the moment of noisy change, armed with the education that they had wondered how they would use, they immediately managed to alter their economic status. If this is true, then the middle-class blacks owe a debt to their poor brothers that mere benevolence cannot repay. The only way to cancel this debt is to try to lead the weary, the dispossessed, out of their morass. I can hear the chorus of middle-class outrage: "Oh, but we have tried. We are the ones who bring the lawsuits, who hold the benefits and the Nights of Excellence for the Urban League." I am not impressed. Though some individuals have, at great personal cost, assumed the mantle of black mass leadership, most bourgeoisie blacks have cloaked themselves in recondite chatter about change and left the hard task of organizing to those less talented than they. They have been seduced by the American myth of individual conquests of poverty.[41]

A deep division, both ideologically and culturally, still exists within our ranks, a division which the new militancy once threatened to heal or eradicate. But the much desired union of the disparate facets of the black American community is no longer imminent. The day of great accord, that memorable day in August, 1963, which marked the March on Washington, when for once all the splintered forces of power in the black community were united all for one and one for all, is now an event that seems long ago and far away. Yet it has been less than a decade since the late Martin Luther King, Jr. thrilled and inspired us all with his "I Have a Dream" speech, a vision of what America seemed then not only capable of becoming, but a vision which in that hour seemed imminently realizable. "Whither is fled the visionary gleam? Where is it now, the glory and the dream?" If the dream has vanished, one inescapable residue of the dream which the new militants foisted on the complacent black middle class is a cloud of unknowing about where blacks really stand in the American scheme of things—all blacks.

Our two great leaders, those who had the capacity and commitment

41. Coombs, pp. 24–25.

to lead and spur us on to an insistence upon the realization of the
American dream for *all*, Martin Luther King, Jr. and Malcolm X, are
dead. SNCC and CORE are names seldom heard, save in academic discussions. SCLC no longer commands the attention nor exerts the leadership influence it had under the direction of Dr. King. The Black Panther Party has retreated into near obscurity since its unsuccessful confrontation with the juggernaut of American's keepers of law and order.
The Black Muslims seem resolved to go their separate way within the
system rather than without. The NAACP and its leaders, despite villi-
fication by some of the more extreme elements among the new militants
as the last bastion of "Uncle Toms" and Negroes, presses doggedly on
toward the mark of the high goal of equal justice under the law, the
right of *every* American citizen.

The new militancy has forced every black American—Afro-Americans,
Negroes, "Uncle Toms," blacks—to hold up the mirror of the American
Dream and see in it the reality of the American experience. The formation of a rejection mentality, where white manners and white education
are concerned, can become a powerful psychological instrument in the
struggle for equality.

The winds of change are blowing in the black American community,
and though its members have not yet become what they shall be, as a consequence of the new militancy they shall never be again what they have
been. Those who have dreamed of an eventual day of liberation and salvation from the shackles of slavery—mentally, physically, socially, politically, economically, spiritually—through the medium of the courts and
the law and the basic goodness of their long-time oppressor, will continue
to dream the dream that seemingly knows no waking. Those who dream
of a new world arising through the passing away or destruction of the
old order, the new militants insist, will continue to hold fast to their
dreams. Dreams and dreamers have an ancient history, and black Americans, past and present, who dream dreams of what they shall or may
become join hands with all the inhabitants of the earth, their brothers,
in such fantasies. "We" (meaning Everyman), said Shakespeare's Pros-
pero nearly 400 years ago, "are such stuff as dreams are made on." If
this be true, and history has proved it is, then black Americans, like
their brothers everywhere, will continue to dream of a new world a-
coming. But the new militancy will not allow the basic dream of equal
justice under the law and the maxim that all men are created equal to
dry up like a raisin in the sun. They have reminded all black Americans (and some whites, too) that the dream some of us have to hold is an
America which, as Hughes said, "has never been — a land where men are

free to grow in spirit and in humanness, to love and know they are loved because they are human beings who have the gift of life to share, a place where the entire design of society is aimed at enabling people to share the laughter and tears and joys of this existence in ever more creative ways."[42]

I am sure that the black middle class would all concur. "The middle-class blacks owe a debt to their poor brothers that mere benevolence cannot repay. The only way to cancel this debt is to try to lead the weary, the dispossessed, out of their morass."[43] Only by so doing will the bitter legal battles of the NAACP during the past 50 years to make real the U.S. Constitution for all black Americans prove worthy of the fight. The sacrifices in lives and property and human worth of the new militants to make meaningful the dream long sought is the charge to the black middle class and intellectuals to do so.

BIBLIOGRAPHY

Aptheker, Herbert. *Negro Slave Revolts in the United States.* New York: International Publishers, 1939.

Brink, William, and Harris, Louis. *The Negro Revolution in America.* New York: Simon and Schuster, 1964.

Browne, Robert S. "A Case for Separation." In Browne, Robert S., and Rustin, Bayard. *Separation or Integration: Which Way for America?—a Dialogue.* New York, 1968.

Casey, Albert E. "Research Activity and the Quality of Teaching in Medical Schools." *Science,* 31 July 1942.

Clarke, John H. *William Styron's Nat Turner: Ten Black Writers Respond.* Boston: Beacon Press, 1968.

Cook, Mercer, and Henderson, Stephen E. *The Militant Black Writer in Africa and the United States.* Madison: University of Wisconsin Press, 1969.

Coombs, Orde. "Soul in Suburbia." *Harper's,* January, 1972.

Cooper, Wayne. "Claude McKay and the New Negro of the 1920's." *Phylon,* (1964): 229–38.

Cruse, Harold. *The Crisis of the Negro Intellectual.* New York: Morrow, 1967.

DuBois, W. E. B. *Dusk of Dawn.* New York: Harcourt, 1940.

Farmer, James. "We Cannot Destroy Segregation With a Weapon of Segregation." *Equality,* 1 (November 1944): 2.

Frazier, E. Franklin. *Black Bourgeoisie.* Glencoe, Ill.: Free Press, 1957.

———. *The Free Negro Family.* Nashville: Fisk University Press, 1932.

———. *Negro Youth at the Crossways: Their Personality Development in the Middle States.* New York: Schocken Books, 1967.

Gloster, Hugh M. *Negro Voices in American Fiction.* Chapel Hill: University of North Carolina Press, 1948.

Graham, Edward K. "The Hampton Institute Strike of 1927. A Case Study in Student Protest." *The American Scholar* (Autumn 1969): 668–82.

42. Hughes, pp. 692–94.
43. Coombs, pp. 24–25.

Green, Vera M. "The Confrontation of Diversity Within the Black Community." *Human Organization,* 29, no. 4 (Winter 1970): 267–72.

Hamilton, Charles V. "An Advocate of Black Power Defines It." *New York Times Magazine,* 14 April 1968.

Harding, Vincent. *Beyond Chaos: Black History and the Search for the New Land.* Atlanta: Institute of the Black World, 1970.

Herskovits, Melville. *The Myth of the Negro Past.* Boston: Beacon Press, 1958.

Hughes, Langston. "The Negro Artist and Racial Mountains." *The Nation,* 23 June 1926, pp. 692–94.

Johnson, Charles S. *Growing Up in the Black Belt.* New York: American Council on Education, 1941.

Killens, John O. "Explanation of the Black Psyche." *New York Times Magazine,* 7 June 1964, pp. 37–38.

Mead, Margaret. "Postscript: The 1969 Demonstrations." *The American Scholar* (Autumn 1969): 682–83.

Meier, August; Rudwick, Elliott; and Boderick, Francis. *Black Protest Thought in the Twentieth Century.* Indianapolis: Bobbs-Merrill, 1971.

Myrdal, Gunnar V. *An American Dilemma.* New York: Harper, 1944.

Osofsky, Gilbert. "Symbols of the Jazz Age: The New Negro and Harlem Discovered." *American Quarterly,* 17 (1965): 229–38.

Park, Robert E. "The Bases of Race Prejudice." *The Annals of the American Academy of Political Science* (November 1928): 20.

Powell, Blanche Ruth. *Attitudes of Middle Class Negroes Toward Separatism in Negro-White Relations.* Washington, D.C.: U.S. Government Printing Office, 1970.

Redding, Saunders. "The Black Youth Movement." *The American Scholar* (Autumn 1969): 584–87.

Reid, Ira De A. "The Negro in the American Economic System." Unpublished manuscript prepared for Gunnar Myrdal's *An American Dilemma,* 1940.

Rose, Arnold. *The Negro in America.* New York: Harper, 1964.

Williams, George W. *History of the Negro Race in America.* Reprint of 1883 ed. New York: Bergman, 1968.

Woodson, Carter G. *The Negro in Our History.* Washington, D.C.: Associated Publishers, 1941.

Wright, Nathan. *Black Power and Urban Unrest.* New York: Hawthorn Books, 1967.

Index

A.M.E. Church. *See* African Methodist Episcopal Church

A.M.E. Institutional Church and Social Settlement, 125

A.M.E. Zion Church. *See* African Methodist Episcopal Zion Church

Abbott, Lyman, 12

Abbott, Robert S., 17

Abolition movement, 3, 117, 171

Abolition Society of Philadelphia, 3

Abolitionists, 4

Abridging the Right to Vote, 182

Abyssinian Baptist Church (NYC), 107, 126

Accommodation. *See* Public accommodation

Acculturation, 64

African colonization, 92

African Free School, 3

African Grove Theater, 64, 79

African Methodist Episcopal Church: British financial support of, 116; colleges affiliated with, 30, 31, 33-34; Committee on Slavery, 111; conferences, 111-12, 117, 120; *Discipline,* 111; education, support of, 121; evangelism, 112-13, 119-20; founding, 107, 109-10; membership figures, 110, 123; slavery issue, 111; social services, 125

African Methodist Episcopal Zion Church: colleges affiliated with, 33;

education, support of, 121; evangelism, 113, 119; founding, 107-10, 118; membership figures, 110, 123; voting rights of women, 109

African Orthodox Church, 130

African Roscius, 64

African step dance. *See* Juba dance

African Union Protestant Church, 118

Afro coiffure, 38

Agricultural Adjustment Administration, 97

Agriculture Department, 161, 186

Air Force, 147

Alabama: black elected officeholders, 180-81, 183; pupil placement laws, 28; voter registration on, 176, 183

Alabama A & M University, 30

Alabama State University, 30

Alabama, University of, 27, 37

Alaska, voter registration, 176

Albany State College, 31

Alcorn College, 16, 18, 32, 41

Aldridge, Ira, 53-54, 64, 67, 79

All God's Chillun Got Wings, 74-75, 77

Allen, Richard, 105, 107, 109

Allen University, 33

Alston, Melvin, 25

American Baptist Home Mission Society, 16, 21

American Baptist Missionary Convention, 123

217